1978

# THE END AND THE BEGINNING
## Pakistan 1969–1971

# THE END
# AND THE BEGINNING

## Pakistan 1969–1971

HERBERT FELDMAN

LONDON
OXFORD UNIVERSITY PRESS
LAHORE   KARACHI
1975

*Oxford University Press, Ely House, London W 1*

GLASGOW NEW YORK TORONTO MELBOURNE WELLINGTON
CAPE TOWN IBADAN NAIROBI DAR ES SALAAM LUSAKA ADDIS ABABA
DELHI BOMBAY CALCUTTA MADRAS KARACHI LAHORE DACCA
KUALA LUMPUR SINGAPORE HONG KONG TOKYO

ISBN 0 19 215809 0

PRINTED IN INDIA
BY P. K. GHOSH, AT EASTEND PRINTERS,
3 DR SURESH SARKAR ROAD, CALCUTTA 14

954.9
F304

# CONTENTS

81400

'. . . I conceive that there are cases in which the true interest of the whole may be promoted by disruption. For instance, where two portions of a State's territory are separated, by a long interval of sea or other physical obstacles, from any very active intercommunication and when, from differences of race or religion, past history or present social conditions, their respective inhabitants have divergent needs and demands. . . . Under such conditions as these, it is not to be desired that any sentiment of historical patriotism, or any pride in the national ownership of an extensive territory should permanently prevent a peaceful dissolution of the incoherent whole into its natural parts.'

(Henry Sidgwick, *Elements of Politics*)


'It is always dangerous for soldiers, sailors and airmen to play at politics. They enter a sphere in which the values are quite different from those to which they have hitherto been accustomed.'

(Winston S. Churchill, *The Second World War*)

# ABBREVIATIONS

*D*   *Dawn*. A daily newspaper published in English in Karachi.

*FCTC*   *From Crisis to Crisis*, O.U.P., London, 1972.

*PO*  *Pakistan Observer*. A daily newspaper published in English in Dacca. It is now known as the *Bangladesh Observer*.

*PT*  *Pakistan Times*. A daily newspaper published in English in Lahore. It is owned by the National Press Trust and is, therefore, at any given moment, a mouthpiece of the Government of the day.

*RiP*   *Revolution in Pakistan*, O.U.P., London, 1967.

# ACKNOWLEDGEMENTS

As always, there are debts of gratitude to be recorded. Once again, I have to thank Major Ibnul Hasan whose knowledge of sub-continental affairs is equalled only by his judgement and penetration. For much of the information about armament, I have relied on the invaluable publications of the International Institute of Strategic Studies in London. Finally, I need scarcely add that for such errors and omissions as may be found, I am entirely responsible.

H. F.
Karachi 1973–4

# Introduction

This book examines General Yahya Khan's administration of Pakistan from 25 March 1969 to 20 December 1971 and is a direct continuation of my two preceding works which dealt with Field-Marshal Ayub Khan's martial law and presidential administrations respectively.[1] However, the subject is approached here from a different standpoint. Since the kind of Pakistan which came into being on 14 August 1947 has given way to something else, many of the considerations which were significant for that Pakistan have either disappeared or have undergone substantial transformation. Thus, the tensions set up by the fact that the old Pakistan was divided into two zones, separated by an unfriendly India, have ceased to be relevant to considerations of policy whether it be in Islamabad, in Dacca, in Delhi or in any other seat of government. So, too, the division of economic responsibilities and liabilities; the disparities in investment and growth rates; the claims of each zone upon the national resources as well as questions of foreign attachments and defence—all have experienced profound alteration.

The focus of this book is Yahya Khan's administration and the events which culminated in the dissolution of the old Pakistan. Questions of economic growth, foreign policy, social and civic affairs find mention only in so far as they are relevant to the main theme. For the same reason, it has not been thought necessary to dwell at great length upon Yahya Khan's purge of the civil services,[2] and other cathartic measures. In these respects, therefore, the construction of the present work differs from its two predecessors.

For the present writer the demise of the old Pakistan was marked by two distinct events: (a) the dissolution of West Pakistan in 1970 into its four former constituent Provinces,[3] and (b) the declaration of an independent Bangladesh in March 1971. It was known from the outset that some people, even in the Muslim League itself, were doubtful about the viability of the Pakistan of 1947. This is said not

---

[1] *Revolution in Pakistan*, O.U.P., London, 1967, and *From Crisis to Crisis*, O.U.P., London, 1972, referred to in this book as *RiP* and *FCTC* respectively.

[2] On this subject cf. *FCTC*, Appendix I.

[3] The consolidation of Baluchistan, the North-West Frontier Province, Punjab, and Sind took place in 1955, not, of course, in 1947.

with reference to the old and now never-to-be-answered question whether the Pakistan Resolution passed on 23 March 1940, with its reference to 'states' was so intended, or whether the resolution passed in 1946 by the Convention of Muslim League Legislators defined the Pakistan that the Muslim League desired. That matter, now, is purely academic and the more important question is: what was in the minds of those who, when the United Kingdom decided on its future relationship with the sub-continent, were to be responsible for the Muslim-majority areas? The fact that some people, at the time of the creation of Pakistan, expressed misgiving proves very little. Nor is it necessary to quote, in this context, the decidedly *ex post facto* statements of Zulfikar Ali Bhutto[4] or of Sheikh Mujibur Rahman,[5] whatever may be the place of those statements in the historical record. Much more to our purpose is to try to ascertain when the prospect of a parting of the ways appeared *after* Pakistan had been established in August 1947. At what point could it have been said, on the basis of the evidence *then* available, that notwithstanding the expressed wish for unity,[6] a separation of the two zones seemed inevitable and, in some quarters, had become firmly desired?

By February 1968, the signs seemed to me to point to an ultimate division and to the probability that Ayub Khan himself felt it to be inevitable, if not sooner, then later. Years afterwards, in an interview reported in the *Daily Telegraph*, London, 1 April 1972, Ayub Khan said he had planned to offer independence to East Pakistan but that 'certain things' came in the way and he could not do it. The disparity between earlier conduct and later profession is extreme, nevertheless it is worth noting that Mr. Bhutto has written: 'Above all, he [Ayub Khan] bore an intense prejudice against East Pakistan.'[7] Having regard to the circumstances of their quarrel, this statement may, itself, not be unprejudiced, but after eight years of close association, Bhutto had ample opportunity to become privy to Ayub Khan's views. Moreover, it must be remembered that as early as 1962, when announcing his constitution, Ayub Khan called for an 'honourable partnership' between the two wings and this, however desirable, was certainly not the same thing as national assimilation.

[4] Notably in *The Great Tragedy*, Pakistan People's Party Publication, Karachi, 1971, p. 66. This 31,000-word piece, largely an exercise in polemics and apologetics, keyed to its time, is useful but must be read with circumspection.

[5] In January 1972, after his return to East Bengal from prison in West Pakistan, Sheikh Mujib repeatedly said that ever since 1947 he had desired detachment from West Pakistan.

[6] It is noteworthy that one of the Dacca newspapers most attached to Sheikh Mujib and his party bore the name *Ittefaq* meaning 'unity'. The use of the word was impressive but equivocal.

[7] Bhutto, op. cit., p. 6.

In addition, there is the *ex post facto* evidence. Bhutto has written: 'A careful examination of his [Sheikh Mujib's] speeches at the time [i.e. during the East Pakistan provincial elections of 1954] would reveal that he was becoming disillusioned. He spoke bitterly of the domination of Bengal. He spoke eloquently and with feeling of the cruel exploitation of his people. His hatred of West Pakistan and particularly the Punjab was taking deep roots.'[8] And again: 'He hated West Pakistan and was totally disillusioned with it.'[9] These passages well exemplify the feeling, in West Pakistan, that Sheikh Mujib was the midwife of a newly gestated Bengali nationalism, a feeling widely held, especially in official circles (where Mujib's name was anathema), leading to a misreading of the situation, and to misconceptions which contributed much to the tragedy of 1971.

It has long been apparent that among the Muslims of Bengal there existed an ambiguous attitude towards the apparently clearer aspirations of the Muslims of the Provinces astride the Indus. Today, it is more than ever noteworthy that the late A. K. M. Fazlul Haq, the man who, at Lahore in 1940, moved the Pakistan Resolution, was also the man to declare, after the East Pakistan provincial elections of 1954 from which he emerged the leading politician in that Province, that one of the first things his (East Pakistan provincial) ministry would take up would be independence.[10] And again, the late H. S. Suhrawardy who, at Delhi in 1946, moved the resolution of the Muslim League Legislators' Convention which purported to define the political form that Pakistan should take, i.e. the form it took in August 1947, was likewise the man who had earlier called for a 'united sovereign Bengal'.[11]

Early in the history of Pakistan itself the people of the eastern Province had begun to feel and to express apprehensions concerning their future. In the latter part of 1950, during the Constituent Assembly debate on the Interim Report of the Committee set up to define the Basic Principles for the Constitution, a member of the House, from East Pakistan, rose to say that this report had aroused grave, even if erroneous, apprehensions in East Pakistan. There was, this member continued, a growing belief that the Interim Report contained princi-

---

[8] Ibid., p. 75

[9] Ibid.

[10] He later denied this, but was confronted with the correspondents of the *New York Times* and of Reuter, who affirmed that they heard him say it and produced their shorthand notes made at the time.

[11] Suhrawardy was far from being alone in this. Many members of the Muslim League from Bengal favoured or sympathized with this idea. It must be remembered that the partition of Bengal and of the Punjab was not the proposal of the Muslim League but of the Indian National Congress. In the present context, the important word is not *united* but *sovereign*.

ples which, if adopted, would reduce the majority population of East Bengal into a minority and would turn East Bengal into a colony. He added that some people considered the Report to be undemocratic, un-Islamic, and reactionary and that provincial autonomy would disappear leaving a unitary government.[12] From words it did not take the people of East Bengal long to proceed to action. In 1952 they succeeded, but only after lives were lost in the course of police firing, in enforcing a decision that Bengali would, along with Urdu, be adopted as one of the two national languages of Pakistan. Shiekh Mujib certainly participated in the agitation, and four members of the Provincial Assembly were arrested for their part in these demonstrations.

The provincial elections, held in East Bengal in 1954, when the Muslim League party was swept from power and office, retaining only nine seats was a drastic revulsion implying a sense of hostility towards West Pakistan, for it seemed as if, through this blow at the Muslim League, East Bengal was registering disapproval of the prevailing state of politics. This point became explicit, a year later, in the Constituent Assembly, when Ataur Rahman spoke as follows: 'Sir, I . . . yesterday . . . said that the attitude of the Muslim League coterie here was one of contempt towards East Bengal, towards its culture, its language, its literature and everything concerning East Bengal. . . . In fact, Sir, I tell you that far from considering East Bengal as an equal partner, the leaders of the Muslim League thought that we were a subject race and they belonged to the race of conquerors.'[13] The boldness of expression is interesting. In 1950 such opinions were guarded, the speaker being careful to suggest that he was simply repeating sentiments uttered by others 'even if erroneous'. In 1954 the speaker was bold enough to present such views as his own and to assert them without equivocation.

One more quotation may suffice. It is from the debate on the 1956 Constitution Bill when Abul Mansur said: 'Pakistan is a unique country, having two wings which . . . differ in all matters excepting two things . . . a common religion and . . . a common struggle. With the exception of these two things, all other factors, viz. the language, the tradition, the culture, the costume, the dietary, the calendar, the standard time, practically everything is different. There is, in fact, nothing common to the two wings, particularly in respect of those things which are the *sine qua non* to form a nation.'[14]

[12] Constituent Assembly *Debates*, vol. VII, no. 6, p. 183. Quoted in Feldman, *A Constitution for Pakistan*, O.U.P., Karachi, 1955. See also Callard, *Pakistan: A Political Study*, Allen and Unwin, London, 1957, p. 172 et seq.

[13] Constituent Assembly *Debates*, vol. I, p. 530, 7 September 1954. Also quoted in Callard, op. cit., p. 72.

[14] *Debates*, vol. I, p. 1816, 16 January 1956. Also quoted in Callard, op. cit.,

The Six Points, so energetically propagated by Sheikh Mujib and his Awami League, were not in fact the basis of the movement which culminated in the sweeping electoral victory of 1970 and subsequent independence. The Six Point manifesto was simply the programmatic expression of a movement which preceded the Six Point formulation by years and had begun to take root as early as 1950. This being so, we may ask whether General Yahya Khan's suppression of the Awami League and its 1970 manifesto had any effect on the roots of the secessionist movement and whether the grievances by which that movement was nourished and through which it grew strong, could thereby have been redressed, much less erased.

If it be true that all this was present to the mind of Pakistan's two military leaders and their advisers then, clearly, they were faced with a cruel dilemma and each of them, although more particularly Yahya Khan, might have said, echoing Sir Winston Churchill, that he had not become the Head of State in order to preside over the dissolution of Pakistan.[15] Still, notwithstanding Ayub Khan's later assertions[16] the evidence shows that in West Pakistan there was negligible understanding of the ferment which led to the break-up of 1971.

The two wings of Pakistan had few political ideas in common. For the people of West Pakistan, and, in particular, of the Punjab, the only imaginable Pakistan was *their* kind of Pakistan which meant one where policies were determined by such questions as Kashmir, the inadvisability of too great an involvement with India—political, cultural, and commercial—and instead a reliance on partnership with Iran and Turkey; an interest, passionately rather than shrewdly felt, in Middle East affairs and, for better security, an understanding with China. The Chinese link excepted, what compatibility with its own interests could East Pakistan discover in an orientation such as this?[17] If the two wings of Pakistan could not reconcile their difference of orientation, then the Pakistan born in 1947 could not be politically viable.

At the time, those in authority chose to overlook these tensions. In

p. 157. And, for good measure, Abul Mansur might have included a passage from a letter, written in 1861, by Ghalib. It reads: 'My friend, Delhi and Lucknow are agreed that *jafa* (faithlessness) is feminine. No one would ever make it masculine except, perhaps, in Bengal, where they make even "cow-elephant" masculine.' Russell and Islam, *Ghalib, Life and Letters*, Allen and Unwin, London, 1969, vol. I, p. 265.

[15] 'I did not become the King's First Minister in order to preside over the liquidation of the British Empire.' Speech at the Mansion House, 10 November 1942. Nevertheless, the Empire was liquidated after all.

[16] See p. 2.

[17] It is worth noting that the first two Muslim countries to recognize Bangladesh were Malaysia and Indonesia.

the speeches and writings of Ayub Khan[18] there is nothing to show that any of these problems worried him. Obviously, a country whose political and economic structure is as unusual as Pakistan's requires for survival men of exceptional qualities of statesmanship. It does not seem that either Ayub Khan or Yahya Khan possessed them.

Undoubtedly Ayub Khan was substantially the abler of the two men, but readers of my book *From Crisis to Crisis* will easily conclude that I hold Ayub Khan to be largely responsible for the dissolution of Pakistan. To have restored the country after Ayub Khan's régime would have required in his successor a measure of political resource, character, and good fortune such as Yahya Khan could never claim. Yahya Khan received into his hands a political and economic *haereditas damnosa* virtually beyond hope of recovery. History may well conclude that it was Yahya Khan's misfortune to have completed what Ayub Khan had launched. Even the Muslim League, sole political party in the country which could reasonably claim to be equally well based in each wing, had been riven by Ayub Khan into two competing parties—his own (Convention) Muslim League and the legitimists, the (Council) Muslim League.[19]

Others made their contribution to the events of 1971 and it is doubtful whether Mohamed Ali Jinnah himself understood the political implications inherent in the Pakistan he eventually accepted. This doubt springs partly from the fact that he appeared to believe in the possibility of imposing Urdu on East Pakistan as the 'state' language of the entire country.[20] Jinnah died before the country's political problems took specific shape but it does seem reasonable to suggest that clear-minded constitutionalist as he was, Jinnah would have understood the overriding importance of getting the constitutional machinery organized and elections held, for without these the nation's

[18] I refer, here, not only to his book, *Friends not Masters* (OUP, London, 1967), but also to the eight volumes of his speeches and writings published by the Government of Pakistan. Ayub Khan might claim that he *did* have these things in mind and he could point to the immense devolution of executive authority from the Centre to the eastern and western Provinces. There is substance in this, but Ayub Khan robbed himself and the country of the advantage of what he had done by introducing in his Constitution of 1962 provisions which enabled him to nullify, in large part, the liberality of his earlier policy. In short, what he had done came to be interpreted by his opponents, particularly in East Pakistan, as sheer bluff. His treatment of Sheikh Mujib, particularly during the closing years of his administration, was ample proof of his inability to understand the real nature of his political problems. However, it is fair to bear in mind what he said in April 1972 (see p. 2).

[19] Later, in Yahya Khan's time, there was to be yet a third—the Quaid-i-Azam Muslim League founded by the North-West Frontier politician, Abdul Qayum Khan.

[20] Address at Dacca University Convocation on 24 March 1948. He said: 'Make no mistake about it. There can only be one state language . . . and that . . . can only be Urdu.' Quoted in Feldman, *RiP*, p. 165. See however, n. 24 below.

political life could not truly begin. Those who came after him did not seem to understand this essential fact.

The man who probably laid the foundations for the demise of the old Pakistan was the late Ghulam Mohamed, a former Governor-General.[21] By his summary dismissal of Khwaja Nazimuddin from the Ministership in 1954, Ghulam Mohamed did four things. First, he convinced many in East Pakistan that West Pakistan and, in particular, the Punjab, intended to keep the reins of government permanently in hand. Second, he demonstrated that *coups* of this sort were possible in Pakistan. Third, he introduced the army into politics with the appointment of Ayub Khan, then Commander-in-Chief of the Pakistan Army, as Minister of Defence. Fourth, to use Callard's words, 'The price of the Governor-General's *coup* was high. Three major conventions of cabinet government had been destroyed or weakened.'[22] Indeed, from this time onward political decline hastened until, in 1958, Iskander Mirza and Ayub Khan tried to cut the tangled skein by recourse to Martial Law.

Allama Iqbal, in his much-quoted speech, delivered in 1930 at the annual session of the Muslim League, in which he called for 'self-governing states', also referred to a 'central federal state exercising only those powers which are expressly vested in it by free consent of the federal states'. Moreover, this was exactly the position of the All-India Muslim League in May 1946.[23] And the Cabinet Mission Plan of 1946, which envisaged an unpartitioned India with a Central Government to deal with Foreign Affairs, Defence, and Communications, was accepted by that same League. It was also accepted by the Indian National Congress but, almost immediately thereafter, Pandit Jawaharlal Nehru, on singularly prevaricating grounds, thwarted it. Thus, it can be argued, with a good deal of force, that the Muslims of the sub-continent would have preferred an undivided India with constitutionally built-in guarantees that would protect their way of life and interests in the face of an overwhelming and permanent Hindu majority.

Because of the Congress attitude this became impossible, and raises

---

[21] This man, probably in his time one of the four ablest in Pakistan, had some serious disabilities: a hasty, choleric temper; absolutely no gift for public speaking; and, above all, no political training whatsoever.

[22] Callard, op. cit., p. 137.

[23] S. M. Ikram, *Modern Muslim India and the Birth of Pakistan*, Sh. Muhammad Ashraf, Lahore, 2nd rev. ed., 1970, pp. 172–3. It seems, however, that at the Round Table Conference held in London in 1930, Iqbal took up a different position. He said that there should be no central government in India, but that the Provinces should be autonomous, independent dominions in direct relationship with the Secretary of State for India in London. He did not, moreover, make any reference to Pakistan as such.

the question whether the Pakistan that emerged in August 1947 was the next acceptable alternative. It is known that after the massacres in Bihar, in 1946, Jinnah took the view that the Muslims must be masters in their own house in all respects. This would involve a partition, but did Muslims desire the kind of partition that was actually created? The answer turns partly on the constitutional structure that was intended but there is very little to show that, at the time, the matter was being considered. Federation, confederation, unitary government, parity between the two wings—none of these seem to have been seriously discussed although they were present to the minds of some. On the whole, it seems fair to say that the kind of Pakistan which emerged in 1947, notwithstanding the many unanswered questions, was acceptable to the Provinces astride the Indus. For East Bengal, it was, at that euphoric moment, acceptable likewise, but many people had doubts and reservations. It was also said that unpublished documents existed showing that Jinnah expressed readiness for East Bengal to form its own independent government but, not surprisingly, very little has ever been remarked on this, much less disclosed.[24] What we do know for certain is that within three years of Pakistan's first emergence signs of discontent in the eastern wing were plain, and that within five years lives were being lost in the course of political controversy.

I conclude this Introduction with some points of explanation. While it is an undoubted advantage to live continuously in a country whose progress through time one desires to observe, the disadvantage to the Pakistan-dweller is that he is cut off from Indian journals and books while those from other countries are expensive and exist under the shadow of the ban. This is less important than the opportunity to become familiar with events as they occur, to meet people, hear their views and witness their reactions and, if only through sheer propinquity, to absorb the prevailing atmosphere, but the want of newspapers and books is certainly felt.

Secondly, in this book, I have used the expressions 'Pakistan', 'the

[24] This 'evidence', which appears never to have been published, achieved an explicit mention in 1972 when the then Minister for Law, Mr. Mahmud Ali Kasuri, addressed a message to the people of East Pakistan. A passage reads: 'There is evidence that when Mr. Suhrawardy suggested to the Viceroy, Lord Mountbatten, that he would try to persuade the Congress and Bengali leadership generally, for a United Bengal as an independent state outside both the Indian Union and Pakistan, the Quaid-i-Azam did not react adversely. Mr. Suhrawardy tried and failed. There can be two inferences from this. One is that the Quaid knew he would not succeed and therefore did not prevent him or Mountbatten from trying. The other is that he gave his blessing to the idea of self-determination by Bengalis.' The message is printed verbatim in *PT*, 16 August 1972. In Ayub Khan's time, Suhrawardy's efforts at constructing a united, sovereign, independent Bengal were adduced as evidence of Suhrawardy's 'disruptionist' tendencies.

old Pakistan', 'the new Pakistan', 'West Pakistan', 'East Pakistan', 'East Bengal', and 'Bangladesh' as appeared to be the most appropriate to the sense of what was being written, as well as to the moment in history to which it related. In the use of these terms, I have been guided simply by questions of clarity and propriety.

Thirdly, readers may discover some overlap between the present volume and its predecessor, *From Crisis to Crisis*. This is not, I think, excessive, but it was necessary for two reasons. It helps to tie the two books together and it is necessary for an understanding of the present narrative.

# I

# Return to Martial Law

The circumstances in which, on 25 March 1969, General Yahya Khan became Chief Martial Law Administrator of Pakistan were different indeed from those in which General (as he then was) Ayub Khan entered upon that office on 7 October 1958.

In 1958 everyone was wearied with the wranglings of politicians; disgusted with the prevalence of corruption, nepotism, and dishonesty; burdened by increasing taxation, rising prices, and black markets; alarmed by the encroachments of the privileged few upon the nation's limited resources; and deeply distressed by recent events in East Pakistan where the Speaker of the provincial legislature was assaulted in the House[1]—all of which combined to arouse in everyone profound relief on hearing President Iskander Mirza's proclamation that Martial Law had been instituted, that the existing constitution was abrogated, that all political parties stood abolished, and that measures would soon be adopted to mitigate the evils which oppressed the people. The appearance of the armed forces upon the political stage, while for many reasons to be deplored, would, it was believed, at least ensure responsible government in which patriotism and dedication would be the most prominent features. These, even if not actual guarantees of prosperity, of progress, and orderly politics, would, it was felt, at least ensure a period of civic tranquillity in which those best qualified to do so could provide a workable constitution for the country, lay the foundations of a sound economy, and raise the national stature in the eyes of the world. In short, on the morning of 8 October 1958, the people of Pakistan, by and large, believed that a new and promising opportunity had been vouchsafed.

When President Ayub Khan relinquished office and, to use the cliché so unhappily familiar in Pakistan, handed over power, people had cause for serious disquiet. Since 8 November 1968

---

[1] He died shortly afterwards, but he was a sick man at the time and it is not clear that his death was attributable to his injuries.

there had been constant rioting, bloodshed, and numerous strikes affecting the public services, education, industry, and commerce. Ayub Khan's administration was gravely discredited along with the man himself. His Basic Democracies system had proved to be a mockery of democracy; corruption had further increased; the privileged few were more securely entrenched than ever; and his much-vaunted constitution had proved to be putty in his hands, to be moulded as he liked.

But although his departure was witnessed with the same relief as had greeted his entry into politics in 1958, by March 1969 people also felt a sense of defeat. A generation had passed since Pakistan first emerged as a nation, master of its own destiny, and the country was again without a constitution. Its political leaders had again failed. Law and order had again broken down with fresh recourse to troops upon the streets, bayonets fixed and light automatics menacingly poised. Most of the grounds for Pakistan's claim to be a well-ordered, dynamic, Islamic, and democratic republic had vanished[2] and so far from having progressed in the evolution of a well-founded polity, it had made no progress at all. Apparently unable to govern itself there had been no alternative but to call in the armed forces. The clock had gone back by more than ten years.

But why suppose the armed forces would respond faithfully to this fresh call? Once before trust had been reposed in them and while no one identified every officer and man with Ayub Khan, experience showed that hopes should not be too high. Yahya Khan might, or might not, escape the temptations to which Ayub Khan had succumbed, but there was no assurance. The fine words with which General Yahya Khan had addressed the nation promised much, but promises had been heard before and had proved empty. What reason was there for supposing they would be more solid this time? Thus, allied to a sense of defeat were doubt and hesitation, together with the growing suspicion that whenever it was felt in General Headquarters that things were not going well or were not going according to the taste and opinion of senior officers, the armed forces (in effect the army alone) would move in or contrive to do so.[3]

[2] It is well to remember that these claims, or the greater part of them, were intended to increase the stature of Ayub Khan.

[3] Hence, perhaps, the title of an editorial in *The Economist*, London, 29 March 1969, 'Tweedle Khan Takes Over'.

Was it not possible that this fresh imposition of Martial Law had been planned so as to thwart the rising opposition of the people to Ayub Khan's masked dictatorship or, alternatively, that it was his 'parting kick' for the politicians who, in the preceding four months, had been harrying and baiting him?[4] By 20 February 1969 rumours of a likely imposition of Martial Law were audible. This was not entirely surprising in view of the evident inability of the civil power to maintain law and order; of the progressive increase in industrial unrest; and of the conflict of opinion between political parties throughout the country. Furthermore, Ayub Khan was plainly fighting for his political life and he might, therefore, in desperation, have recourse to this way of maintaining his authority for, were he to lose it, his life and property, and the lives and properties of members of his family could be in peril. On the other hand, resumption of Martial Law had grave dangers, particularly in East Pakistan. Moreover, a resumption of Martial Law would simply proclaim Ayub Khan's political insolvency and the failure of all he had attempted.[5] But in a special broadcast at 5.30 p.m. on 21 February 1969 Ayub Khan declared that he would not offer himself as a candidate at the next presidential election, to take place in January 1970. The decision, he said, was final and irrevocable. It was generally described as a wise step but while it offered the prospect of Ayub Khan's withdrawal from politics, it did nothing to calm the situation or quieten the now very voluble political leaders.

Meanwhile a rumour was circulating about the movement of troops to East Pakistan. Although the Government of Pakistan always seeks to draw the veil of secrecy over such matters, certain facts could not be suppressed. Railway wagons suddenly became scarce in West Pakistan and space in coastal ships plying between Karachi and Chittagong was not easily available for merchants. In short, it seemed clear the Government of Pakistan had taken the decision to run, and if necessary meet, the risk of trouble in East Pakistan should it be necessary to fall back on Martial Law.

In March 1969 the situation deteriorated further. In Dacca alone, from 7 to 21 March, thirty-nine people were killed in

---

[4] The question whether there was a *coup* or a conspiracy to impose Martial Law is discussed in Appendix H to *FCTC*.

[5] The degeneration of law and order, as well as of Ayub Khan's personal authority in the country, from 8 November 1968 onwards, is described in Ch. XIV, *FCTC*.

various affrays. About the middle of the month, at Laksam in East Pakistan, an officer in charge of a police party and three of its constables were beaten to death.[6] In a severe clash at Jamalpur, in the same Province, seven persons were killed and two were roasted alive.[7] At Parbatipur, in Dinajpur District, the army was called out in aid of the civil power after five people had been killed.[8] In Karachi industrial unrest had reached the point at which, on 20 March, the President of the Federation of Pakistan Chambers of Commerce and Industry asked the Government to deploy troops in industrial areas in order to protect factory premises and their contents. It was also noticed, in West Pakistan, that troops had been posted at key establishments such as radio stations. This at once strengthened rumours that Martial Law could be expected soon, but it was promptly denied by the Governor of West Pakistan, Mr. Yusuf Haroon,[9] who explained that this deployment of troops was simply to free the police for other tasks. Such were some of the circumstances preceding the announcement of Martial Law.

The announcement itself took the form of Ayub Khan's radio address on the evening of 25 March, along with the appearance on the streets of armed soldiers. Next morning the newspapers contained Ayub Khan's letter of 24 March to General Yahya Khan, requesting him to execute his 'legal and constitutional responsibility to defend the country not only against external aggression but also to save it from internal disorder and chaos.' The letter continued: 'The nation expects you to discharge this responsibility to preserve the security and integrity of the country and to restore normal social, economic and administrative life.' The newspapers also contained Yahya Khan's proclamation of Martial Law, the first batch of Martial Law Regulations, and the first four Martial Law Orders. On the same morning, i.e. 26 March, Yahya Khan briefly addressed the nation by radio.

Ayub Khan began his letter by saying that 'with profound regret', he had come to the conclusion that all civil administration and constitutional authority in the country had become ineffective. He regarded himself as having no option but to 'step

[6] *PO*, 17 and 18 March 1969.
[7] *PO*, 18 and 20 March 1969.
[8] It should be mentioned that these violent outbreaks had much to do with the local tyrannies exercised by Ayub Khan's Basic Democrats.
[9] His appointment lasted four days.

aside and leave it to the Defence Forces of Pakistan which today represent the only effective and legal instrument to take over full control of the affairs of the country'. He claimed, 'time will show that this turmoil was deliberately created by well-tutored and well-backed elements'. His radio address was in somewhat similar terms. He sought to justify the course he had adopted and tried to cast the blame on others, principally, it is significant to note, those whose demands 'would have spelled the liquidation of Pakistan'. Yahya Khan's proclamation began with the interesting recital, 'whereas a situation has arisen in the country in which the civil administration cannot effectively function . . .' —an obvious parallelism with the phraseology used by Ayub Khan.

Much can be said about the language employed in these documents and explanations. For example, what was meant by the statement that Ayub Khan found no option but to step aside? Nothing in his Constitution provided him with any such option. Indeed, under that Constitution, he could:

(a) have vacated office in the first place by refusing to take the prescribed oath;

(b) vacate office by dissolving the National Assembly;

(c) resign;

(d) be removed by impeachment;

(e) be removed on grounds of incapacity as defined.

But nowhere does it say he could 'step aside' and what that phrase was supposed to mean is likely to remain for ever unexplained.[10]

Again, what was the authority for saying that Yahya Khan had a 'legal and constitutional responsibility . . . to save it [the country] from internal disorder and chaos'? What was the ground for thinking that the nation, as distinguished from Ayub Khan, desired Yahya Khan to discharge that responsibility, assuming it to exist? Clearly, the nation had never been consulted since everything had been discussed and prepared behind closed doors. No doubt, since 20 February, there had been talk of Martial Law, but this did not mean that the nation either desired it or had been informed of it. Indeed,

---

[10] Of course, he could also die but that contingency scarcely called for constitutional provision. Years later, the Supreme Court of Pakistan discussed these events in Miss Asma Gilani vs. The Government of Punjab and Anor., P.L.D., 1972, vol. xxiv, pp. 139–225. In this case, the Supreme Court held that General Yahya Khan had all along been a usurper and that his régime had been totally unconstitutional.

there were grounds for supposing the nation did not desire it, for even if troops may usefully be employed in the aid of the civil power or to protect important installations, that is quite different from supposing that the armed forces are qualified to 'restore normal social, economic and administrative life'. On the contrary, Pakistan had reason for thinking that when the armed forces become occupied with such matters, the result is to create a class of inferior civil servants and worse politicians, while military efficiency may be impaired.

In the Constitution promulgated by Ayub Khan and in force when he 'stepped aside', the Defence Services (not Forces) are mentioned exactly five times, as follows:

(a) Article 6 states that the fundamental rights of citizens cannot be invoked against the Defence Services when acting in performance of their duties;

(b) Article 17 states that the supreme command of the Defence Services is vested in the President and is to be exercised by him subject to law;

(c) Article 98 touches on the jurisdiction of the High Courts with respect to the Defence Services;

(d) Article 176 relates to tenure of service;

(e) Article 238 states that for a period of twenty years from the commencement of the Constitution, the Defence Minister shall be an officer of the rank of lieutenant-general or equivalent.

There were some ancillary references in: (i) the Third Schedule which stated that the Central Government had exclusive power to make laws relating to the defence of Pakistan; (ii) in the Fifth Schedule which stated that reservists of the Defence Forces were not disqualified from being members of the National or Provincial Assemblies; and (iii) Article 220 prohibited the raising of 'private armies'.

Evidently there is not much here which reposes 'constitutional authority' in the Commander-in-Chief of the Pakistan Army to save the country from 'internal disorder and chaos'. Of course, it was open to either Ayub Khan or Yahya Khan to invoke the maxim *salus populi supreme lex*, but neither of them did and, probably neither they, nor any of their advisers, thought of it, although in the case-law of Pakistan there existed a notable instance in which this doctrine had been invoked, apparently with success.[11] Finally, if the Constitution of 1962 did in fact arm the Commander-in-Chief of the army with a 'constitutional responsibility' such as Ayub Khan had mentioned, Yahya Khan himself disposed of it by abrogating that very Constitution in his Martial Law proclamation.

There is evidence to suggest that as the movement against Ayub Khan intensified, he considered the possibility of using Martial Law himself to silence those agitating against him. But it also seems probable that he discovered he could not long rely on the armed forces to keep him in power.[12] Moreover, Ayub Khan had also to consider the fact that a reversion to Martial Law would emphatically demonstrate the bankruptcy of his administration.[13]

If the decision to re-impose Martial Law was taken after the breakdown of the Round Table Conference that would have left eleven days before the day that Martial Law was actually announced. This would be consistent with the following facts: (a) that no sooner had the Martial Law administration displaced Ayub Khan's government than the machinery of Martial Law, in the form of twenty-five Regulations and four Orders, was made available to the press, and (b) that the first 'hatchet list' was ready.[14] On 4 April the Provisional Constitution Order was issued by which, subject to the supervening authority of Martial Law, the country was to be governed as nearly as possible in accordance with the Constitution of 1962. This did not mean the retention of that Constitution which had already been abrogated. The Order simply meant that the machinery of government, as set out in that Constitution, would be employed. The courts of law had no authority with respect to the Martial Law administration and

[11] Maulvi Tamizuddin Khan's Case, P.L.D., 1955, Federal Court, p. 240. At any rate, the doctrine was invoked by Counsel for the State, Kenneth Diplock, Q.C.

[12] Yahya Khan had ambitions of his own and had drawn a circle of officers round him (see Ch. XIII).

[13] In Pakistan, it has not hitherto been the custom for a political leader who has failed in his office to resign. In such cases the individual simply changed the policy, or altered his decision, and carried on. The question of any convention in this respect did not, therefore, trouble Ayub Khan. All he had to worry about was what people were saying and what they might do.

[14] This phrase signifies the lists of officials whose conduct had invited unfavourable notice. In D, on 12 April, it was stated that five members of the Civil Service of Pakistan were under investigation. On 18 April Mr. N. A. Farooqi, C.S.P., Chief Election Commissioner, was relieved of his duties with immediate effect.

certain fundamental rights, guaranteed by that Constitution, were set aside.

While this recourse to Martial Law had a good deal of deliberation about it, it is not clear that those who planned its re-imposition had given much thought to its likely consequences, which appeared to be as follows:

(a) In the eyes of the world, Pakistan would lose much of its credibility as a stable political entity.

(b) The gap between the two wings would immediately widen and become, perhaps, finally unbridgeable.

(c) Progress in all departments of national activity would slow down and, in some instances, possibly stop altogether. This idea was based on the anticipation of various purgations and the 'cleaning up' of the administration.

(d) Foreign private investment might be adversely affected.

(e) The Kashmir problem would again go into cold storage.

(f) India would become noisily critical and could be expected to point the finger of scorn at this further political breakdown.

We will return to these conjectures shortly. Meanwhile, it is important to consider what Yahya Khan had to say to the nation on the morning of 26 March. The specific points were:

(a) Field-Marshal Ayub Khan had taken all possible steps to arrange a peaceful and constitutional transfer of power.

(b) Ayub Khan failed in these efforts and had called on Yahya Khan to carry out the prime duty of protecting the country from utter destruction.

(c) The armed forces had hoped sanity would prevail and that this extreme step would not be necessary.

(d) Yahya Khan's sole aim in imposing Martial Law was to protect the life, liberty, and property of the people and to put the administration back 'on the rails'.

(e) There had been too much administrative laxity and chaos and this was 'not to be repeated'.

(f) Every member of the administration was advised to take serious notice of this warning.

(g) Yahya Khan had no ambition other than the creation of conditions conducive to the establishment of constitutional government. (He added that it would be the duty of the people's elected representatives to give the country a workable constitution and find a solution for all other political, economic, and special problems.)

(h) At the same time he was conscious of the pressing needs of various sections of Pakistan society, notably students, labour, and peasants. He added that his administration would make every endeavour to solve these difficulties.

(i) The armed forces belong to the people and have no political ambitions.

From this statement, it appeared that Ayub Khan had made an honourable attempt to arrange a peaceful and constitutional transfer of power and had failed from no fault of his own. Apparently, it was the administration which had gone off 'the rails', not Ayub Khan. This was a clear attempt to exculpate Ayub Khan and to lay the blame on unnamed persons and on the people in general. Similarly, Yahya Khan could not be blamed since he was acting in obedience to his 'prime duty'. It could also be deduced that the armed forces were the best judges of what was sane and what was not, and, therefore, on them lay the task of restoring sanity. There was no mention of East Pakistan's discontents or of the possible consequences to the nation of this further constitutional breakdown.

There was immediate reaction in East Pakistan. As soon as the news was heard, people came on to the streets in protest. After some arrests were made it was reported that all had become quiet, but although news of continued unrest did not appear in the newspapers, rumour persisted that East Pakistan was far from tranquil. Reports brought by visitors confirmed the rumours about the Province's resentment and mistrust of Yahya Khan. Nothing of this was published for several months, but the evidence of discontent could not be obscured.[15]

Yahya Khan's address to the nation made no mention of East Pakistan's grievances, but he and his administration were alive to them. By 7 May, changes in the top civil service posts

[15] In particular, Mr. Rehman Sobhan, an economist and intellectual of considerable standing, who later became prominent in the Bangladesh movement, published an article entitled 'What Follows Ayub's Abdication', in the *New Statesman*, London, 28 March 1969. He scouted the theory that Martial Law had become necessary and maintained that it was the same story as in 1958, i.e. a conspiracy between the men in power and the army to thwart the democratic aspirations of the people. This assertion is controversial but, in other respects, there was much in what he said.

resulted in six senior civil servants from East Pakistan holding the rank of secretary to government.[16] One of these was Mr. Syud Ahmed who became the civil service head of the Ministry of Information and Broadcasting. This appointment deserves notice because it had some importance in relation to events in March 1971.

Thus, on the morning of 26 March 1969, the people of Pakistan had ample reason to feel sad and dispirited, with a haunting sense of failure. The material fact was that the preceding four months had wrought grievous political and economic damage and that, with or without the armed forces, strenuous measures would be needed to repair it. If the country had suffered a severe political reverse, the fact had to be accepted and the remedies found. The immediate consolation was that the new Chief Martial Law Administrator had promised an early return to the kind of democratic political institutions which the nation evidently favoured.

---

[16] A secretary to government in this particular hierarchy is the highest rank to which a civil servant can aspire, excluding a judgeship in the Supreme Court. A secretary to government in any ministry is, in fact, the permanent civil service head of that ministry.

# II

# Initial Measures

But however disturbed and angry the nation might feel, the renewal of Martial Law was greeted by expressions of relief. Even Mr. Bhutto considered that the Martial Law authorities had acted wisely.[1] Some District Magistrates issued sternly phrased warnings to hoarders and black-marketeers. The police, with the armed forces behind them, became tough and resolute in the performance of their duties, so enthusiastic indeed that by the end of the month people were complaining of their conduct. In the streets there was the repetition of patrolling soldiers, in battle-dress and bearing arms. The word 'discipline' acquired a refreshing popularity and people were discouraged from urinating on foot-paths and from other un-hygienic, anti-social practices. Very soon there was to be an impressive demonstration of the cleaning-up of streets and the repainting of traffic signs. Much more to the public advantage was the re-opening of schools and colleges in West Pakistan.

On 1 April 1969 General Yahya Khan assumed the office of President of Pakistan. On 4 April it was ordered that the picture of Ayub Khan be taken down in all public offices and replaced by that of the new President. In this sense it could be said that Ayub Khan's disappearance from public life was complete.

On 28 March news reached Karachi from Islamabad at about 11.45 a.m. that Mr. Fida Hasan, Vice-Admiral A. R. Khan, and Mr. Arshad Hussain had been appointed Administrative Adviser, Defence Adviser, and Foreign Affairs Adviser, respectively, to the new Chief Martial Law Administrator. They were being retained, in effect, in the capacities in which they had served Ayub Khan at the time of his fall. This could only be interpreted as meaning that the old administration was continuing, but under another name. An hour later it

[1] In an interview with British Independent Television, reported in the Pakistani newspapers on 6 April 1969.

was learned that this news was incorrect, and there was much speculation as to how such a suggestion was ever made.[2]

The mystery seems never to have been solved but at the time many prominent people were deeply concerned for their future. After all, in Ayub Khan's Martial Law régime politicians had been expelled from public life and hundreds of civil servants had been summarily 'screened'. Was it not possible that the new administration might display the same cathartic zeal? Most of the politicians had deserted Ayub Khan and in the preceding weeks his Basic Democrats had been resigning in droves, but there remained some, especially in the Civil Services, who had served Ayub Khan with impressive devotion and, indeed, a stern fate did overtake some of them.[3] Perhaps a bold attempt had been made to insure against such eventualities.

On 10 April Yahya Khan addressed his first press conference, at which only Pakistani journalists were present. The reason for excluding foreign journalists was unclear but possibly the new President felt that his first meeting with the press should be confined to his own countrymen. He made the following points:

(a) He had not come to stay. The use of the Constitution of 1962 was simply to meet administrative necessities.

(b) Political parties had not been abolished but for the time being their activities were restricted. There would be a restoration of political activity as soon as possible.

(c) The question of regional autonomy would be one for the representatives of the people to decide.

(d) The administration was to be cleaned up.

(e) No censorship of the press had been imposed.[4]

(f) Machinery had been set in motion to work out a proper method of dealing with educational problems.

[2] The fact that this news was broadcast by the BBC and by All-India Radio indicates some official origin and there is ground for thinking that the author was one of the three persons named. On 31 March the retirement of Fida Hasan was announced.

[3] For the fate which overtook civil servants in Pakistan after 25 March 1969, see *FCTC*, Appendix I, entitled 'The Fate of the "303" '.

[4] Nevertheless, the newspapers became sterile, partly through a self-imposed censorship and partly because of that spirit of the *claque* which infects Pakistani journalism. It must be added that later in Yahya Khan's administration writing became very free and journalists experienced a liberality of atmosphere they had not known for many years.

2

(g) Experts had been commissioned to work out a fair wages policy.
(h) Peasants' needs would have to be met.
(i) Concrete proposals had been ordered to establish reasonable prices for essential commodities.
(j) The utmost importance was attached to a solution of Indo-Pakistan disputes on an honourable and equitable basis.

If this statement was intended to clarify further the new President's radio address and the motives he had expressed, it cannot be said to have been reassuring. Indeed, there had appeared a duality of purpose which might—as later proved to be the case—well be a source of confusion.[5] It could be deduced that there would be no immediate move towards elections and that the new government regarded itself as more than a caretaker until such time as the people's elected representatives were able to prepare a new constitution. If Yahya Khan and his colleagues had no other object in promulgating Martial Law than the protection of the life, liberty, and property of the people, if there were no other purpose than to put the administration back 'on the rails' and to create conditions conducive to the establishment of constitutional government, why was this administration concerning itself with far-ranging social questions and matters of foreign policy? We shall return to this point.

Meanwhile, in the same month of April, fourteen more Martial Law Regulations were issued and it could be seen that, as Mr. Sobhan phrased it, the story was to be the same. It is worth noticing that, among other things, crimes so difficult to establish as nepotism, were created.[6] Another peculiar offence was created by a Regulation dealing with what was described as the improper acquisition of property.[7] Clause 4(a) stated: 'A person who owns . . . property or assets which he has reason to believe have been acquired by unlawful or improper means or by means of bribery, corruption, jobbery,

---

[5] With deliberation, I use the word 'duality' and not 'duplicity'. As we shall have much occasion to notice, these men did not have clear minds.
[6] Martial Law Regulation No. 29. The maximum punishment was fourteen years' rigorous imprisonment. One wonders whether the crime was, in fact, limited to nephews or, if not, to relationship in what degree?
[7] Martial Law Regulation No. 37.

favouritism, nepotism, wilful maladministration, wilful misapplication or diversion of public money, or by abuse of whatever kind of official power or position shall surrender such properties and assets in favour of the Central Government. . . .' Acquired by whom? And when? It is impossible to imagine anything more vague or more confused.

It would be interesting to know how many people actually went to prison for the crime of nepotism and how many people surrendered property which they had reason to believe had been acquired by a grandfather, twenty years before, by means of abuse of whatever kind of official power or position. All this was doubtless a matter of over-enthusiastic soldiers fired by reforming zeal, but the dangers inherent in this kind of legislation are obvious. How much property the Central Government acquired in this way is not known. Probably none. Further, one wonders how many a worthy civil servant was denied promotion because the person empowered to authorize it was a second cousin by marriage?

Much more sinister was Martial Law Regulation 31,[8] the first section of which required that any person 'who comes to know of any case of bribery, smuggling, black-marketing, hoarding or of anyone having illegally acquired foreign exchange . . . or of anyone having acquired movable or immovable property by unlawful means . . . shall furnish information as soon as possible to . . . the nearest police station.' Section Two provided that a person convicted of any such offence may, in addition to any other punishment, be fined and the court may order that a sum not exceeding half the fine shall be given to the 'informant'[9] as a reward. However, Section Three provided that if the information were found to be false and 'reflective of *mala fide* intent', the informant would be punished in his turn. It is clear that the drafting of some of these Martial Law Regulations was appalling, and positively hazardous to the citizen.

What is conspicuously bad about this legislation was not that informers were encouraged because, distasteful as their existence is, no police force in the world could manage without

---

[8] Replacing Martial Law Regulation No. 30.

[9] With commendable delicacy the Regulation did not use the smearing word 'informer'.

them. The grave defect lay in the supervening vagueness which opened the door to all kinds of abuse and harassment. How can 'blackmarketing' or 'hoarding' be satisfactorily defined for the purposes of such Regulations and where were they defined? How is anyone to show that information is 'reflective of *mala fide* intent' even assuming he understands what this phrase means? In short, after careful study of these Martial Law Regulations, it is evident that they created a good deal of what might be called martial lawlessness.[10]

Reminiscent of Ayub Khan's methods were Regulations Nos. 32, 33, 34, and 35 which covered false declarations relating to income and other taxes, as well as to money and movable assets held abroad secretly. Since these Regulations yielded sums believed to be in the order of Rs. 11 crores as regards income tax and Rs. 2·75 crores as regards foreign exchange held abroad, it cannot be said they were unprofitable to the state, but whether such laws bring about a reform in behaviour is doubtful. Probably, such peremptory measures only teach greater ingenuity in evading taxes and keeping undetected assets abroad.[11]

There were Regulations against adulteration of foodstuffs (up to fourteen years' rigorous imprisonment or a fine or both); against kidnapping (maximum penalty, death); against publications offensive to Islam or 'disrespectful to the Quaid-i-Azam' (up to seven years' imprisonment); and more besides. A curious aspect of these Regulations is that often many of the crimes already had their place in the criminal law and if these Regulations seemed necessary, along with Military Courts for their application, the inference was that previous governments had not been able to enforce the law. But this was damaging to the idea of Martial Law itself for it showed that Ayub Khan had done no better than his civilian predecessors. Hence the doubts about the ability of Yahya Khan's Martial Law administration to achieve any lasting improvement in civic discipline.[12]

---

[10] I keep well in mind that had it not been for Yahya Khan's military courts, many crimes would probably have gone unpunished, as in the case of the girl Khanum. See *FCTC*, p. 250. Still, the point is that the criminal law is not the proper vehicle for the correction of the kind of anti-social activity with which these Regulations purported to deal.

[11] Indeed, having had two experiences of this kind in ten years, it might be said that well-to-do Pakistanis who had not learned their lesson did not deserve to be well-to-do.

[12] These Regulations possess a curious feature. Those issued by Yahya Khan were numbered serially from 1 to 98 and all are available to the public except

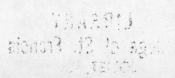

Further, if Ayub Khan's efforts to purge public administration of the evils of corruption, inefficiency, and so on had failed in their purpose, as Yahya Khan had said, what faith could be placed in the latter's assurance that the administration would be 'put back on the rails' and cleaned up?

Yahya Khan's first step to clean up the administration was taken in June 1969. He called upon senior government servants and other officials to submit declarations of their assets on prescribed forms of the most detailed character. One question asked: Do you have any carpets worth more than Rs. 1,000? If the answer to any such question was affirmative, details had to be supplied. This investigation did not, however, apply to officers of the armed forces, a much resented circumstance since the reputation of some senior officers was by no means untarnished. There was also doubt as to how these question-naires should be completed, and lawyers reaped a quite satis-factory harvest from troubled clients in the civil service. The judges of the High Courts informed the Chief Justice of the Supreme Court that they must decline to make such declara-tions since if their integrity could not be assumed, they should not be retained on the bench. This submission was first treated in brusque, cavalier manner by the Martial Law authorities, but later the judges were accommodated and their integrity was assumed.

The next step was publication of Martial Law Regulation No. 58 entitled 'Removal From Service (Special Provisions) Regulation'. Having defined what was meant by a person in the civil service of Pakistan, the Regulation stated that where in the opinion of the authority (defined as the President in the case of a central service official and as the Governor in the case of a provincial service official) a civil servant was ineffi-cient, guilty of misconduct,[13] corruption, had assumed a style

Regulation No. 55. No. 54 is dated 1 September and Regulation No. 56 is dated 27 October 1968 (a misprint for 1969). Between these dates nothing appeared. It is improbable that this is a simple error in numbering, and the question arises: Where and what is Regulation No. 55? Possibly, it provided for a successor in the event of Yahya Khan's demise but why the secrecy? Few people in Pakistan seem to have noticed the omission to publish Regulation No. 55. This fact, in itself, is an example of the irresponsibility that usually accompanies power un-restrained by constitutional safeguards or faithfully observed convention. And if Regulation No. 55 did not deal with the question of a successor in the event of Yahya Khan's death while in office, then what did it deal with?

[13] The definition of 'misconduct' is revealing. It begins: ' "Misconduct" means

of living beyond his means, or was engaged (or was reasonably suspected of being engaged) in subversive activities,[14] he might be dismissed or removed from service, or reduced in rank, or prematurely retired.

Section 3(2) stated that no action should be taken against any person 'except after informing him of the reason' and giving him an opportunity to show written cause why action should not be taken and also an opportunity of being heard in person by a tribunal which, according to the Regulation, would consist of one or more officers of the armed forces.

It could be said that these arrangements were an improvement on the methods of Ayub Khan. Yahya Khan's Regulation No. 58 suggested some kind of system, slender as it was, but there was no machinery by which the public could be assured that it was fairly and efficiently operated. Moreover, it was not known to what extent the answers given in the questionnaires formed the basis on which action was taken.

As in the case of the procedure adopted by Ayub Khan, no one knows how, for what reason, and with respect to what charges, members of the civil services were selected by Yahya Khan's administration for suspension from duty and subsequent action. The number of persons so dealt with was 302 although it is believed some 1,700 names were initially listed. Why the number was so limited and why some notoriously corrupt officials were excluded may never be known although the familiar argument was heard that if too many persons were removed, the public administration might be crippled (as if corruption itself would not cripple it).

Thus, Yahya Khan's machinery was far from satisfactory. Section 3(2) states that no action shall be taken in respect of any persons against whom the authorities had formed an adverse opinion, except after informing him of the 'reason' for it, and from this it seemed that opinion and reason could be equated. Even less satisfactory was the arrangement whereby the fate of a civil servant might rest in the hands of one officer of the armed forces. There was no reason to suppose that such

and includes conduct prejudicial to good order or service discipline, conduct unbecoming to a gentleman, or being involved in industry, trade, or speculative transactions. . . .' The resemblance to Army Regulations is unmistakable and leads to the suggestion that much of this drafting was done by army officers.

[14] The reference to 'subversive activities' is as peculiar as it is vague.

an officer would not be a fair-minded, just, and penetrating judge, but equally there was no reason to assume he would be, and since no one knows who these officers were, the whole business remains shrouded in mystery. Moreover, the Regulation seemed based on the assumption that among the armed forces there was no inefficiency, misconduct, or corruption.

The Regulation said nothing about any explicit publication of: (a) the nature of the adverse opinion formed against any civil servant; (b) the reasons for the action taken against him; (c) his replies to the charges made against him; (d) the name(s) of the officer(s) forming the tribunals; and (e) publication of the proceedings of these tribunals. Everything was done *in camera* and remains secret to this day.

Of course, the familiar argument was heard that in the matter of corruption and misconduct in the civil services the ordinary law had failed. No doubt, prosecutions for corruption were rare and convictions rarer still, especially in the case of senior officials whose power and influence enabled them to destroy evidence, suborn witnesses, and obstruct the enquiries of the police. While this may be true and while it may be the case that the men dismissed were, in the main, deserving of their fate, this is irrelevant to the problem and its solution. No law can be effective if influential people are determined to obstruct it. It follows that in the presence of such a determination the *ad hoc* form of peremptory measures, witnessed in Pakistan three times in fourteen years, has proved as powerless to induce reform as have been the older statutes.

The most solid criticism to be made of these measures is that they have done nothing to purify the civil administration or to discourage the evils they sought to cure. The fact that this method of summary purging grew in frequency is the most eloquently adverse testimony of all. The reason is simple. Such methods are themselves bad, unsystematic, exposed to abuse, liable to error and the negation of justice. An honest man runs the risk of victimization; a corrupt official simply leaves the service, free to live in undisturbed comfort upon his ill-gotten gains. Not only can there be no confidence in such haphazard administrative reform, there can be no incentive in the services to raise standards. On the contrary, with the knowledge that some such fate may await him, there is ample temptation for a civil servant to make the most of it until the axe falls. The solution lies of course in the character of the nation itself, but then character is not built either by passing acts of parliament or by summary purges.

# III

# Initial Political Developments

The new administrative structure, at the top level, resembled that adopted by Ayub Khan in 1958, with the three service chiefs, Lieut.-General Abdul Hamid Khan of the Army, Vice-Admiral S. M. Ahsan of the Navy, and Air-Marshal Nur Khan of the Air Force as Deputy Chief Martial Law Administrators. Between them, they divided the ministerial portfolios.

Lieut.-General Hamid Khan was Yahya Khan's *alter ego* in many ways, beginning with the time when they were contemporaries at the Indian Military Academy from which they were both commissioned into the Baluch Regiment. Both served in the Western Desert during World War II and both were made prisoners of war. This parallelism in their careers did not, however, reflect itself in their personalities and abilities. Hamid Khan was the abler man with considerable intellectual resources in the profession of arms. Ayub Khan reposed great faith in him and when Hamid Khan was appointed Director of Military Training, a brigadier's appointment, the name of the post was changed to Director-General, thereby justifying Hamid Khan's advancement to the rank of major-general. He was on terms of close friendship with Yahya Khan who, while not credited with Hamid Khan's ability, had in some respects a stronger personality or, at any rate, saw his own purposes more clearly. It seems that in later years Hamid Khan's grip on his professional life began to falter. Various reasons have been suggested for this, not excluding the influence of Ayub Khan's administration. It is certain, however, that with the onset of Martial Law in 1969 he was a person on whom Yahya Khan could rely without having to fear any ambition dangerous to himself.

Of the three men, Vice-Admiral Ahsan was, in many ways, the most interesting. He had served with distinction in the Royal Indian Navy during World War II and had been decorated with the Distinguished Service Cross. Later, when

Lord Mountbatten became Viceroy, Ahsan was appointed an aide-de-camp, an association which did not serve him well in Pakistan where Mountbatten's name was anathema. When independence came, Ahsan continued for a time as an A.D.C., serving Jinnah in that capacity. Even in those days Ahsan was regarded as one of the Pakistan Navy's most promising officers and was confidently spoken of as a future Commander-in-Chief. Unfortunately, he was born in the Deccan which did not commend him to some of his Punjabi service rivals and they managed to get him posted to jobs which minimized his time with the fleet and at sea. Thus, he served on the staff of SEATO and, for several years, was Chairman of the Inland Water Transport Authority in East Pakistan, an experience which brought him into close contact with the people of that Province with whom he became popular because of his ability, integrity, and unaffected courtesy. When the time came to consider his appointment as Commander-in-Chief, there were determined efforts to thwart it and it goes to Ayub Khan's credit that he would not deny so competent an officer his just opportunity.

Air-Marshal Nur Khan was a man cast in very different mould. An Awan from Campbellpur District in the Punjab, he was an efficient, aggressive officer with a touch of showmanship. He had the reputation of being tough and competent, with no patience for sluggards or backsliders. He was, for some time, managing director of Pakistan International Airlines and was credited with having done the job well. In the new set-up of March 1969 he was also regarded as the loner, the masterless man. It was noticed that he had taken the portfolio relating to social service—education, labour, public health—and this was interpreted, no doubt correctly, as evidence of political ambition, since through these he could make the most impression with the masses.

Premonitions concerning Air-Marshal Nur Khan soon seemed justified. Within three months of his appointment as Deputy Chief Martial Law Administrator rumours were circulating that substantial differences had cropped up between Yahya Khan and himself. It appears he was creating administrative problems by highly personal methods of working which included the introduction of a few young men from outside the civil service as personal advisers. Already people were expressing the view that he would not last much longer. It was known he had been exerting himself to influence the Annual Budget but had not been able to persuade the Finance Secretary to make such provision for social welfare as he, Nur Khan, desired.

However, Nur Khan was not discouraged. Between 3 and 6 July 1969 he held press conferences to publicize his new policies on labour and education. The principal feature of his labour policy was to fix a minimum wage of Rs. 140 a month for unskilled workers in industrial establishments with not less than fifty employees and located in the Karachi area.[1] Restoration of the right to strike, or to impose a lock-out, abrogated when Martial Law was imposed, was also promised and this promise was kept in the following November. Clearly, the overall impact of this policy, judged from any point of view, was not staggering, and industrialists took the point that unless there were an improvement in productivity, the result would simply be higher prices. Nur Khan himself made reference to industrial inefficiency, but although he described the workers as lazy, he did not exonerate management either.

His educational policy, which appeared in the newspapers of 5 July, was equally limited in scope and was mainly concerned with what were called 'educational objectives', which could be described as an emphasis on technical and analytical skills. One peculiar aspect of Nur Khan's views lay in the statement that, as soon as possible, Pakistan must give up English and have recourse to the national languages.[2] Without their adoption, he claimed, Pakistan could not survive.[3] He underlined the point by reference to the very limited number of people who knew English, by which he seemed to be saying that with so few people understanding it, its utility was clearly limited and could therefore be dispensed with. But, by a parity of reason, it could also be said that if English occupied so small a place, the emphasis on recourse to national languages was unnecessary since national languages were already widely

[1] Equal, at the then official rate of exchange, to slightly less than US $30. This equivalent was illusory since, by reason of the Export Bonus Voucher System, the rate of exchange was artificial.

[2] At that time, Bengali and Urdu.

[3] *D*, 24 July 1969. The language problem is far more complicated in Pakistan than Nur Khan seemed to understand. Events since December 1971 have shown how complicated it is.

used. The point is not simple, and Nur Khan was careful to mention that English would retain its importance.

In West Pakistan, apart from English and the national languages, there were the regional languages. If English were dispensed with in the administration, the higher courts of law, and the universities, would Baluchistan, the North-West Frontier Province, and Sind accept Urdu in its place? Moreover, in commerce and industry generally the most important language after English was, and is, Gujerati. Moreover, there were other disadvantages. The Soviet Union, for example, publishes in English a wide range of cheaply priced text-books covering many branches of study—the humanities, science, technology —and from this it might be inferred that instead of discouraging English, the best course was to encourage as many people as possible to learn it. There is, perhaps, some sentimental aversion to English since it may be a reminder of British rule, but Americans might say the same. However, we have drawn attention to this issue not to argue whether and to what extent the retention of English is desirable, but to demonstrate the kind of confused thinking that became so characteristic of the Yahya Khan régime.

Even if the régime had had its purposes clearly in mind at the outset (which is unlikely) grounds already existed for suspecting it was losing sight of them. Certainly, in his address to the nation Yahya Khan had made special reference to the grievances of labour, of students, and of the peasants and if his Government was attempting some redress, it could not reasonably be said he was trespassing outside the brief he had prepared for himself. At the same time, it seemed that under pressure from Nur Khan he was impetuously embarking on social reforms at a time when his Martial Law administration was barely three months old and when its principal concern should have been civic pacification, the restoration of public confidence, and the production of an acceptable constitution or machinery for that purpose. Air-Marshal Nur Khan was simply creating a distraction from the main tasks. While these premature announcements did not make any significant contribution to the eventual breakdown of Yahya Khan's administration and the dissolution of the old Pakistan, they certainly helped to raise doubts as to the singleness of purpose of the administration. It is strange indeed that elaborate statements on social policy should have been thought necessary at a time when the very existence of a united Pakistan seemed gravely imperilled.

To be sure, there was need for social reform and Nur Khan, with others who thought with him, could well argue that without it the other purposes of the régime could not be achieved. The real criticism lay in the emphasis, the orientation, and the timing. At the moment when Yahya Khan was saying that there was as yet no consensus on the constitutional issue,[4] he was also embarking on reformist legislation of far-reaching character which raised the question whether he and his colleagues intended to remain in power long enough to ensure its implementation. Indeed, he was asked this very question in Dacca. He answered that the next government could change the laws if it wanted to.[5] General unease increased with the departure of Nur Khan on visits to China and Iran. The real object of these visits, it was said, was to get Nur Khan out of the way since Yahya Khan was wearying of his reforming zeal.

Early in that month of July it was learned that Yahya Khan intended to appoint a Council of Ministers or Advisers. People asked how he would succeed in finding members for that Council from East Pakistan, a speculation which itself proves that the state of feeling in that Province was well known. The announcement of a Council was made on 5 August and it comprised:

| | |
|---|---|
| Dr. A. M. Malik (East Pakistan) Health, Labour, and Family Planning | An ophthalmic surgeon by profession, long a placeman in the public life of Pakistan. A faithful work-horse of the Central Government, he accepted any appointment whether of minister, governor, or ambassador whenever the Centre desired to please East Pakistan by throwing something in that direction. |

[4] In Dacca, *D*, 11 July 1969.
[5] Yahya Khan often displayed an unguarded tongue and he was given to replying to a question in a slightly flippant, evasive manner which suggested that he did not know the answer.

| | |
|---|---|
| Sardar Abdul Rashid<br>(North-West Frontier<br>Province)<br>Home and Kashmir Affairs | A retired Inspector-General of Police who had also been involved in politics before the advent of Ayub Khan. |
| A. K. M. Hafizullah<br>(East Pakistan)<br>Industries and Natural<br>Resources | A retired civil servant who had also accepted a ministership during Ayub Khan's Martial Law administration. |
| Nawab Muzaffar Qizilbash<br>(Punjab)<br>Finance | Kinsman and clansman of Yahya Khan. Belonged to the old class of landed magnates. Prominent in politics before the advent of Ayub Khan. |
| N. S. Haq<br>(East Pakistan)<br>Education and Scientific<br>Research | An academic. |
| Nawabzada Major-General<br>Sher Ali Khan<br>(Punjab)<br>Information and<br>Broadcasting | Previously Chief of the General Staff until he quarrelled with Ayub Khan who sent him abroad as an ambassador. Yahya Khan served under him as Deputy Chief. In some ways the ablest of this group, Sher Ali's views on social status and religion clouded his mind. |
| Ahsanul Haq<br>(East Pakistan)<br>Commerce | Another placeman. Son of a distinguished Bengali, Ahsanul Haq was a person of no distinction. He had been Pakistan's ambassador in Indonesia and was afterwards a Director of the Pakistan Tobacco Company Ltd., subsidiary of the British American Tobacco Company Ltd. |

It was quickly noticed that no one from Baluchistan or Sind had been named but, on 15 August, Mr. Mahmood Haroon, member of a well-known Karachi business family, was appointed Minister of Agriculture and thus represented Sind and Baluchistan. In this way representation in the Council between the two wings was equalized, but there was a ninth person to reckon with, namely Yahya Khan, who had reserved for himself the portfolios of Defence, Foreign Affairs, Economic Affairs, and Planning. Thus, not only were there five West Pakistani votes in the Council but all the decisive portfolios were held by West Pakistanis.

The description of these men as mediocrities is not unfair, but Yahya Khan may have found it difficult to discover men to accept office so long as his Martial Law hierarchy remained in being, along with Yahya Khan himself as Chief Martial Law Administrator. In such circumstances, many men would be reluctant to accept an appointment such as Yahya Khan was offering since it might easily turn out to be a form of political suicide, because of the stigma of being associated with a Martial Law administration and also because it had been clearly stated that persons who accepted membership of this Council of Ministers would not be permitted to stand for election to the new Assembly.

Of all the appointments made by Yahya Khan at this time, that which gave the most satisfaction was that of Mr. Justice Abdus Sattar of East Pakistan as Chief Election Commissioner, but the satisfaction was moderated by Yahya Khan's further statement that elections would not be held for twelve to eighteen months. Indeed, there was ample reason to suppose he was in no hurry.[6] During his tour of the country in April 1969 when he met political leaders,[7] Yahya Khan had been extremely non-committal with respect to his political intentions, although he had much to say about cleaning up the administration. Until that had been done, he claimed, free and fair elections would not be possible. His election plans became more specific however, when, in August 1969, he announced

---

[6] To a well-known Sindhi political leader, Mr. M. A. Khuhro, Yahya Khan had said, in July 1969, that elections would be held at the end of 1970.

[7] But not Maulana Bhashani who coyly avoided a meeting by announcing beforehand that he was suffering from blood pressure and had been recommended complete rest.

that the electoral lists were to be ready by June 1970.[8] In the following October he issued a statement in which he said that he would soon declare his views, and repeated his assurance of elections within twelve to eighteen months.[9]

[8] *D*, 31 August 1969.
[9] *D*, 25 October 1969.

# IV

# The Situation in East Pakistan

It has been said earlier that the proclamation of Martial Law in March 1969 was badly received in East Pakistan. The question arises: What was the intensity of that feeling? In attempting some answer it has first to be said that: (a) Sheikh Mujibur Rahman was not exonerated from blame for what had happened, and (b) many East Pakistanis, for reasons we shall discuss, did not desire a complete separation.

Throughout the country it was widely felt that Sheikh Mujib had contributed much towards the imposition of Martial Law because of his hasty pronouncement, on return to Dacca immediately after the Round Table Conference, that the decision to revert to parliamentary government and to direct universal suffrage would not suffice for East Pakistan. He was, in effect, saying that nothing less than autonomy based on the Six Point Programme must be conceded. It was considered that in this way he played into the hands of the army and facilitated their plans for a resumption of military rule. Certainly, as it appears to me, his real error was to reiterate the Six Point Programme immediately upon reaching Dacca.[1] If Sheikh Mujib did make this contribution to Martial Law, he had, by inference, helped to widen the gap between Pakistan's two wings.

The question follows: Did he desire to widen the gap? The view, then held by informed observers in Pakistan, accredited diplomats, and the like, was that since the Sheikh had every prospect of becoming Pakistan's next Prime Minister, he would naturally prefer to govern a country of 120 millions rather than one of only sixty-five millions.[2] Moreover, there were

---

[1] *PO*, May 1969. See, also, the rambling but nevertheless important statement of Nawab Nasrullah Khan, leader of the Pakistan Democratic Movement. *Leader*, Karachi, 17 and 19 May 1969.

[2] Sheikh Mujib's ambitions were, however, for East Bengal, not for Pakistan, and in West Pakistan he had no interest at all. This explains what he really meant when he said he did not want the capital transferred to East Pakistan (*D*, 3 May

ambitious East Pakistanis who, with Sheikh Mujib as Prime Minister of an undivided country, could expect to rise quickly in the administration or, if in industry and commerce, reap many benefits. Why should they wish to see the country split and their own prospects limited to East Bengal? Such hopes were held by many and it was among them that criticism of Sheikh Mujib was heard.

In August Sheikh Mujib visited Karachi with the numerous entourage he affected. The importance of his visit lay not in the prospect of talks with Mr. Bhutto, but with G. M. Syed, the Sindhi leader who, after years of political obliteration,[3] had emerged as a leader of the Sind United Front with a pro-gramme more or less confined to the dissolution of West Pakis-tan into the old Provinces. On 8 August Sheikh Mujib made a highly significant speech in Karachi. He adhered firmly to the Six Points and then returned to the Lahore Resolution of March 1940 with its, by now, familiar reference to states in the plural. He claimed he did not seek the break-up of Pakistan but, on the contrary, a way to make it strong and enduring. Thereafter, it was observable that the Sheikh was getting closer to the Sind United Front and was making challenging speeches reviving old controversies touching the Constitution of 1956 and suchlike matters. When, in the middle of August, the Sheikh returned to East Pakistan, it was evident he had made contacts very satisfactory to himself, not only with the Sind United Front but with leaders such as Abdus Samad Khan Achakzai who also desired the dissolution of West Pakistan into Provinces.

Meanwhile, in the eastern Province events were disquieting. Not only did resentment over Martial Law continue to smoul-der, but food prices were rising menacingly and in July rice was selling at Rs. 55 a maund, close to a famine price. On 7 August the anniversary of the death of Rabindranath Tagore was observed in as ostentatious a manner as possible and in the Province both Radio Pakistan and television gave pro-

1970), but the remark was then interpreted in a diametrically opposite manner. Still, it is also true that the then editor of the *Pakistan Observer* said to a West Pakistani journalist: 'Till now, West Pakistan has exploited us. Now, we will exploit West Pakistan.'

[3] Before partition, G. M. Syed was a member of the Indian National Congress. After partition he was a political détenu for years or was otherwise not permitted to leave his ancestral village.

minence to the occasion.[4] In West Pakistan not even the newspapers made the slightest mention of it, an interesting aspect
of the cultural gap.

The established politicians in East Pakistan were evidently
losing influence and their leadership was passing more and
more into the hands of younger people mostly drawn from the
professional and student classes, with some representation from
the industrial proletariat. Not only was this trend irreversible
but these newly emerging people had clear and new ideas
about political orientation, i.e. leftist and nationalist, and by
'nationalist' Bengal was meant. Student elements were particularly aggressive, In fairness to Yahya Khan, however, it
should be said that the seeds of discontent had been sown long
before, perhaps on the day that Jinnah informed the people of
East Pakistan that Urdu, and only Urdu, would be the national
language of Pakistan.

Dacca University was seriously affected by circumstances
special to itself of which the most conspicuous arose from the
extraordinary factionalism which had overtaken Ayub Khan's
own party, the (Convention) Muslim League, in East Pakistan.
So serious had this become that, in February 1969, twenty-
three members of the party issued a statement condemning
the actions of the East Pakistan Government and appealed to
Ayub Khan to intervene.[5] Considering the moment, it may be
that those members, in asking for Ayub Khan's intervention,
were looking to the future and were creating for themselves an
alibi. This is possible, but there can be no doubt about the
fierceness of the long-standing rivalry between them and the
Governor, Monem Khan.

Seeking student support, the factionalists spread their activities to Dacca University where violence erupted between opposing groups, and a state of gangsterism developed. Later
the *Pakistan Observer* remarked that the University campus had
been reduced to 'an intellectual slum'.[6] The circumstances
prevailing in the University had much to do with the opposition felt towards Monem Khan personally.[7] Such, indeed, was

[4] *PO*, 7 and 8 August 1969. In the preceding May Tagore's birthday anniversary had been celebrated, and East Pakistani newspapers said that Tagore's great-
ness had been obscured in Pakistan on political grounds (*PO*, 8 and 9 May 1969).
[5] The statement appeared in *PO*, 2 February 1969.          [6] 6 March 1970.
[7] In *FCTC* I described Monem Khan as the most execrated man in the country.

the animus that the students refused to accept their degrees from his hands, as Chancellor, and after his departure convocations were held on 8 and 22 March 1970, the first in five years, when some 12,000 degrees were conferred.

In September 1969 occurred a real confrontation in Dacca between students and the Martial Law authorities, and it ended in a complete victory for the students. The trouble began when students announced a meeting to be held in the University, whereupon the Inspector-General of Police announced that for the purposes of Martial Law Regulations, the Dacca University campus would be deemed a public place.[8] The students took up the challenge and said that not only would they hold their meeting but that, thereafter, they would march in procession to the Shaheed Minar, a memorial to those who died in 1962 when protesting against the Report of the Commission on Education. The Inspector-General responded by saying that the University authorities would be expected to report any breach. The atmosphere became feverish, but the Government finally gave permission for the meeting and for the procession (at the same time upholding the Inspector-General's ruling, by inference) but chose to ignore, it appears, student demonstrations occurring elsewhere in East Pakistan.

Not surprisingly, the students took fresh courage. Defiance became more explicit and the cry went up: 'We do not want Agha Shahi', meaning 'We do not want to be ruled by the Agha'.[9] At student meetings, it was openly declared that the right slogan for the Province was no longer *Pakistan zindabad*;[10] that the Islamic emphasis was no longer necessary since in politics the doctrine would be socialism. The military authorities were now in a quandary and it became difficult to enforce

On 14 October 1971 two men went to his house and shot him. He died next day and his murderers seem never to have been apprehended. Perhaps little effort was made.

[8] At that time it was an offence under Martial Law to hold meetings in public places without prior permission.

[9] There is a *double entendre* here. *Agha* is a Persian word meaning 'chief' or 'master'. It is a term of respect. Yahya Khan's full name is Agha Mohamed Yahya Khan Qizilbash and the intention of the slogan is obvious enough. However, at that time Pakistan's Permanent Representative at the United Nations was named Agha Shahi so that if objection were taken to the slogan it could be said the last named was meant.

[10] Meaning 'Long live Pakistan'.

the ban on meetings. Maulana Bhashani said he would take out a procession on 3 October to protest against the killing of Muslims in India.[11]

It was decided to continue the policy of conciliation. On 3 October Yahya Khan's statement appeared excusing students who 'since 15 September' had broken or ignored Martial Law but he added that the Government would not tolerate such conduct indefinitely. The students graciously responded by calling off a strike fixed for 6 October. Shortly afterwards schools and colleges in Dacca were closed for two months and the Governor of the Province, Vice-Admiral Ahsan, went to Rawalpindi.[12] It had become clear that many among the younger groups had decided to disobey Martial Law and that leftist opinion was intensifying. It was also said that illicitly procured arms, manufactured in China, were falling at an increasing rate into unauthorized hands. The visit of Lieut.-General Hamid Khan to Peking was linked by some to this disturbing news and it was believed he was carrying some form of protest. Clearly, there was enough to justify the Governor's visit to Rawalpindi to attend the President's conference on law and order.[13] About this time Sheikh Mujib went to London where he met Mr. Yusuf Haroon and Mian Mumtaz Khan Daultana, President of the Council Muslim League.[14]

East Pakistan's heated atmosphere soon erupted into violence. On 2 November a *hartal* (strike) was called for that day. It ended in rioting in which, according to the official communiqué, six persons were killed, but the communiqué was written in very guarded language and it was not clear whether the firing was that of the police or the army. Incidents continued for the next two or three days and the total number of killed was estimated at twenty-two. It transpired that the

[11] In the preceding month there had been serious communal riots in Ahmedabad in which some 400 Muslims were killed. Of course, Bhashani's real purpose was that as he was in opposition to Sheikh Mujib he had to make his own showing against Martial Law.

[12] The circumstances in which he became Governor of East Pakistan will be related in the next chapter.

[13] *Daily News*, Karachi, 21 October 1969.

[14] This meeting became famous as the First London Plan. Whether there was any plan and what it amounted to is unclear, but there is no doubt that Sheikh Mujib was seeking a political alliance with one of the West Pakistan parties. We shall come to this when considering the question of the dissolution of West Pakistan into its old constituent Provinces.

riot was a clash between Bengalis and Biharis because the Biharis claimed that election registration forms should be printed in Urdu as well as in Bengali. The fact that Urdu was one of Pakistan's two national languages lent substance to this claim, but the Bengalis would have none of it. Sheikh Mujib, who returned from London as soon as the riots occurred, said that *muhajirs* (refugees) who had migrated to East Pakistan must 'Bengalize' and that the only language for East Pakistan was Bengali, and he objected to the use of Urdu in the election registration forms to be used in the Province.[15] These events could only be construed as a rising tide of Bengali nationalism[16] and none of it augured well, more particularly when, in December, Martial Law Regulation No. 60 was issued which stated that on 1 January 1970 full political activity in Pakistan could resume.

[15] In an interview reported in the *Daily News*, Karachi, 22 October 1969.

[16] After March 1971, much was heard of the Biharis, the antagonism felt towards them by Bengalis and their sufferings in Bangladesh where, after December 1971, about 250,000 Biharis are supposed to have expressed the wish to migrate to Pakistan.

The problem goes back to 1946 when fearful communal riots occurred in Bihar and Muslims suffered appalling loss of life. In consequence, many Bihari Muslims fled to Bengal expecting a welcome from their co-religionists. They were not refused but, after independence, community differences soon became apparent and the Biharis were either unassimilable or did not wish to assimilate. They maintained a provincial character, did not use Bengali, and preferred to use Urdu. Social contact was limited and inter-marriage negligible. More important, the Bihari proved to be an enterprising, industrious person and a good worker. Employers showed a marked preference, which created fresh resentments. In 1953 occurred the murderous riots in the Adamjee Jute Mills, Dacca, in which several hundred Biharis—men, women, and children—were slaughtered.

This incident did not, by itself, create any breach (for that already existed), but it did much to widen it. In the period which culminated in Sheikh Mujib's great election victory of 1970, and the events which followed, the Biharis, for the most part, allied themselves with Yahya Khan's government, probably in the belief that the army would prevail. It was an error of judgement in which the Biharis were not alone but they, perhaps, paid more cruelly than others.

# V

# Political Developments at the Centre and in West Pakistan

As we know, at the Centre and, by the same token, in West Pakistan, the most conspicuously active figure was Air Marshal Nur Khan. He was trying to force the pace of social reform, only to be sent on trips abroad because Yahya Khan found him a nuisance. It appeared that he was trying, in the Martial Law Council of Administration, to force himself into second place after Yahya Khan, and that he would like to find his way still further. There were even rumours that Yahya Khan might step aside in his favour.

Early in August 1969, however, the speculative tone changed and it was thought that Nur Khan might shortly become Governor of West Pakistan, with Admiral Ahsan going to East Pakistan as Governor. These ideas had their logic because people hoped that, with his strong personality, Nur Khan would be able to defeat the movement for the dissolution of the western Province; and Ahsan was the most acceptable non-Bengali candidate for the Governorship of East Pakistan. On 15 August these appointments were announced. However, the administrative consequences were far from clear. Would these new Governors continue as Deputy Chief Martial Law Administrators and, if not, what would be their position *vis-à-vis* the Martial Law Administrators in their respective Provinces? This the general public did not know. Neither did the new Governors[1] and the position remained obscure for a fortnight.

Eventually it became plain that there was no point in relying on Nur Khan's powerful personality. He had been cut down to size. As Governor of West Pakistan he was no longer at the Centre; he ceased to be Commander-in-Chief of the Air Force

---

[1] See Vice-Admiral Ahsan's interview reported in *D*, 18 August 1969. Air Marshal Nur Khan remained silent, a significant posture for him at that time.

when he became Deputy Chief Martial Law Administrator, and on 1 September he ceased to hold the latter appointment also.[2] These important changes were the outcome of a meeting at Abbottabad, immediately prior to 15 August, attended by Nur Khan, Ahsan, and a number of senior army officers, and presided over by Yahya Khan. The situation in the country was discussed; the question of how long Martial Law should be retained was examined; and, it seems, disagreement over policy was plentiful. Nur Khan played a perhaps too prominent part, opposing himself vigorously to the ideas of others and just as vigorously advancing his own. A decision to reduce his power was taken by the army, but the Air Marshal was not so easily crushed even if, in the end, he had to go.

On 7 November the right to strike, impose a lock-out, and conduct labour agitation was restored,[3] and the externment order served on the well-known woman socialist and labour leader, Qaniz Fatima, was withdrawn. Perhaps the hand of Nur Khan, as Governor of West Pakistan, was visible in this, although it may well have been an attempt by the Central Government to appease West Pakistan's industrial workers among whom unrest had reappeared. Even before 7 November the law had been flouted with agitation and mass-meetings. At the premises of Packages Ltd. in Lahore the managerial staff in the factory had been besieged,[4] physically assaulted, with two victims badly injured. Strikes proliferated, trouble brewed, and men were arrested for inciting others to violence. By 18 November fifteen strikes had started in Karachi and five in Lahore. There were scuffles with the police, and the West Pakistan Government issued a warning to those guilty of arbitrary strikes and lock-outs. On 19 November Qaniz Fatima arrived in Karachi and was given a tremendous ovation. Thereafter it was but a matter of time for the situation to worsen, and on 22 November the police were compelled to fire on a destruction-bent crowd in Karachi's principal industrial area.[5] At the end of the month ministerial and cleri-

---

[2] So, too, did Vice-Admiral Ahsan.
[3] Except in the case of eight specified public utilities.
[4] Well-known as the *gherao*.
[5] The official hand-out said it was an 'organized band of hooligans'. In fact, it was a crowd of some 2,000 workers who had assembled, while the police were about forty in number.

cal staff of the Central Government in Karachi struck but there was no mention of it in the newspapers. The situation had become serious enough for the President to call an emergency meeting of the Cabinet and of the two provincial Governors.

Industrial disputes continued into the New Year and their effect began to be felt. There was a shortage of postage stamps because Security Printing Corporation workers had been on strike for several weeks. Well-known agitators were hard at work, and a West Pakistan province-wide strike was threatened for 3 February. About 8,000 workers were in virtual occupation of the Dawood Textile Mill at Landhi, some eighteen miles from Karachi, and no less than twenty other major industrial establishments were on strike. On 21 January 1970 it was recorded that on the preceding day no less than sixty-five strike notices had been served in Karachi alone.

On 1 February 1970, only one month after full political activity had been resumed in the country, Nur Khan resigned and was replaced by Lieut.-General Atiqurrahman. The parting between Yahya Khan and Nur Khan was not happy and Nur Khan was required to leave Government House in twenty-four hours.[6] Evidently resignation was a euphemism for dismissal. A rumour circulated widely that Nur Khan had been planning some sort of *coup*, smarting under the treatment he had received from the army. Quite possibly he nourished some such idea, but the explanation seems to lie in his statements on the subject of national languages. It was reported that on 28 January, when addressing the Government College Students' Union in Lahore, he had said that it had been decided to give up English and, by 1975, to change over to Bengali and Urdu. This, he had added, was the first time a specific deadline had been fixed for such a change.[7] It seems Nur Khan was later informed that the question of national language was one for the Central, not the provincial, Government, to which Nur Khan replied that being unaccustomed to reprimands of this sort, he preferred to resign. It is certain that he was uncomfortable with Yahya Khan and, no doubt, Yahya Khan felt the same about him. The question of Nur Khan's views on

---

[6] He packed his bag and crossed the road to the Intercontinental Hotel.
[7] Nur Khan afterwards claimed he had been misreported (*D*, 30 January 1970).

national languages provided Yahya Khan with a convenient opportunity. After Nur Khan had left office, the press was instructed, or advised, not to quote him, and none of his utterances was seen in the newspapers for several months.

As Governor of West Pakistan Nur Khan had continued a policy of ingratiating himself with the labouring and student classes. At a conference of Divisional Commissioners, he gave instructions that no labour-leader or student-leader was to be arrested without his prior approval. These orders alienated the magistracy and the police, and contributed to the increasing civic unrest. It explains why, on assuming office, General Atiqurrahman announced that his administration was determined to maintain law and order. Nur Khan made no further public appearance until his press conference on 2 June 1970, an undistinguished performance conveying the impression of a man untrained in politics and public life.

Within a short time after the re-imposition of Martial Law a distinctly obscurantist tendency had begun to develop. This had much to do with an unconstructive harping on Islam, and during the ensuing months it seemed as if no one could talk about anything else.[8] In July Martial Law Regulation No. 51 appeared which included the specification of a maximum penalty of seven years' rigorous imprisonment for any person who published, or was in possession of, any book, pamphlet, etc., which was offensive to the religion of Islam. How anyone was to decide what was, or was not, offensive to Islam does not seem to have been considered. For example, are views held by Shi'as offensive or intolerable?[9] And what of the views of the Qadian community? Moreover, there already existed abundant legislation on blasphemy, on offending the susceptibilities of classes of persons, etc.

July was fertile in this kind of legislation. The West Pakistan Publication of Books (Regulation and Control) Ordinance was promulgated. This stated that any book previously printed or

---

[8] This must be attributed mainly to the Information Minister, Sher Ali Khan, who confused religion with politics. On one occasion he declared that persons who professed to be socialists were *kafirs* (heretics or unbelievers).

[9] Ibn Khaldun refers to the 'wicked interpretations' which Shi'as put on the traditions. *The Muqqadimah*, translated by Franz Rosenthal, Bollingen Series, XLIII, vol. 1, p. 403. This idea has endured to the present day, and in Pakistan differences between Sunnis and Shi'as lead regularly to bloodshed.

published in another country could not be printed in West Pakistan without the prior permission of the provincial Government—a neat form of censorship. The import of all books, newspapers, etc., originating in India was prohibited throughout the country, and on about 12 July Dr. Fazlur Rahman's book on Islam was banned.[10] Banning books has long been a favourite pastime of officialdom in Pakistan although it must be conceded that in circumstances of widespread illiteracy the Government is faced with a difficult problem. Any book which happens to offend any sectarian prejudice may easily lead to riot.[11] Thus, it is often safer to ban the book than allow it to become an excuse for violence and looting. Still, such expedience is a surrender to ignorance and, in the end, intellectual gagging leads only to disaster.

Other aspects of this tendency boded ill. In West Pakistan a symposium to discuss academic freedom reached the consensus that such freedom must be allowed but only to the extent that it did not conflict with the ideology of Pakistan. It is not necessary to comment upon the hopeless lack of realism in such pronouncements nor on the dangers inherent in them. What is interesting is to compare the attitudes prevalent in the East and West wings for, in the former, there was never an overt and exuberant profession of religious fervour or a use of Islam as a rallying-cry. Thus, in a study of student political activists in both wings in 1968 it was ascertained that of the students questioned in East Pakistan only eight per cent of the total and twelve per cent of the politically competent took pride in Islam and Islamic nationalism, whereas in West Pakistan the corresponding figures were seventeen and thirty per cent. Even in West Pakistan the results are unimpressive, but they nevertheless provide another instance of disparity in outlook between the two wings.[12]

At the same time a familiar target such as free-masonry became the subject of official enquiry and there was talk of banning it. Xenophobia renewed its popularity, particularly

---

[10] See *FCTC*, p. 122, n. 66.

[11] Even the supposed existence of a book may suffice to start a riot. See p. 102.

[12] Talukdar Maniruzzaman, 'Political Activism of University Students in Pakistan', published in the *Journal of Commonwealth Studies*, Leicester University Press, vol. IX, no. 3, p. 239. It is not clear to what extent Hindu students in East Pakistan were involved in this study.

as regards the United States, and in July 1970 there were some
mendacious attacks on American diplomats in Pakistan.[13] These
trends may seem trivial but they are the product of rearward-
looking, narrow, and introverted intellectual tendencies which
have done great damage to Pakistan and have contributed to
a marked decline in educational attainment.

This period of ill-will towards the United States coincided
with Pakistan's flirtation with the Soviet Union and with
Yahya Khan's fresh incursion into foreign policy when he
briefly visited Moscow in June. The communiqué published
afterwards was in the usual lukewarm language but it contained a virtual promise of a steel mill which greatly warmed
the Pakistani heart. Yahya Khan evidently felt he had achieved
a masterly stroke although it was plain enough that all was
contingent upon a settlement with India, a view soon confirmed when, in July, negotiations resumed between the two
countries on the Farrakka Barrage.[14] The foundations of Yahya
Khan's negotiations with the Soviet Union are unclear although
the initiative probably came from the Soviet Union which,
since Tashkent, had become the arbiter of the sub-continent.
Mr. Bhutto rightly observed at the time that every phase of
the Soviet steel mill project could be used 'as a massive lever
to exert pressure on Pakistan and curtail her relations with
China'.[15]

Towards the end of October, Yahya Khan indicated that
he would soon state his views on domestic politics, and he
repeated the promise of elections within twelve to eighteen
months. Accordingly, on 28 November he addressed the nation.
Beginning with such familiar topics as economic problems, and
speaking in his usual deliberate, tight-lipped manner, he went
on to announce his decision to dissolve West Pakistan into its
four former constituent Provinces. He also stated that parity

[13] About that time, Pakistani newspapers were publishing accounts of how the
American ambassador in Pakistan, Joseph Farland, had earlier been associated
with political disturbances in Indonesia, the suggestion being that he might be
up to the same kind of mischief in Pakistan. In fact, up to that time, Farland had
never been to Indonesia. Again, the then American consul-general in Karachi,
Hobart Luppi, paid a visit to the Sind leader, G. M. Syed, not an unusual or
unreasonable thing for him to do at that juncture. This event was also used to suggest all kinds of sinister implications.
[14] See, e.g., *PT*, 4 July 1970, on the next talks with India. The tone was distinctly amicable.
[15] Address to lawyers in Lahore on 6 August 1970.

of representation in the National Assembly, as between East and West Pakistan, would be abandoned and the principle of 'one man one vote' would be adopted, thus giving more seats in the Assembly to East Pakistan than all the four western Provinces combined. He said that elections for a National Assembly would be held on 5 October 1970 and that the Assembly would be required, within 120 days of its first sitting, to draft a new Constitution.

This address was well received in so far as it appeared that Yahya Khan meant business, but the decision to break up West Pakistan sounded ominous. How, it was asked, could Yahya Khan make this decision himself? Was he not making a decision that really belonged to the National Assembly in its constitution-drafting capacity? If so, why was Yahya Khan making this decision in advance? Would not this dissolution place grave limitations on the Assembly's work and thwart whatever might be the majority view on so important a subject? Did not this decision open the door to political mischief, whether in East or West Pakistan, or both? And did not this decision have a bearing on the forthcoming elections? To these penetrating questions many people in West Pakistan added a hearty dislike and intense suspicion of the adoption of the 'one man one vote' principle.

As a first step, on 21 December 1969, Yahya Khan signed Martial Law Regulation No. 60 which authorized resumption of political activity on 1 January 1970. The Regulation stated that no political party 'shall propagate any opinion or act in a manner prejudicial to the ideology or the integrity or the security of Pakistan'. Violence, attempts to seduce members of the public services, exertion of undue pressure on newspapers, interference with the activities of other political parties, possession of weapons at public meetings, propagation of slogans inciting people to hatred for other communities, obstruction of political meetings, processions, etc.—all were made punishable. In particular, Section 10 made provision by which those persons who had been removed from the public service, either by dismissal or compulsory retirement, were debarred from membership of any political party. They were prevented from holding public meetings, taking out processions, etc. The force of this was to be felt later in the year. A further Martial Law

Regulation, No. 61, cancelled Regulation No. 21 which had placed restrictions on public meetings. Thus was the nation poised to resume political life.

# VI

# The Dissolution of West Pakistan

Although there are many in Pakistan[1] who would disagree, I hold that the dissolution of West Pakistan into its four former constituent Provinces was, apart from the shattering calamities of 1971, the biggest single political disaster that the old Pakistan experienced during its troubled existence. By the time Yahya Khan undertook the responsibilities of office the consolidated West Pakistan, clumsily known as the 'One Unit', may have become burdensome for many. Some had never accepted it and others became hostile to it. Moreover, in the closing period of Ayub Khan's administration, it had become evident that irrespective of what he might say,[2] the continuance of the One Unit had become a dominating political issue.

Its urgency was well illustrated when, as early as February 1969, five members of Ayub Khan's own party, the (Convention) Muslim League, all of them members of the National Assembly and all belonging to Sind, requested him to dissolve West Pakistan into its former Provinces.[3] In earlier days such temerity would have received a dusty answer, but the times had changed. A few weeks later Hyder Baksh Jatoi, a leader of Sind's impoverished peasantry, was released by Supreme Court order after thirteen months of detention. This release, considered in relation to the grounds for his detention, was a noteworthy event, occurring a few days before Ayub Khan's departure. The document ordering Jatoi's detention had stated

---

[1] Perhaps also in Bangladesh but for different reasons which we shall come to.
[2] On one occasion, Ayub Khan said that those who spoke of dissolving the One Unit were 'wasting their breath'. See *FCTC*, p. 204.
[3] See *FCTC*, Ch. XI, in which the circumstances are narrated. For the background to the creation of the One Unit, see Callard, *Pakistan: A Political Study*, 1957, Ch. V; Wayne Ayres Willcox, *Pakistan: The Consolidation of a Nation*, Columbia University Press, New York, 1963, and Feldman, *A Constitution for Pakistan*, O.U.P., Karachi, 1955.

he was an 'irreconcilable opponent of the One Unit'.[4] His attitude had never been in doubt, for prior to his detention and during Ayub Khan's Martial Law régime, he had been prosecuted for agitation against the consolidation and had served a three-year sentence. Soon after his release in March 1969 Jatoi, at a press conference, unrepentantly declared that, before all else, the One Unit must go.

He was by no means the only person to oppose the consolidation nor was he the only man to suffer imprisonment for it. Again, in Ayub Khan's time, the Baluch leader, Ghaus Baksh Bizenjo, had been sentenced, at a *jirga* trial held in Quetta Jail, to a fourteen years' term and a fine of Rs. 5,000.[5] Others could be named. Jatoi's release focused attention afresh on the subject and it continued to be agitated after Yahya Khan became President. It was further emphasized when G. M. Syed, another irreconcilable, announced the formation of his Sind United Party which some Sindhi politicians promptly joined. It was with G. M. Syed that Sheikh Mujib had most to do when he visited West Pakistan in August 1969 and it was during that month that Abdus Samad Khan Achakzai, a leader of the Pathan community of Baluchistan, proposed that the Provinces of Pakistan be organized on a linguistic basis.[6]

The part, regrettable and political, played by Sheikh Mujib on this question deserves close consideration. He had early revealed an interest in it and had publicly stated his disapproval of the consolidation. Why did Sheikh Mujib disapprove? And were the grounds of his disapproval related to the causes of discontent among those in West Pakistan who desired the break up?

The answer turns upon the reasons which led three of West Pakistan's Provinces to seek dissolution. It was possible for Sheikh Mujib to argue that, on general constitutional grounds, the consolidation was undesirable and that it therefore concerned East Pakistan, but the more important issue was whether East Pakistan's opposition to the One Unit was founded upon theoretical questions of political structure or upon material

---

[4] Other grounds for detention were that he had called Ayub Khan's government a 'dictatorship' and that he had spoken of Indians 'with some regard'.
[5] See *FCTC*, p. 201.
[6] *Daily News*, Karachi, 16 August 1969. Achakzai was chief of the Pakhtoonkhawa National Awami Party. He was assassinated, in his house in Quetta, in December 1973.

considerations. There is no doubt that the three minority Provinces of West Pakistan, i.e. Baluchistan, the North-West Frontier, and Sind, believed that the material considerations were the most pressing. Their complaint was that the Punjab, as the wealthiest, the most educationally advanced, and the most populous of the four Provinces—its total population exceeded the three others' put together—had used its advantages to the detriment of the rest. The Punjabis got the best jobs, easier promotion, and the best money-making opportunities. Very little had been done to encourage the advancement of the three other Provinces, much less give them their due share in the public administration, in the sweets of office, and in such economic progress as there was. Of course, the Punjab had its answer ready[7] but the main question here is: how could it be said that East Pakistan shared in these disadvantages and how was the alleged selfishness of the Punjab impinging upon East Bengal? Of course, the eastern Province had its own complaints but they were very different, and would probably continue with, without, or in spite of, the One Unit. Thus, the substance of the three minority Provinces' grievance was not relevant to East Pakistan and could not be shared by that Province. With its own sense of unfair exploitation, East Pakistan might express sympathy for the aggrieved Provinces in the west. It might wish them release from the yoke under which they claimed to suffer, but it did not share that yoke.

It was open to Sheikh Mujib to say that, as a Pakistani, the country's constitutional structure was as much his concern as that of anyone else and, further, that the structure of West Pakistan was a constitutional matter of the first importance. But for him to add that the reasons which led the minority western Provinces to seek dissolution had direct relevance to East Pakistan was an impermissible exaggeration.

Sheikh Mujib could not claim that Punjab hegemony in the One Unit lent to it any further accretion of strength at the Centre since, even if the hegemony be admitted, the principle of parity existed at that time to limit its potency. Moreover,

---

[7] See a very interesting, unsigned article on the financial implications of the One Unit in *PT*, 6 February 1970. Probably written by a senior Punjabi civil servant, it shows how important was the financial contribution the Punjab was making to the West Pakistan Province as a whole. This has serious implications following the dissolution in 1970.

3

when Yahya Khan announced that the principle of parity would be given up, then the Punjab, with or without that hegemony, must yield to East Pakistan so long as the latter's representatives in the Assembly worked together.

The reason for Sheikh Mujib's objections was the matter of the party line-up in the National Assembly when the time came. This was a highly speculative matter for Sheikh Mujib could scarcely have foreseen that in the coming elections, his party would gain an unprecedented victory. As matters then stood, Mujib could confidently expect to win a large number of National Assembly seats in East Pakistan, but he could not be certain of any in West Pakistan, much less could he rely on winning so many seats as to give his party an overall majority in the House. In East Pakistan he had an active rival in Maulana Bhashani and there were other parties such as the (Council) Muslim League, the (Convention) Muslim League, the Jama'at-i-Islami, and others which, while posing no serious threat, might well capture a few seats between them.

What really interested Sheikh Mujib was the party complexion of the Assembly after the elections, and he was right in supposing that it might wear a much more favourable aspect if West Pakistan had already been dissolved into its old, constituent Provinces. The reason is clear enough. Such a dissolution would limit, even if it did not entirely remove, the ability of the Punjabis to influence the course of elections throughout the western Province. Since Sheikh Mujib could not be sure of obtaining a clear majority in the House from East Pakistan alone, it was to his advantage to have some affiliation with a West Pakistan party, especially one which had opposed Ayub Khan and the One Unit. But no such affiliation would serve his turn unless that party could be sure of getting seats in the House and he judged, no doubt rightly, that the prospects for any such party would be enhanced if West Pakistan were broken up.

When, in August 1969, Air Marshal Nur Khan was appointed Governor of West Pakistan, it was vaguely hoped by those who desired a continuance of the One Unit that he would prove strong enough to hold the Province together. This hope proved illusory and Nur Khan neither distinguished himself in the governorship nor did he get along with the Centre. Indeed, agitation against the One Unit consolidation increased in intensity and a former Chief Justice of Pakistan, who was advising Yahya Khan, was reported as having said that the One Unit question must be resolved first and other constitutional issues afterwards.[8] This was a disquieting and confusing statement. Did it mean that Yahya Khan and his advisers should settle the One Unit problem themselves and then proceed to other constitutional matters, or did it mean that the National Assembly, when elected, would be required, willy nilly, to settle the One Unit problem first and, thereafter, proceed to other constitutional business? The answer to these questions was provided by Yahya Khan himself when, about a month later, he announced his decision that the One Unit would be dissolved.

This announcement, on 28 November 1969, was not the dissolution itself, but only of an intention to dissolve. Consequently, the matter was in some ways still an open question, and public opinion was still far from appeased—on either side. Although little newspaper publicity was allowed to be given to the subject the One Unit problem was becoming more urgent both in Sind and Baluchistan. The temperature of public opinion was rising and there were clear indications of a propaganda war, underlined by the appearance of a long article on the One Unit written by Chaudhry Mohamed Ali,[9] a former Prime Minister and one who was not only wedded firmly to the One Unit consolidation but was among those instrumental in bringing it about.

In Sind, particularly, the problem had acquired sinister overtones so that it ceased to be a simple matter of dissolution. In Sind, the situation, briefly stated, was:

(a) the influx in 1947 of people from other parts of the sub-continent had wrought great alteration in Sind's population with respect to community and language;

(b) Karachi grew rapidly from a city of 400,000 to one of nearly three million, equal to about one-quarter of Sind's entire population;

(c) after partition, agricultural land in Sind was acquired by non-Sindhis in unfair disproportion.

[8] *D*, 30 October 1969.          [9] *PT*, 3 January 1970.

In 1947 Karachi's population comprised two main linguistic communities—Sindhi-speakers and Gujerati-speakers, with a sprinkling of others. In 1961 the Census showed a population of 2·048 million, of whom 838,499 had migrated from India. Linguistically, the population now divided as follows:

| | |
|---|---|
| Urdu speaking | 1,101,776 |
| Punjabi speaking | 260,747 |
| Sindhi speaking | 174,823 |
| Gujerati speaking | 152,471 |

In short the character of Karachi had undergone profound change and was totally untypical of Sind for, in the rest of the Province the total number of Urdu-speakers was 669,966 and Punjabi-speakers numbered 448,649. Of course, all were Muslims and all Pakistanis but, as the history of the country has shown, these considerations have never so far been enough to create a unified nation.

Moreover, Karachi's expansion in all other respects has given it a place in Sind, not to mention the rest of Pakistan, which is quite exceptional. It is a disproportionately large reservoir of political strength and source of revenue. In 1972, out of a total Central Budget of Rs. 875 crore approximately, Karachi contributed (a) Customs Duties of Rs. 162 crore; (b) Sales Tax Rs. 17 crore; (c) Export Duties Rs. 3·5 crore; and (d) Income and Corporation Tax Rs. 9 crore; i.e. about 22 per cent. For Sind, in 1971, out of taxes and excise collected amounting to Rs. 11·15 crore, Karachi contributed no less than Rs. 8·48 crore.

Lastly, there is the question of rural land in Sind which bears heavily on the question of agriculture. There has long been a stream of Punjabi settlers, mainly from Campbellpur and Mianwali Districts where the land is poor and water is scarce, but the process of Punjabi settlement was stimulated very suddenly in the 1950s when land commanded by the newly constructed Kotri Barrage was being allotted to army pensioners, of whom most were Punjabis, owing to Punjabi predominance in the army. These new settlers also included retiring civil servants whose selfishness was such that scandals ensued and the auction or grant of land to them was suspended.

A similar story can be told of land commanded by the

Guddu Barrage in Sind, completed in 1962. The figures are revealing. Out of 2·934 million acres commanded by the barrage, 598,525 were reserved as state land for disposal on permanent tenure, and part of this area was sub-allotted as follows:

| Allottee | Allocated (acres) | Disposed of by 1971 (acres) |
|---|---|---|
| Defence Forces | 79,500 | 70,797 |
| Local peasants | 272,365 | 185,606 |
| Persons displaced by reason of the construction of the Mangla Dam in the Punjab | 20,351 | 20,351 |
| Persons displaced by reason of the construction of the new capital at Islamabad in the Punjab | 17,229 | 17,229 |
| Frontier tribesmen | 1,656 | 1,656 |
| Retired Government servants | 33,926 | 32,440 |

*Source: Sind Annual 1971.* Published by the Government of Sind, Films and Publications Department, December, 1971

As in the case of Kotri Barrage land, attention was first given to military personnel and civil servants and, as before, allocations to civil servants became so questionable that the scheme was eventually withdrawn. It is worth noticing that whereas, nine years after completion of the Guddu Barrage, areas reserved for military personnel and retired civil servants had been allocated as to 89 per cent and 90·6 per cent respectively, the allocation of land reserved for local peasantry had reached 68·5 per cent. Moreover, the land provided for displaced persons from Mangla and Islamabad went, in the nature of things, to Punjabi-speakers.

These figures apply only to the 598,525 acres reserved for allotment on permanent tenure and, as has been seen, the total area commanded by the Guddu Barrage was intended to be nearly three million acres. However, the area does not come into use as soon as the barrage is finished. There remains the task of completing the canal system, especially the distributaries and minors, as well as land clearance and levelling, road construction, and so on. The point is that when these barrages were completed the first allocations went largely, if not entirely, to non-Sindhis and thus discontent was nourished.

The decision to dissolve the One Unit did not allay all feelings on the subject, and in Sind, particularly, the jealousies, suspicions, and resentments created by the great convulsion of 1947 were still strongly felt. Eventually these smouldering emotions burst into flame. In Hyderabad, in January 1970, serious rioting occurred and the army was called in. Twenty-one people were said to have been injured by bullets, stabbing, etc., but this was an official figure and it may well have been more. Shops were set afire, motor-scooters were damaged, cinemas and petrol service stations attacked. The press note issued by the Hyderabad District administration said that the trouble was between 'local and non-local students', language which is clear enough. It was between Sindhis and non-Sindhis. These events were the outcome of three days of preparation. The Sindhis had been reinforced by armed men coming in from the countryside and they made a full-scale attack on Punjabis and Pathans. The latter joined forces in a Punjabi–Pathan front, and battle was joined.

The Hyderabad trouble continued with a *hartal* on 27 January and with various recriminations against the Deputy Commissioner, the City Magistrate, and the Vice-Chancellor of Sind University who were in various ways accused of taking sides. Maulana Ehtishamul Haq, a Muslim divine and refugee-leader from India, asserted that the Hyderabad riots had exceeded, in their violence, atrocities committed by the Hindus upon Muslims.[10] On 29 January a ban was imposed on public meetings, but the infection spread and a similar ban was necessary in Nawabshah where schools were also closed. Two days later, two Sindhi leaders, Kazi Akbar and Hafiz Syed Mustafa Shah, were arrested for prejudicial activities.

On 30 March 1970 Yahya Khan promulgated the Province of West Pakistan (Dissolution) Order and on 30 June/1 July 1970 the Province ceased to exist. The four former Provinces were re-constituted under their familiar names. In addition, certain centrally administered areas were specified—the

---

[10] *D*, 29 January 1970. The Maulana was given, at times, to language as exaggerated as it was indiscreet. See *RiP*, p. 153.

Islamabad Capital Territory and the Centrally Administered Tribal Areas. The word 'dissolution' rang ominously and it is surprising that a word of better import could not be found but probably no one thought it necessary. One hardy soul, Mir Riasat Ali, Convener of the All-Pakistan Non-Party Political Workers' Group challenged the Order in the High Court, but his petition was dismissed and with the liquidation of the old West Pakistan people were now heard talking sardonically of the day when Pakistan itself would be broken up. Whatever the constitutional *impasse* a few years before, it would have been impossible to have heard such sentiments and, for those with ears to hear, it did not sound well.

The Dissolution Order contained some reservations comforting those who viewed the break-up with dismay. Thus, the Pakistan Western Railway, the West Pakistan Water and Power Development Authority, the West Pakistan Industrial Development Corporation, and the West Pakistan Agricultural Development Corporation all came under the control and direction of the President of Pakistan and since the economic role of these organizations was so prominent, the effect of the dissolution was mitigated, along with the financial implications, since from these organizations large sums accrued to the Government. But this was a transient situation and, having gained so much, why should not the new Provinces ask for more? In due time, after the departure of Yahya Khan, they did so.

The administrative complications which the One Unit consolidation sought to remove immediately reappeared. West Pakistan, instead of being one Martial Law Zone, became four, each with its own Martial Law Administrator and each with its separate administrative hierarchy, whereas East Pakistan, with a population exceeding that of the four new Provinces combined, had only one such administration. Promotions proliferated, as did staff appointments, and the cost of administration increased. In due time, the same was to be true of the civil administration.[11]

As might be expected, the dissolution, far from satisfying those who had clamoured for it, merely encouraged fresh aspirations. Two months after the Dissolution Order, the Syndics

[11] See *FCTC*, Ch. XI.

of Sind University passed a resolution that Sindhi should become the University's official language. A month later a book
appeared, written in Urdu by one Abubakar Khan Magsi,
entitled *Arabic—Pakistan's National Language*. It was a violent
attack on Urdu which the author described as a 'minority'
language associated with the Aligarh Movement and he referred to Aligarh University as an agent of British imperialism.[12]
Much more serious was the controversy between Sind and
the Punjab over the division of Indus water, a dispute only
made possible by the dissolution and by the fact that the Indus
Waters Scheme, a necessary result of the Indus Waters Treaty
with India, was planned at a time when West Pakistan was a
single administrative unit. The urgency of this problem obliged
Yahya Khan to set up an Inquiry Commission but, as with
other inter-provincial disagreements, the problem continued
long after Yahya Khan ceased to hold office.

One of the most distressing aspects of the dissolution was the
chorus of sycophantic praise which accompanied it. Those men
who had 'hailed' the consolidation when it came, now congratulated Yahya Khan on its disappearance. Those newspapers which, in their time, had reserved some of their most
caustic vituperation for men like Hyder Baksh Jatoi and Ghaus
Baksh Bizenjo, now related scandals which attended the unification of West Pakistan. An article entitled 'Let Break-up
Lay the Ghost of Provincialism' actually began with these
words: 'Dismemberment of the administrative One Unit does
not mean the disintegration of West Pakistan.'[13] No doubt, much
depends on what was meant by 'disintegration' but however
much people might find comfort in such ratiocination, the fact
was that the dissolution had given fresh stimulus to every kind
of regional aspiration which, in due course, would find a voice
in demands for autonomy and the claim that the new Pakistan
comprised four nations.

It may be asked, what justifies the description of the One
Unit dissolution as the biggest political disaster prior to 1971?
The reply lies in the reasons which led Yahya Khan to make
this decision and in the consequences of it. His reasons have

[12] *Star*, Karachi, 24 September 1970. Magsi's remarks about Aligarh are worth
comparing with what Dr. Rajendra Prasad wrote in *India Divided*.
[13] *PT*, 1 July 1970.

not been made explicit but some guesses may be hazarded. It seems Yahya Khan was impelled by pressure from all the Provinces except the Punjab. Ayub Khan's inability or unwillingness to recognize the problem had intensified regional and clan loyalties[14] and his relentless pursuit of those opposed to the One Unit had created equally relentless determinations among those who sought to end it. The vehemence with which those who desired the break-up urged it upon Yahya Khan must have suggested a threat of civil disobedience to enforce it. Secondly, there was the idea that if there were no such dissolution, in West Pakistan, the coming elections would be fought on the Punjabi vs. non-Punjabi issue, obfuscating all else[15] and, of course, helping to open the door to an East Pakistani dominated National Assembly.

The first misfortune was that no one's purpose, neither the Provinces' nor Yahya Khan's, seems to have been achieved. Thus:

(a) Sheikh Mujib had no need of any West Pakistan alliance because of his sweeping electoral victory;

(b) The dissolution, far from removing discontent in West Pakistan, only opened the door to fresh controversies;

(c) The desire for provincial autonomy in West Pakistan instead of being assuaged was further stimulated;

(d) In the post-electoral confrontation between East and West Pakistan the western Province no longer spoke with one voice.

By the time Yahya Khan acquired office the possibility of retaining the One Unit had perhaps passed. It is the present writer's view that had the difficulties and discontents been recognized in time, the dissolution would have been unnecessary and the agitation against it neutralized. All that can be said now, however, is that the dissolution opened the door to a myriad of political and constitutional difficulties which did not cease when the country divided in 1971.

---

[14] In 1971, the Baluch leader, Sardar Akbar Khan Bugti, remarked to the present writer that, in Baluchistan, family planning means doubling the Baluch population. (With an area of 125,000 square miles, Baluchistan has a population of about two millions, but this comprises Brahuis and Pathans, as well as Baluch.)

[15] It appears this view was urged by Air Marshal Nur Khan.

# VII

# The Legal Framework Order

The Legal Framework Order (for convenience referred to hereafter as 'the LFO') was promulgated on 30 March 1970 simultaneously with the Order dissolving West Pakistan. It begins by saying that on 26 March 1969, in his first address to the nation, Yahya Khan pledged himself to restore democratic institutions. It goes on to say that he reaffirmed this pledge on 28 November 1969 when he asserted that polling for a general election would commence on 5 October 1970 for the National Assembly and on 22 October for Provincial Assemblies. The last recital states that 'it is necessary to provide for the constitution of a National Assembly of Pakistan for . . . making provision as to the Constitution of Pakistan *in accordance with this Order* . . .' (my italics).

The LFO, therefore, was the first expression of those pledges and it was specifically linked, by recitals, to the Order dissolving West Pakistan. The dissolution Order also stated: 'Whereas for the purpose of making provision in the said legal framework for elections to the Provincial Assemblies and delineation of constituencies for such elections it is necessary to provide for the dissolution of the Province of West Pakistan and the constitution of new Provinces in its place.' The obscurity of this drafting, its incompatibility with such reasons as had been given for dissolving West Pakistan, and the poverty of its thinking deserve notice. It has already been said that at an early stage in Yahya Khan's administration there was cause to doubt his clarity—some said purity—of purpose, and publication of the LFO did much to reinforce such doubts.

On 28 November 1969 Yahya Khan said his intention was to transfer power to the people and he went on to state the possibilities he had considered in order to do this. They were:

(a) The convening of a Constituent Convention to draft a Constitution and then dissolve itself. He, Yahya Khan, regarded this solution as neat but had two objections:

(i) two elections were required, one to provide members for the Constituent Convention and the second under the Constitution evolved, and (ii) all this would delay the transfer of power.

(b) The revival of the Constitution of 1956. He rejected this because, at the time, there had been much objection to it. In this he was right. When that Constitution was passed, the East Pakistan Assembly members walked out.

(c) He could draft a Constitution and take a national referendum on it. He considered this difficult because 'a simple "yes" or "no" cannot possibly be given by the people to such a comprehensive document as a Constitution.'

(d) He could 'evolve a Legal Framework for general elections on the basis of consultation with various groups . . . as well as a study of past Constitutions. . . . The proposal from me would only be . . . a provisional Legal Framework.'

He went on to say: 'After careful thought, I have decided to . . . evolve a Legal Framework for holding elections to the National Assembly.'

These possibilities, and the reasons for Yahya Khan's choice deserve notice:

(a) Yahya Khan assumed that after the Constituent Convention had done its work, it *must* dissolve itself. But what was the ground for this assumption? Could not the Constitution have provided that once the draft was approved, the Convention could transform itself into a legislature and carry on? In fact, this is exactly what Yahya Khan proposed in his LFO, the only difference being that in his case the expression 'Constituent Convention' was not used and the constitution-making body began life as a National Assembly. Mr. Bhutto would have preferred a *Constituent* Assembly.

(b) No doubt Yahya Khan was right in rejecting the 1956 Constitution and, in any case, it was inconsistent with his decision to abolish the principle of parity.

(c) As to holding a referendum on a draft prepared by him, it may well be that a simple 'yes' or 'no' would have been difficult, but there were other possibilities. He could have drafted a constitution and presented it to the elected representatives of the people for their approval or amendment.

(d) As regards the legal framework by which elections were to be held, some advance planning would have been necessary. But what was meant by 'provisional framework'? How provisional? As things worked out, it was not provisional at all, but a kind of steel structure within which the National Assembly was expected to work, thus limiting its freedom of action and incurring the risk of conflict with the electorate's expectations.

The LFO was a document of great importance and occupies a vital place in the history of this period. Its salient features were that:

(a) The proposed National Assembly was to consist of 313 members of whom 300 would occupy general seats and thirteen seats would be reserved for women. Of these, 162 general seats and seven women's seats were allocated to East Pakistan and the rest were divided as follows:

| Province | General | Women |
|---|---|---|
| Punjab | 82 | 3 |
| Sind | 27 | 1 |
| Baluchistan | 4 | 1 |
| North-West Frontier Province | 18 | 1 |
| Centrally Administered Tribal Areas | 7 | 1 |

(b) Each Province was to have a Provincial Assembly with membership as follows:

| Province | General | Women |
|---|---|---|
| East Pakistan | 300 | 10 |
| Punjab | 180 | 6 |
| Sind | 60 | 2 |
| Baluchistan | 20 | 1 |
| North-West Frontier Province | 40 | 2 |

(c) The membership of these various Assemblies was based, as to general seats, on the Census of 1961, and the principle of election would be direct voting based on universal adult franchise. Women's seats would be filled by members of each Assembly voting for candidates nominated.

(d) A member could resign his seat by notice in writing to the Speaker of the Assembly of which he was a member, i.e. *after* the Assembly had met and elected a Speaker.

(e) A member who failed to take the prescribed oath within seven days of the Assembly's first meeting would be deemed to have vacated his seat unless good cause were shown.

(f) The National Assembly would be summoned, for the purpose of framing a Constitution, by the President on such day and at such time as he decided.

(g) Sections 20, 21, and 22 of the Order read as follows:

20. The Constitution shall be so framed as to embody the following fundamental principles:

(1) Pakistan shall be a Federal Republic to be known as the Islamic Republic of Pakistan in which the Provinces and other territories which are now and may hereafter be included in Pakistan shall be so united in a Federation that the independence, the territorial integrity and the national solidarity of Pakistan are ensured and that the unity of the Federation is not in any manner impaired.

(2) (i) Islamic Ideology which is the basis for the creation of Pakistan shall be preserved; and
(ii) the Head of the State shall be a Muslim.

(3) (i) Adherence to fundamental principles of democracy shall be ensured by providing direct and free periodical elections to the Federal and the Provincial legislatures on the basis of population and adult franchise;
(ii) the Fundamental Rights of the citizens shall be laid down and guaranteed;
(iii) the independence of the judiciary in the matter of dispensation of justice and enforcement of the fundamental rights shall be secured;

(4) All powers including legislative, administrative and financial shall be so distributed between the Federal Government and the Provinces that the Provinces shall have maximum autonomy, that is to say maximum legislative, administrative and financial powers but the Federal Government shall also have adequate powers to discharge its responsibilities in relation to

external and internal affairs and to preserve the independence and territorial integrity of the country.

(5) It shall be ensured that
    (i) the people of all areas in Pakistan shall be enabled to participate fully in all forms of national activities and
    (ii) within a specified period economic and all other disparities between the Provinces and between different areas in a Province are removed by the adoption of statutory and other measures.

21. The Constitution shall contain in its preamble an affirmation that:
    (1) the Muslims of Pakistan shall be enabled individually and collectively to order their lives in accordance with the teachings of Islam as set out in the Holy Quran and Sunnah; and
    (2) the minorities shall be enabled to profess and practise their religions freely and to enjoy all rights, privileges and protection due to them as citizens of Pakistan.

22. The Constitution shall set out directive principles of State Policy by which the State shall be guided in the matter of
    (1) promoting Islamic way of life;
    (2) observance of Islamic moral standards;
    (3) providing facilities for the teaching of Holy Quran and Islamiat to the Muslims of Pakistan; and
    (4) enjoining that no law repugnant to the teachings and requirements of Islam as set out in the Holy Quran and Sunnah is made.

(h) The Constitution was required to provide that the National Assembly constituted under the LFO would be the first legislature of the 'Federation' for the full term, and a similar provision was made for the Provincial Assemblies.

(i) Section 24 stated: The National Assembly shall frame the Constitution in the form of a Bill to be called the Constitution Bill within a period of one hundred and twenty days from the date of its first meeting and on its failure to do so shall stand dissolved.

(j) Section 25 stated: The Constitution Bill as passed by the National Assembly shall be presented to the President for authentication. The National Assembly shall stand dissolved in the event that authentication is refused.

(k) Section 27 provided that the interpretation of the provisions of the LFO would rest with the President and that he, not the National Assembly, would have power to amend it.

The LFO also contained a Schedule III comprising forty-eight Rules of Procedure by which the National Assembly was required to conduct itself, but notwithstanding the elaboration of these Rules, there was a notable omission. They contained nothing about voting procedure in the House. They did not specify by what majority the Constitution Bill must be passed—simple majority, a majority calculated with respect to provincial considerations, or a specified majority of all members present and voting. As Mr. Bhutto afterwards remarked: '. . . even in its attempted comprehensiveness the Order failed. There was a patent void as to voting procedure . . .' and Mr. Bhutto concluded that this was, 'as a favour, left to the Assembly to decide.'[1]

Whether, as Mr. Bhutto thought, the matter of voting procedure was left to the decision of the Assembly as a favour, or whether it was left to the Assembly out of sheer mischief in the belief that most of the 120 days allowed would be consumed in arguing over this very topic may never be known, but the omission was certainly deliberate because Section 17(2) states: '. . . in particular the National Assembly shall decide how a decision relating to the Constitution Bill is to be taken.' What reason led those responsible for the LFO to leave this decision to the Assembly may also never be known, but it is certain that if, for example, the LFO had specified a two-thirds majority, it could not have been said there was anything unfair or unusual. A Constitution Bill is no ordinary piece of legislation and nothing could be more appropriate than that such a Bill should enjoy a wider consensus than a simple majority of one.[2]

Moreover, such a provision would have ensured that both wings of the country participated in the majority and the threat of domination by one wing over the other would have been eliminated. But the omission to specify voting procedure, if not rectified immediately, could not be rectified at all, for as soon as the elections were in train, any amendment to

---

[1] *The Great Tragedy*, 1971, p. 58.
[2] The Assembly prescribed by the LFO had 313 seats so that, with all members present and voting, the House could divide 157 against 156.

the LFO relating to decision-taking or majorities would have at once evoked charges of gerrymandering. And if no such specified majority could have been obtained, then it is just as probable there would have been no agreement in the National Assembly on voting procedure and decision-taking.

Since the National Assembly never met to produce a Constitution for the old Pakistan, it will never be known whether, and how far, Yahya Khan's plans, as they appeared in the LFO, would have operated, but it is certain that the Order was no contribution to a solution of the constitutional problem. Quoting Mr. Bhutto again: '. . . the Order contained inherent contradictions'.[3]

Although, in his address on 28 November, Yahya Khan said he would provide a scheme 'in the nature of a provisional framework for holding elections to the National Assembly', the LFO, as finally promulgated, was anything but provisional and went a great deal further than offering a framework for election-holding. It was highly mandatory and purported to set out a number of constitutional matters on which the Assembly was *instructed* what it must do. The LFO stated it had been made by the President 'in pursuance of the Proclamation of 25 day of March 1969 and in exercise of all powers enabling him in that behalf'. Moreover, interpretation of the LFO was a matter for him alone and no Court had power to question his decisions. Only he had power to change the Order and the President reserved the right to authenticate any Constitution Bill the Assembly might agree upon.[4] If authentication was refused, the Assembly would stand dissolved. It appears that it was not necessary for the President to assign any reason for a refusal to authenticate but the LFO is unclear on this point. Mr. Bhutto was probably right when he wrote on this aspect: 'Perhaps it was not appreciated at the time that it would not have been possible for an individual, no matter how great his power, to reject without democratic sanction the decision of the National Assembly.'[5] Still, affronts to democracy were of a piece with the thinking of Yahya Khan and his advisers, and the tenor and spirit of the LFO were entirely

[3] *The Great Tragedy*, p. 57.

[4] Cf. the preamble to the Indian Constitution which states '. . . we the people of India give to ourselves this Constitution'.

[5] *The Great Tragedy*, p. 57.

consistent with what eventually happened in East Pakistan. It is not surprising that the protest which the LFO provoked owed much to the agitation initiated by Sheikh Mujibur Rahman's demand for a withdrawal or amendment of Sections 25, 26, and 27.

From the LFO, it was clear the National Assembly would not be a sovereign body. Its decisions were subject to the approval and authentication of a President who was also Chief Martial Law Administrator. It was just as clear that with respect to certain matters the National Assembly had no choice even if its own views on those matters and the views of the electorate differed from the provisions of the LFO. Thus, for example, Section 20 which states that 'the Constitution shall be so framed as to embody the following *fundamental* principles' (my italics). Some of these principles, allegedly fundamental, are worth looking at.

(a) Section 20(1) required that 'Pakistan shall be a federal republic.' It may be asked, what is fundamental about a federation? Suppose the electorate had desired a unified structure? With what authority did Yahya Khan seek to impose a federal structure? With what purpose? It is true that in previous constitutions the federal structure had been formally adopted but a formal statement is one thing and the implementation of it is another. Thus, Ayub Khan's Constitution of 1962 stated that the territories of Pakistan should form a Federation with the Provinces 'enjoying such autonomy as is consistent with the unity and interest of Pakistan as a whole' but, as was pointed out by a former Chief Justice of Pakistan, the system actually set up by Ayub Khan was not a federation but a decentralized, unitarian government.[6] And, since these attempts had failed, the Assembly might have liked to try something else. Its hands should not have been tied by something which was certainly not fundamental.

(b) The LFO prescribed that 'Islamic Ideology' should also be provided for, as being fundamental. Probably there are people who, holding to a faith or ideology, regard it as fundamental and worthy of some kind of political expression. This is a view to which no one can object. But by no means every-

---

[6] M. Munir, *The Constitution of the Islamic Republic of Pakistan*, All-Pakistan Legal Decisions, Lahore, 1967, p. 70.

one, or even a majority, in Pakistan held that view. Sheikh Mujib's party, for example, desired a secular constitution and when, later, Bangladesh came into existence, the secular position was adopted as one of the four principles of state policy. Thus, even on the issue of Islam, there was no unanimity within the country, and to call for some importation of it into the Constitution was certainly not 'fundamental' for everyone. Similar points can be made about Section 22 which mentioned promoting the Islamic way of life and the observance of Islamic moral standards. Since the vast majority of the National Assembly would inevitably consist of Muslims, Assembly members would hardly be ignorant of these matters or be in need of a reminder about them. By introducing these subjective, indeterminate, and controversial issues, the LFO was simply provoking disputation to no effective purpose.

(c) Much more serious was the provision, in Sections 24 and 25, that if the Assembly failed to frame a Bill within 120 days or if authentication were refused, the Assembly would stand dissolved, while on the important question of what would happen then, the LFO was silent. Whether there would be fresh elections or whether Yahya Khan would prepare his own draft, no one knew. The curious point about this omission, intentional or not, is that in the address to the nation on 28 November 1969, Yahya Khan, speaking with reference to the 120-day period, said: 'I would be happy if they [i.e. the National Assembly] can finalize it before the expiry of this period. If, however, they are unable to complete the task by the end of the stipulated period, the Assembly would stand dissolved and *the nation will have to go to the polls again*' (my italics). Thus, although the omission was not fatal, in that it did not actually prevent the Assembly from completing its task, it provided a source of suspicion as to Yahya Khan's real intentions, especially when it was remembered that in November 1969, he had said there *would* be fresh elections. These circumstances acquired a grimmer hue when, in a radio address on 3 December 1970, just before the elections, Yahya Khan said that if no Constitution were evolved, Martial Law would continue. He may have meant Martial Law would continue until fresh machinery for constitution-making were worked out, but he did not say this.

(d) Perhaps the most important material defect of the LFO was the creation of Provincial Assemblies and arrangements for provincial elections. What purpose this served at that juncture, it is impossible to understand. On the face of it, these provisions showed that Yahya Khan and his advisers had no grasp of their task (always assuming, of course, the purity of their motives and the sincerity of their intentions). The creation of Provincial Assemblies was entirely irrelevant to the purpose of the LFO, which was to provide organization for elections and a National Assembly whose business was to draft a Constitution. Arrangements for Provincial Assemblies at that moment were useless. Who could say what provisions the new Constitution would make for the Provinces? What would be the arrangements for national administration? What reservations and delegation of powers would the new Constitution contain? For not only did the LFO impose limitations on the Assembly's work, but the Assembly could not be sure that its decisions would be authenticated and take effect. The LFO made reference to 'Provinces' but did not specify that, in the new Constitution, Pakistan *must* be divided into Provinces. Following India, the Assembly might have chosen the word 'states' or, in the interests of unity, it might have ventured upon an entirely fresh constitutional structure.

Since the Constitution had not been drafted, no one knew what the powers and duties of the Provincial Assemblies would be. On this issue, therefore, an elector would not know how to vote. In the case of the National Assembly the elector knew, or thought he knew, what sort of Constitution he wanted but as regards Provincial Assemblies the elector would be voting in a vacuum. Reasons for the apparently confused LFO provisions can be suggested:

(i) It was reasonable to anticipate that the National Assembly would provide for Provinces and provincial governments in the new Constitution.

(ii) No injury would be done if provincial elections were held at roughly the same time as the National Assembly elections, and there were certain advantages in doing so: First, there would be a saving of money since arrangements for the National Assembly elections would answer for the provincial; second, the holding of provincial elections would reinforce the promise of a return to democracy and the transfer of power.

(iii) The elections would give substance to the re-emergence of West Pakistan's four Provinces.

(iv) It is possible Yahya Khan agreed to hold provincial elections in response to the inevitable clamour of those with a desire to be elected to something or anything.

(v) The country would be spared a second bout of election fever.

Among the reasons listed above, only one carries any serious weight—the last. In Pakistan, elections tend to be an over-heated experience and the political state of the country suggested the desirability of limiting that experience. The remaining reasons possess little cogency and two of them—the question of expense and of providing opportunities for those seeking prominence—are hardly praiseworthy.

It has been suggested here that in making provision for Provincial Assemblies, the LFO did something both superfluous and irrational. Two more points must be added. The first is that with the election of Provincial Assemblies, impotent as they would be until the Constitution was approved, Yahya Khan nevertheless created additional pressure groups, additional platforms from which distracting and unnecessary political activity could emanate. The second involved a danger that had probably not been foreseen. When Sheikh Mujib asked for power to be transferred to the Provinces, Yahya Khan was able to reply that the suggestion was premature, impolitic, impractical, undesirable, prejudicial to the integrity of Pakistan, and so on. But he could not say that the apparatus did not exist, for he himself had provided it.

The foregoing criticism of the LFO seems to me incontrovertible, but there are other objections which are open to dispute. They are as follows:

(e) In providing for elections on the basis of population, Yahya Khan abandoned the principle of parity of representation in the National Assembly as between East and West Pakistan. So doing, he gave up what, in West Pakistan and particularly in the Punjab, was regarded as fundamental and irrefragable and although East Pakistan had previously accepted the parity principle, it had done so with reservations which developed into grievances. Of course, if democratic representation means anything, it must mean representation directly proportional to population. The parity principle meant, in effect, the disfranchisement of a number of East Pakistani electors. In giving up this principle, Yahya Khan was not only acting in accordance with the democratic idea, he was also answering an East Pakistani grievance. Nevertheless, many in West Pakistan saw grave danger in abandoning the parity principle. It would lead, they argued, to a permanent majority for East Pakistan in the National Assembly, enabling it to carry all measures it desired, with West Pakistan powerless to resist. Therefore, measures unfavourable to West Pakistan or disliked there would in turn become grievances dangerous to national unity. This assumed that all East Pakistan members would work together and vote *en bloc* and that an overall majority of twenty-five in the House would always provide East Pakistan with a working margin. However, it must be added that not all West Pakistanis shared this view and some held that giving up the parity principle would mitigate East Pakistan's grievances.

(f) Mr. Bhutto afterwards suggested that other methods could have been adopted. Either the principles of a new Constitution could have been determined by discussion among political leaders and confirmed by a national referendum, whereafter a Constitution Commission could have been appointed to prepare a draft; or the principles, likewise determined, could have found constitutional form through a Constituent Assembly.[7] Whether these ideas, interesting as they are, would have facilitated agreement on principles and on the question of autonomy (to which Mr. Bhutto made special reference) it is impossible to say. It must be remembered that Mr. Bhutto wrote this *after* 25 March 1971 when East Pakistan was virtually lost. As to agreement between political leaders on the basis for a constitution, Sheikh Mujib had made it clear that he would not give way over the Six Points. The expression 'Constituent Assembly' certainly appears more appropriate than the name used in the LFO, but 'Constituent Assembly' had ominous undertones for Pakistan. It called up memories

[7] *The Great Tragedy*, p. 59.

of those pre-1958 men who, for eleven years, did little except perpetuate their existence.

(g) It was also Mr. Bhutto's opinion that to leave the question of autonomy undecided was a serious mistake.[8] He rightly argued that the election in East Pakistan was allowed to be fought on this divisive issue and it was obvious that the question of provincial autonomy ranked high in everyone's mind. Yahya Khan might well have replied that his LFO made specific reference to maximum autonomy for the Provinces and, further, that he had taken precautions to ensure that no solution of the autonomy problem would be acceptable unless the result conformed to Section 20 of the LFO. But there is much substance in what Bhutto wrote because there is a vast gap between stating 'all powers shall be so distributed . . . that the Provinces shall have maximum autonomy' and working out the mechanics of that distribution.

(h) Soon after the LFO was promulgated, it was said that instead of requiring the National Assembly to prepare a Constitution Bill for submission to him, Yahya Khan should have had a Bill drafted and placed before the Assembly as a basis for discussion, with liberal powers of amendment. On this, Yahya Khan's purpose seems clear. He did not want it said that he was, in the least degree, following his predecessor. The National Assembly should be free to decide what it wanted with no pressures of any sort from him.[9] The idea was not unworthy and had its roots in Pakistan's history, but it was unsound. A leader with political responsibilities must lend a sensitive ear to the people's voice—and this is probably true even in the most naked of tyrannies—but a leader must also lead and there are moments when leadership is more important than accommodation to popular sentiment. In a situation calling for such discrimination, the choices may be very delicately balanced and it is easy to choose wrongly as, in the present instance, Yahya Khan did. Proof of this error lies in the fact that, in the end, Yahya Khan found himself obliged to produce his own draft. Allowing the liberal powers of amendment already mentioned, it does not seem that Pakis-

---

[8] Ibid.
[9] Bearing in mind the terms of the LFO, the measure of freedom in this respect may be doubted.

tan's democratic aspirations would have suffered unduly had Yahya Khan produced a draft Constitution Bill because (a) his own LFO indicated clearly the kind of constitution he would be likely to produce; (b) he knew, roughly, the kind of parliamentary system that would be acceptable; and (c) there is, after all, a great deal in any constitution which automatically writes itself—mechanics of government, judiciary, civil services, election.

Such, then, was the LFO, the 'provisional framework' through which Pakistan was to enjoy, for the first time, general elections based on universal adult suffrage, with representation based on population. It was an ill-conceived, ill-thought-out, rickety affair. One of its main blemishes was the suspicion, which its terms created, that the National Assembly was not intended to succeed in its task. The prospects of a happy outcome were small and the promise of fierce controversy ample.[10]

[10] Of course, Yahya Khan was dependent on others for advice, especially on legal and constitutional matters. It is evident that some of this advice was poor. One instance may suffice. The National Press Trust, created by Ayub Khan, was disliked by the public and by the profession of journalism because it was a combination of newspapers controlled by the Government. A notorious part of Ayub Khan's propaganda machine, it was hoped that with Ayub Khan's departure it would be dissolved. In Dacca, in January 1971, Yahya Khan was taxed with this and he replied that the National Press Trust was a charitable trust established under the law and that the Government had no power to 'disband' it. He added that the National Press Trust had nothing to do with the Government. At this conference, Mr. Syud Ahmed, Secretary, Ministry of Information, said that this opinion had been given by the Ministry of Law.

Whether or not Yahya Khan, as President, could be equated with the Government, it is strange that a man with powers enough to dissolve the One Unit and promulgate an LFO which purported to direct the National Assembly as to the form and content of the Constitution had no power to dissolve the National Press Trust or, it seems, any means by which such powers could be acquired or created. The National Press Trust was apparently beyond the reach of Pakistan's sovereignty.

# VIII

# The Party Line-up—
# Electioneering, 1970

After the 1970 elections it became customary for Mr. Bhutto
to refer to three parties in Pakistan—Sheikh Mujib's Awami
Party, his own Pakistan People's Party, and the armed forces
as represented by the Martial Law administration. More than
once he said that if agreement were possible between President
Yahya Khan, Sheikh Mujib, and himself, 120 days would not
be needed in which to complete a new Constitution.[1] In treat-
ing the armed forces (which, as we have said, meant the army),
as politically involved, Mr. Bhutto had ample justification, but
his explicit references to this and to the necessity for agreement between Yahya Khan, Sheikh Mujib, and himself, instead of just Mujib and himself, was perhaps unwise. While the
political involvement of the armed forces could not be gainsaid,
the emphasis he put on it by himself without Mujib's endorse-
ment was unfortunate. We will discuss this later.

Our immediate concern here is with the complexion of politics by reference to the party contestants and to others who
entered the field when full political activity resumed. There
are various ways of grouping them. One is by territorial status,
i.e. by the influence wielded by the party in either or both
wings of the country. Another is by the number of candidates
fielded. Yet a third is by the colour of the party manifesto.

At the beginning of 1970 these matters were largely conjectural. The political outlook of each party could be estimated
with fair accuracy, but what territorial status and what strength
in the constituencies the principal parties actually possessed
could not be known until nomination day. We will anticipate
these discoveries since, with the knowledge nomination day
provided, it became easier to interpret what happened in the
months preceding.

[1] *D*, 14 January and 1 February 1971.

When nominations for election to the National Assembly were received, no less than twenty-five different parties were represented. To these must be added 319 independent candidates of whom 210 were in West Pakistan and 109 in the eastern Province. In the western Provinces there was a total of 901 candidates for 138 seats and in East Pakistan there were 769 candidates for 162 seats (women's seats excepted). In the western Provinces the eagerness of independents was quite remarkable. Thus, in the Provincial Assembly elections in the Punjab there were twenty-three independent candidates in Bahawalpur II (Constituency No. 164) out of a total of twenty-five. Of the twenty-five parties nominating candidates for the National Assembly, thirteen fielded less than ten candidates and of the other twelve, the maximum number of candidates put into the field by any party was that of Sheikh Mujib's Awami League which nominated 169. Thus there was not a single party going to the poll with anywhere near one candidate for every Assembly seat. In earlier months this was not known but when nominations were received it became obvious at once that there was no possibility of any party securing an overall majority in the House based on national territorial status.

This question of territorial status deserves further examination. The nomination figures are interesting and, as events proved, were prophetic.

| Party | Candidates in E. Pakistan | Candidates in W. Pakistan |
| --- | --- | --- |
| Awami League | 162 | 7 |
| Jama'at-i-Islami | 69 | 79 |
| Convention Muslim League | 93 | 31 |
| (Qayum) Muslim League | 65 | 67 |
| Pakistan People's Party | nil | 119 |
| Council Muslim League | 50 | 69 |
| Pakistan Democratic Party | 81 | 27 |
| Jama'at-i-Ulema-i-Pakistan | 13 | 90 |
| National Awami Party (Wali Khan Group) | 36 | 25 |
| National Awami Party (Bhashani Group) | 15 | 5 |

From these figures, it is clear that the only parties that could claim an equal interest in both wings were the Jama'at-i-Islami, the Council Muslim League, and the Qayum Muslim League. There were others with as many or more candidates seeking election, but every one of them was regional with no strong attachments in all Provinces. The division between East and West was marked and ominous. Clearly, these observations apply with special force to the two parties which emerged victorious—the Awami Party in the East and the Pakistan People's Party in the West. To some extent, this situation was due to the splitting of the Muslim League by Ayub Khan[2] for had this not happened it is certain that the League, a party rooted in both wings of the country, would have enjoyed a far greater presence in the elections than did the splinter groups into which the League had more or less degenerated. Indeed, during the months preceding the elections, the possibility of a unification of these groups was hoped for by many as it was thought that a unified Muslim League would have a far-reaching impact.[3]

The distribution of candidates was a fair guide to assessing the territorial status of the parties and to their prospective strength in the Assembly, since the number of candidates fielded would have a bearing on representational strength. The third criterion was the colour of the party manifesto which requires some detailed consideration.

(a) *Awami League*: Sheikh Mujib was considered to be a middle-of-the-road man. He had connections with business and was reputed to enjoy the friendly interest of the United States of America.[4] However, as earlier mentioned, politics in East Pakistan were changing, with a drift to the left and the Awami League was no exception.

(b) *Jama'at-i-Islami* and *Jama'at-i-Ulema-i-Pakistan*: Their policies were founded upon Muslim orthodoxy and the drift was conservative and rightist.

(c) *Convention Muslim League, Council Muslim League, Pakistan Democratic Party*: Middle-of-the-road. Conventional politics.

[2] See *FCTC*, pp. 19–21.
[3] *Pakistan Economist*, Karachi, 20 March 1971, p. 20.
[4] In Dacca, in March 1970, it was said that U.S. Embassy officials were speaking openly in favour of Mujibur Rahman.

(d) *National Awami Party* (Wali Khan Group): Leftist with Moscow leanings. Secular in outlook.

(e) *National Awami Party* (Bhashani Group): Leftist with Peking leanings. Bhashani's movement was rooted in East Pakistan's peasantry but although he had a great gift for organizing 'movements', his position on nomination day revealed unexpected weakness.

This leaves us with the Pakistan People's Party founded by Zulfikar Ali Bhutto and the Muslim League founded by the North-West Frontier politician, Abdul Qayum Khan.

(f) *Pakistan People's Party* was founded in November 1967 by Mr. Bhutto with the name 'People's Party'. The word 'Pakistan' was added later. After his differences with Ayub Khan, Bhutto remained quiet for some time and his political future was the subject of speculation. The obvious move would have been to join some party in opposition to Ayub Khan but, eventually, he launched his own Party with the slogans:

> Islam is our Faith
> Democracy is our Polity
> Socialism is our Economy
> All Power to the People

With a characteristic display of energy, flamboyance, and vehement oratory Bhutto rapidly made an impact in West Pakistan, but made little progress in the eastern wing. On 9 March 1969, only a short time before Yahya Khan announced a resumption of Martial Law, Bhutto and East Pakistan's Maulana Bhashani signed an agreement to work together for, *inter alia*, the establishment of socialism in conformity with the ideology of Pakistan and the elimination of foreign interference, which would include withdrawal from SEATO and CENTO. The arrangement was soon revealed as a dead letter. The emergence of the People's Party as the pre-eminent political organization in West Pakistan will be considered later.

(g) The Muslim League founded by Abdul Qayum Khan in May 1969 was first called the Quaid-i-Azam Muslim League. When setting up this new League, he invited to Abbottabad, in West Pakistan, such disparate ele-

ments as Hasan Mahmood of Bahawalpur; Qazi Qader
and Wahiduzzaman, both of East Pakistan and both
inveterate enemies of Monem Khan, former Governor
of that Province; Pir Pagaro of Sind; Fakhruddin Valika,
a prominent Bohora businessman of Karachi; and lesser
personalities. There are grounds for supposing (and further reference will be made to them) that Qayum Khan
was acting at the behest of the Martial Law administration, the purpose being to bring about the amalgamation of the three Leagues. Thus, without openly coming to terms with the (Council) and (Convention) Muslim
Leagues, parties which the Martial Law administration had by implication denounced, the same administration hoped to create a unified Muslim League with
all the nationwide political advantages accruing from it.
Thus, at a very early stage in the history of his new
party, Qayum Khan called for an amalgamation of the
three Muslim Leagues, but aware of the ascendancy he
was likely to enjoy by virtue of his association with
Yahya Khan's administration, notably in the person of
Nawab Muzaffar Khan Qizilbash and General Sher Ali
Khan, the two older Leagues hesitated.

In Qayum Khan, a seasoned politician, Yahya Khan's administration hoped to find a personality who might revivify the
Muslim League and build up a countrywide party whose policy
would be moderate, rightist, and devoted to the idea of a
firmly integrated Pakistan. For this reason, and with such support, it appeared that although he failed to engineer a unification Qayum Khan was able to field, on nomination day
some seventeen months later, no less than 132 candidates. But
all this required money. The question of the origins of the funds
then arose, which, in turn, raised the question of the considerable sums accumulated by Ayub Khan's (Convention) Muslim
League.[5]

In Martial Law Order No. 14, Yahya Khan's Government
stated that there was reason to believe these funds were being
misused, and as the Order was dated 12 June 1970, i.e. in the
middle of the election campaign, the inference was that the
money was being used to influence the elections in a way the

[5] See *FCTC*, p. 75.

administration did not like. The Order proceeded: 'No person
shall henceforward operate the accounts of the said funds *except
in accordance with orders issued by me*' (i.e. the Chief Martial Law
Administrator) (my italics). Order No. 15, dated 3 August 1970,
appointed a Committee to enquire into the 'affairs of the funds
of the Pakistan Muslim League commonly known as the Convention Muslim League'. The outcome of this enquiry seems
not to have been made public but members of the League
tried, through the courts of law, to ascertain what was being
done with the money. The inference was that the funds were
neither completely frozen nor totally inaccessible but were, in
terms of Martial Law Order No. 14, at the disposal of the Chief
Martial Law Administrator. The nature of any disposition remained concealed. The outcome of these legal proceedings is
obscure and what has happened to the money since remains
unknown.

It is certain that Yahya Khan's administration sought funds
for political purposes and, in this, the name of Major-General
Ghulam Umer was often mentioned. A former Director of Military Intelligence and, in Yahya Khan's administration, Chairman of the National Security Council, Ghulam Umer played
an intensely political, and rightist, role. In doing so, he succeeded in making himself hostile to Bhutto. Ghulam Umer
belonged to that school of senior officer which *desired* political
involvement in the sincere belief, perhaps, that only thereby
could Pakistan and its ideology be truly secure.

There were other considerations. Sheikh Mujib was suspect
and the Six Points utterly unacceptable. The fact that Ayub
Khan had been compelled to withdraw the Agartala proceedings[6] did not, to the armed forces, suggest innocence. Indeed, those three members of the Civil Service of Pakistan who
had stood trial in that case and had been released along with
the others, were nevertheless compulsorily retired by Yahya
Khan in a Martial Law Order dated 30 July 1970, again, it
will be noticed, during the election period.

The administration was hostile to Zulfikar Ali Bhutto and
his People's Party with its slogan 'Socialism is our economy'.
At the outset of the political campaign Bhutto and his party
were disfavoured and it is clear the administration never fore-

[6] See *FCTC*, p. 189.

saw with what energy and success Bhutto would build up his organization. Possibly, in the early days of 1970, Bhutto himself did not expect such rapid progress and it is also possible that, in those days, the prospect of October elections did not appeal to him. That a campaign against him had been organized soon became apparent. At the beginning of March 1970 113 of Pakistan's *ulema* published a *fatwa* that socialism was *kufr*.[7] This drew from J. A. Rahim, a founder-member of the People's Party, a retort condemning the *fatwa*, describing it as part of a Jewish conspiracy to undermine Islam.[8] But the campaign against socialism continued and slogans appeared on the walls such as *Socialism kufr hai. Muslim millat ek ho*.[9] The anti-left movement continued, quite clearly with official sanction.[10]

As Minister of Information, Sher Ali Khan was able to influence the Press and, in particular, the National Press Trust —the Government-controlled group of newspapers—which came directly under his jurisdiction. Sher Ali desired to make certain staff changes which the Chairman of the Trust—Aziz Ahmed, a retired civil servant—was not prepared to carry out. Aziz Ahmed was replaced by a former Chief Justice of Pakistan, S. A. Rahman, known for his strong attachment to the Jama'at-i-Islami. His views were much more congenial to the Minister and, in April 1970, an opportunity to prove this occurred in West Pakistan when a strike was organized by journalists. It was an ill-conceived, ill-organized, ill-contrived affair and resulted in an anti-left purge under S. A. Rahman's direction.

By contrast, others were making great play of Islam and, in May, on the occasion of *'Id-i-Milad* (the birthday of the Prophet) Yahya Khan issued a statement calling on everyone not to injure the ideology of Pakistan by word or deed. This was followed, a week later, by Shaukat-i-Islam Day (Glory of Islam), organized by the Jama'at-i-Islami. A great procession was taken out and the perceptible targets were Zulfikar Ali

[7] *Fatwa* means an interpretation of the religious law, a juris-consult. *Kufr* means heresy, unbelief.

[8] *Daily News*, 3 March 1970.

[9] Socialism is heresy. Let the Muslim people remain one.

[10] Later, Mr. Bhutto openly charged Sher Ali Khan and Mahmood Haroon, both Ministers in Yahya Khan's Government, with 'working openly against the yearlong election campaign' (*The Great Tragedy*, p. 61). Relations between Bhutto and Sher Ali were particularly harsh and, having the nimbler tongue, Bhutto rarely missed the opportunity of a telling gibe.

Bhutto and Maulana Bhashani. In West Pakistan reports of this occasion were given headline treatment, but in East Pakistan newspapers were distinctly moderate.[11]

Such were the prevailing attitudes. It is important to trace the course of developments as parties made their appeal to the electorate and fought their tactical battles. Not surprisingly, Maulana Bhashani provided the most extreme and the most colourful performance, largely a repetition of his tub-thumping, arm-flourishing technique in the last days of Ayub Khan's administration. Conscious of the essential weakness of his position and his inability to field a politically effective number of candidates, Bhashani inaugurated a peasants' conference at Tangail, in East Pakistan, with the slogan 'Food before elections'. At this conference, a Peasants' Volunteer Movement was established. Two of its features were that members wore red caps and raised the slogan 'We want red Islam'.[12] Three months later, Bhashani visited West Pakistan and, on arrival at Lahore, declared all wealth must be nationalized with not a penny in private hands.[13] His themes increased in severity and even if his election prospects remained obscure, there could be no doubt about the interest he attracted.

Having toured West Pakistan in a special train, called the *Kisan* (peasant) *Express*, he held a meeting at Toba Tek Singh, drawing a crowd of some 40,000 which, for Toba Tek Singh, is a big crowd indeed. Clearly, people had flocked from the countryside to hear this fiery and bearded friend of worker and peasant. Bhashani reiterated his theme of 'Food before elections' and said that if the Government tried to force elections on the people, he would start a guerrilla war for which purpose he claimed to have 30,000 armed men.[14] He called for a nationwide strike on 20 April to condemn American imperialism, feudalism, capitalism, *and* the work of Indian agents in Pakistan. He wanted factories, farms, etc., to be handed over to the people and demanded 85 per cent of the seats in the National Assembly for the peasants, ten per cent for urban workers, and the rest 'he was not troubled about'. The entire

---

[11] See, e.g., *PO*, 1 June 1970.
[12] During the labour disturbances in Karachi in 1972 workers greeted each other with the words *Surkh salaam* meaning 'red salaam'.
[13] *D*, 22 March 1970.
[14] See reference to import of arms from China into East Pakistan in Ch. IV.

performance, ludicrous and irrelevant, was intended to demonstrate his personal hold on the people, although, at the same time, Bhashani desperately hoped the elections would not be held since his defeat in East Pakistan by Sheikh Mujib was certain.

In the following month Bhashani announced a *jehad* (holy war) for socialism. 'Don't burn the Adamjee jute mill!' he exhorted the workers. 'Burn Adamjee!'[15] However, notwithstanding his attachment to socialism, Bhashani did not neglect Islam and his next publicity-winning manoeuvre was an appeal for funds for his Islamic University of Santosh, East Pakistan. In September Bhashani paid a sudden visit to West Pakistan where he met Yahya Khan. This, and the mystery surrounding his visit, aroused many suspicions among those who remembered Bhashani's performances in the days of Ayub Khan.[16] Certainly from the point of view of Yahya Khan's administration it was unwise since Yahya Khan was at once thought to be seeking means of countering Sheikh Mujib. The entire affair drew bitter comment from Bhutto.[17]

What Yahya Khan desired of Bhashani seems to be unknown, but Bhashani is supposed to have said that as an old man, well past eighty, who had made his contribution to the Pakistan Movement and to Pakistan, he was not interested in the elections. All he wanted was food, clothing, shelter, and employment for the poor and, as usual, there was a special word for the peasants among whom he desired land to be distributed. If, and so long as, the armed forces worked for these objectives, he would be ready to co-operate and any fighting words about strikes, *gherao*, etc., should be treated as ordinary political window-dressing. None of this has been publicly documented and the best that can be said about it is that it is entirely consistent with Bhashani's simplistic attitude to politics and to his suspect approach during the Ayub Khan era and even before.

Some months later Bhashani somersaulted again, calling for an independent, sovereign East Bengal. This, coming on the

---

[15] The name refers to a pre-eminent family group of industrialists. Their jute mill in Dacca is one of the largest in Asia. It was afterwards nationalized by the Bangladesh Government.

[16] Cf. *FCTC*, pp. 71–2.

[17] *PT*, 1 October 1970.

eve of the elections, was clearly intended to steal some of Mujib's thunder. It availed him nothing and he was crushingly defeated, but by no means silenced. He continued to clamour for East Pakistan's independence with the threat that until it was won, he would campaign for the boycott of goods manufactured in West Pakistan. Eventually, in the fateful month of March 1971, Bhashani pledged full support for Sheikh Mujib but it is improbable that anyone was taking any notice. His true importance, and for whom, may be judged by the fact that in spite of his inflammatory calls for violence in both East and West Pakistan and the fact that he was the first to raise the cry of independence for East Bengal, he was neither molested nor arrested.

Although in all this Bhashani cuts no admirable figure, he was not quite so inconsiderable in politics as may appear. The truth is that he was no politician, in so far as that means organizing a party with an apparatus and a programme. A pietist of altruistic temper, he was deeply imbued with a sense of the miseries of the poor and the selfishness of the rich. Although not without a certain craft himself, it is probable he was exploited by self-seeking persons. His temperament combined simplicity with cunning and a love of self-advertisement. He was never able to achieve office and was crushed by Mujib, but he was never inconspicuous and he played an important role in creating—in the masses and especially among the rural poor—a political awareness with particular reference to 'socialism' which they had not previously possessed.[18]

When political activity resumed on 1 January 1970 the parties at once flung themselves into unrestrained political conflict, but they still did not know Yahya Khan's mind for although he had promised elections in October, the LFO had not yet been published. Quite possibly he noticed with dismay that from the outset the interparty going promised to be rough. Within a couple of weeks of resumption of political life, the note of vilification between parties became evident and seemed likely to rise in acerbity. Fazlul Qader Choudhury, who inherited Ayub Khan's mantle as leader of the (Convention) Muslim League, complained of accusations against his party

---

[18] About Maulana Bhashani, see also *FCTC*, pp. 174–5. The word 'socialism' is put in inverted commas here as it is not clear what the Maulana meant by it.

concerning the huge funds it had collected and said that 'a certain gentleman addressing big meetings' had received a sum of Rs. 1·17 lakhs from (Convention) Muslim League Funds.[19] Next day, Bhutto denied ever having received any such amount from those funds. Shortly after this, physical violence began when, in Dacca, there was a collision between Jama'at-i-Islami workers holding a meeting at the Paltan Maidan, and those who objected to criticism of Sheikh Mujib and Maulana Bhashani. One person was killed and about 400 injured. Next day, 19 January 1970, there was the usual protesting *hartal* and one more person died.

As time passed the situation became less and less assuring. Wrangling and bickering, in which attacks on personalities predominated, grew in intensity and the familiar cry went up that foreign Powers were interfering in the elections. On 1 April, at Sanghar, some followers of Pir Pagaro attacked a People's Party procession led by Bhutto, and one man died of gunshot wounds. Bhutto claimed his life had been spared by a miracle showing that Allah intended him 'to serve his people' but the press note issued by the West Pakistan Government put it rather differently. It said that when violence broke out, Mr. Bhutto had already been put in a police jeep on its way to Shahdadpur. However, it was admitted that the driver of a vehicle a little way behind that of Mr. Bhutto's was hit by a bullet and died. From this it could be inferred that the shooting was deliberate and that Bhutto was the target. Still, this was by no means the only recourse to arms. On 7 May a procession of National Awami Party workers (Wali Khan group) returning from Saidu Sharif was fired upon and two persons were killed.

In 1970 the monsoon in East Pakistan was particularly severe and by the beginning of August serious floods were experienced. They became the object of incessant reporting and so intense did this reporting become that two probable aims seemed to be behind it: (a) to enforce a decision to postpone the elections and; (b) to persuade foreign countries to provide relief in cash or kind.

In the middle of the month it was announced that because of the floods in East Pakistan the elections would be postponed

[19] *D*, 14 January 1970.

until 7 December in the case of the National Assembly and, in the case of the Provincial Assemblies, until a date not later than 19 December, and that there would be corresponding postponements of nominations. The reception to this announcement was decidedly mixed. Neither Sheikh Mujib nor Zulfikar Ali Bhutto had any immediate comment to offer, but the general public seemed to feel this was a decided reverse for Yahya Khan, damaging his image and credibility. It was thought that this decision had been forced upon him by such men as Muzaffar Qizilbash, Sher Ali Khan, and Mahmood Haroon. Yahya Khan had also come out with a statement that there would be no dissolution of his Cabinet before the elections. His reason for this was that his Ministers were doing a 'dedicated job'. They were not, he explained, representatives of the people but, rather, his representatives. 'Leave my Cabinet alone', he concluded.[20]

Unfortunately Sher Ali Khan increased public doubt about Yahya Khan's sincerity by announcing that Government would soon order a ban on the flying of party flags on rooftops. Coming from him, this was indeed meaningful since his indulging in party affairs, notably in support of the Jama'at-i-Islami, was widely believed, and the party with the most flags visible was certainly not the Jama'at. It was Bhutto's People's Party.[21] A few days later Sher Ali Khan was obliged to eat his words. He said there would be no restriction on the display of party flags 'so long as there is no law and order problem',[22] but as the subject had been launched those parties with fewer flags flying pursued it. The general theme was that the parties whose flags were seen most were paying people to hoist a flag. One Major Aslam Khan, a supporter of Qayum Khan, said 'one political party was spending a colossal amount of money on hoisting flags'.[23] On his side, Bhutto claimed that the elections had been postponed merely to provide time in which the three Muslim Leagues, along with Air-Marshal Asghar Khan's Tehrik-i-Istiqlal, could amalgamate to form a solid, right-wing front against him. The suggestion was not implausible.

By this time Bhutto was displaying a marked hostility to-

[20] *PT*, 17 August 1970.
[21] My own travels in West Pakistan, at the time, confirmed this.
[22] *PT*, 23 August 1970.
[23] *D*, 25 August 1970.

wards the administration. In an angry speech at Rawalpindi on 30 September he referred to the many arrests of his party men and went on to say that if he were alive 'and not in jail', he would make public certain matters within his knowledge. The reference was evidently to the meeting between Bhashani and Yahya Khan. He added that the way political events were shaping gave rise to the possibility of civil war.[24] Many people considered this speech and these references highly irresponsible but, as events were to show, Bhutto did not speak without reason. Quite apart from political intervention by such men as Sher Ali Khan and quite apart from party strife in West Pakistan, there had been serious incidents in East Pakistan. On 14 August, in Dacca, when the Independence Day Football Match took place, there was a serious riot. Four persons were killed and 200 injured. The newspaper reports of this affair were thoroughly tendentious, as they aimed to show proof of police brutality while minimizing the circumstances in which the violence started. The police had in fact lost all sense of self-restraint and so, too, had the mob.

In the autumn of 1970, immediately prior to his departure on a visit to Nepal, Yahya Khan addressed the officers of General Headquarters. He reviewed the country's situation and at the close of his address he invited questions. He was asked whether, in the event of civil commotion, the armed forces would be called upon to maintain order.[25] Yahya Khan's reply was that neither he nor the senior officers of the armed forces desired to be charged with the political management of the country. He and they hoped that as soon as possible the nation and its political leaders would carry their due share of responsibility. He added, however, that so long as he and the armed forces carried the burden of administration in the country and of maintaining law and order, everyone should bear in mind that, in the pursuit of these duties, nothing would be left unused, not even force if it were necessary.

[24] It was often stated that if the arrested members of the People's Party were not released, the Party might boycott the elections. This was one of Bhutto's main themes in the inflammatory speeches he was making at that time. One reason was the trial and conviction by Summary Military Court No. 1, Hyderabad, of Ali Ahmed Khan Talpur. He was sentenced to one year's rigorous imprisonment.

[25] Had the questioner in mind, here, the last phase of Ayub Khan's administration? See *FCTC*, Ch. XIV.

This answer was fully consistent with the publicly stated attitude of Yahya Khan and his administration. Elections would
be held. The National Assembly would frame a constitution.
Power was to return to the people. Whatever the disclaimers,
however, Yahya Khan's administration was to some extent
politically involved, and this involvement could not be shed
lightly. The reasons for this assertion have already been discussed and they can be charitably summarized by saying that
Yahya Khan and his colleagues confused their duty with their
predilections, a confusion made worse by their ignorance of
politics and the ways of politicians. No doubt the most neut-
rally dispassionate Chief Martial Law Administrator cannot
be expected to stand aside to watch his country torn to pieces,
its ideology subverted, the foundations of its existence razed.
But what the people want they will eventually get, and the
quickest, easiest and most convenient way of achieving it is by
the ballot box. It seems unnecessary to elaborate the point
here, yet the LFO shows that Yahya Khan and his advisers
did not understand this. Hence the bloodstained consequences.

Meanwhile preparations for the elections were in train. Near
the end of September it was announced that all educational
institutions in the country, including universities and religious
*madrassahs* would close from 23 November to 1 January 1971.
The object was to prevent student involvement in politics and
to enable the schools and other buildings to be used as polling
stations. It was asked, how would the student relieved of his
studies be precluded from involvement in politics when on the
contrary, such freedom appeared to facilitate it?

The activities of the main parties were following predictable
lines. Sheikh Mujib was assiduously preaching his Six Point
programme, affirming that nothing less would satisfy East
Pakistan. In October he outlined a programme of provincial
autonomy, and it was plain that were such a programme
implemented it would be the end of Pakistan.[26] Again, at a
press conference in Dacca on 26 November he said he wanted
maximum autonomy, not secession, and when asked about
independence, he replied 'No, not yet'.[27] There is not much
more to be said about the work of the Awami League. The

[26] The speech is reported verbatim in *D*, 29 October 1970.
[27] *PT*, 27 November 1970.

appeal was popular in the eastern Province and it was certain the party would do well there.

Undoubtedly the party which made the most unexpected impact, establishing itself as a major factor in the country's political life, was Bhutto's Pakistan People's Party. First announced in November 1967, it took shape as an aggressive, energetic, political organization and it owed these attributes to the example of its leader. There could be no doubt about Mr. Bhutto's extraordinary vitality as he travelled the country, mostly in West Pakistan, making as many as half a dozen speeches a day. That he was doing well could not be doubted and, as time went on, ambitious persons, sensing the progress he was making, deserted their existing political affiliations and joined him, bringing fresh accretions of strength. Nevertheless, there were disquieting features. The first was that in the determination to stir the voters and gain their support, the People's Party candidates were making extravagant promises to the voters, especially to the poorer classes. Secondly, the party membership, and more particularly the candidates, were a strangely assorted lot. They included members of the landed aristocracy, well-to-do and not so well-to-do professional men, businessmen, labour leaders, and people of leftist tendencies from pink to scarlet. What commonly held principles and emotions united this heterogeneous collection were far from clear. There was, certainly, the party manifesto. There were the slogans about Islam, democracy, socialism, and power to the people but whether they meant the same thing to all those who, under the People's Party tri-colour, hoped for election to the National Assembly or to a Provincial Assembly, was uncertain.

While it is certain that some persons in or connected with Yahya Khan's administration disliked Mr. Bhutto and his party, there is an air of equivocation about relations between the administration and Mr. Bhutto. In the election year, as late as September, Bhutto was accusing the administration of victimization and even claimed that manoeuvres were afoot to create a party that could effectively oppose him. On the other hand, Bhutto stated, some months after March 1971, that 'according to the régime's [i.e. Yahya Khan's administration's] calculations' the People's Party was not expected to get more than twenty seats in the National Assembly.[28] If, indeed, that was the expectation, it is curious that, rating Bhutto's prospects so low, the administration should have felt it necessary to go to the lengths of which Bhutto complained. I shall attempt to explain these contradictions later. The question also arises as to the political distance which actually separated Mr. Bhutto from Yahya Khan's government. We have it on Mr. Bhutto's own authority that 'a few months before the elections', he had a discussion with Lieut.-General Peerzada, Principal Staff Officer to the President, who asked Mr. Bhutto outright what he thought were Sheikh Mujib's true intentions. Without hesitation Mr. Bhutto replied: 'Separation'.[29] What is meant by 'a few months' can be argued, but the recorded fact is that prior to the general elections of 1970 Mr. Bhutto concluded that Sheikh Mujib desired East Pakistan's separation from West Pakistan, and Mr. Bhutto communicated this opinion to the existing government. Mr. Bhutto claimed that in spite of this he made every effort, after the election, to arrive at a political settlement in the context of one Pakistan 'knowing as I did that the alternative would be bloodshed and slaughter'.[30]

In October nominations were filed for 300 seats in the National Assembly and for seats in the Provincial Assemblies. For East Pakistan's 162 National Assembly seats there were 870 nominations, and for West Pakistan's 138 seats nominations were 1,070. In Karachi alone there were 73 candidates for seven seats. Even after less enthusiastic aspirants had dropped out, no less than 1,570 candidates went to the National Assembly polls. For Provincial Assemblies, nominations were just as numerous. In East Pakistan 2,121 persons filed papers for 300 seats, while in West Pakistan 3,500 persons filed papers for the 300 seats of the four Assemblies. For fifteen Karachi seats in the Sind Assembly, there were 360 nominations. However, when the elections were held, East Pakistan candidates had fallen to 1,868, and candidates in West Pakistan to 2,386. From these figures it appears that the people of West Pakistan showed greater appetite for public life than did those of East Pakistan, with the promise, at the same time, that loss of deposits would

[28] *The Great Tragedy*, p. 62.
[29] *The Great Tragedy*, p. 75.
[30] Ibid.

prove more lucrative to the state in the western provinces. Equally, it might be argued that in East Pakistan people were more alive to Sheikh Mujib's prospects of success. Meanwhile there was a lot of educational propaganda on the screen, radio, and television teaching people how to vote and behave at the polling stations, and the stage seemed well set.

Then, a tragedy of horrifying magnitude overtook everything.

In the middle of November, the tornado-ridden land of East Pakistan was visited with a cyclone of unparalleled fury, accompanied by a tidal wave which swept inland for miles, annihilating all before it. Who and what were not destroyed by the hurricane were lost in the raging waters. It was estimated that one million persons lost their lives, while the damage to countryside, crops, and cattle was incalculable since all administration in the devastated areas broke down completely. Yahya Khan proclaimed a national calamity. Assistance from many countries in the shape of money, medicines, food, and other necessities was at once promised and soon delivered. Officers and men of the Royal Marines arrived to lend practical help.

This disaster which fell upon the country after the previous postponement of elections because of the monsoon floods seemed like the work of some malign fate; and although it was plain that where the cyclone had struck further postponement was unavoidable, the question of delay elsewhere raised difficult questions. If elections proceeded in the rest of Pakistan, their results could easily influence subsequent elections in the stricken areas. The objections in principle were clear but, on the other hand, West Pakistan was not affected and any postponement there, as in the rest of East Pakistan, might provoke adverse interpretations. As it was, the calamity had far-reaching consequences. It was later said that the provision of relief goods from abroad was used as a cover for bringing in weapons and ammunition to be used by secessionists. The truth of this has never been proved, but there were many in Pakistan who believed it and many still do.

On 29 November Yahya Khan announced that, except in the cyclone-torn areas, elections would go ahead. In the devastated districts elections would be held later as if they were by-elections. It was the right decision, but the salutary effect was lessened by the further statement that if the Legal Framework Order were violated, Martial Law would continue. People read many meanings into this cryptic assurance.

On the evening of 3 December Yahya Khan addressed the nation by radio. Much of his address was familiar, but totally irrelevant to the juncture and the hour—foreign affairs, economic situation, and so on. On the constitutional situation, he had these points to make:

(a) Martial Law is supreme.
(b) Elections were being held under Martial Law.
(c) The new constitution must be drafted within the prescriptions of the Legal Framework Order.
(d) If no new constitution were evolved within those prescriptions and within the time allowed, Martial Law would continue.
(e) The Government would adopt all measures necessary to ensure orderly and peaceful elections.

The measures to ensure peaceful and orderly elections soon became apparent. Troops were on the streets, and Section 79(a) of the Election Order was invoked to prohibit processions or public meetings for a period extending from 48 hours before the elections to 48 hours afterwards. In Karachi and other places in West Pakistan, Section 144 was enforced to prohibit the carrying of weapons for a period of one month. Election days —7 and 17 December—were declared public holidays and on the afternoon of 5 December—as the hour of prohibition on public meetings drew near—party workers rushed round the cities with public address equipment, loudly and repetitiously exhorting the people to support *their* man.

In Karachi, on 7 December 1970, the city wore much the same aspect as any Sunday. Shops were closed. Restaurants and liquor stores were open. There was little traffic about and little sign of people streaming to the polls. Some military presence was visible including at least one mobile military court to deal with trouble-makers on the spot. On the basis of what was seen at 10 a.m., it appeared elections would pass off without trouble and polling would be low. There were serious complaints about the indelible ink used to mark thumbs of persons who had voted so that they would not try a second time. It was said the ink washed off in water and so the purpose was defeated. One suspected a venal purchase officer and a dishonest supplier.

The most important factor was the astonishing victory of Sheikh Mujib's Awami League. Out of East Pakistan's 169 seats (including those reserved for women) in the National Assembly, the Awami League secured 167. In West Pakistan, Mr. Bhutto's party emerged first with 88 seats out of 144 (likewise including women's seats).

A word must be said about the voting itself. Taking the country as a whole, about 50 per cent of the electorate voted. In Baluchistan and the North-West Frontier Province voting was poor, owing mainly to a widely scattered population, very cold weather, and poor road communication. The possibility of malpractice cannot be excluded. In West Pakistan the effect of road communication was a distinct feature of the results. So, too, literacy and urbanization. Thus, in the case of the People's Party, its share of votes, cast in nine Districts with 586 persons to the square mile, a road mileage of 13·5 per 100 square miles of area, a literacy percentage of 15·1, and an urban population of 25·9 per cent, was 52 per cent. However, in ten other districts with 185 persons to the square mile, a road mileage of 7·9 per 100 square miles of area, a literacy percentage of 7·9, and an urban population of 14·1 per cent, the same party secured only 25 per cent of the votes cast. The bearing of these factors on the appeal made by this Party was therefore obvious.

These data help to explain why Bhutto, a Sindhi, was able to do so well in the Punjab. Between the two Provinces relations were not entirely amicable owing, in part, to old resentments felt towards Punjabi settlers in Sind and, in part, to the contribution made by some Sindhis to the break-up of the One-Unit. Thus, it can be seen that Bhutto's party did best in those districts of the Punjab where literacy was highest and road communication better. In a Province where political awareness was more intense than elsewhere in West Pakistan, such factors would work in favour of a highly articulate man speaking the language of progressive change. But this, alone, does not answer the question why Bhutto gained so much Punjabi support. It can be attributed, firstly, to the fact that the Province's own political leadership was scarred with a long and dismal record of failure. Secondly, Bhutto's firm stance towards India had won for him much Punjabi admiration. In addition to all this, he enjoyed the sympathy and liking of younger people with whom he had always sought to identify himself, particularly among the student groups.

In East Pakistan Sheikh Mujib's spectacular victory made all such analysis unnecessary. Efforts were made later to attribute much of that victory to the Hindu community and its sinister purposes. Since that community represented about 15 per cent of the population of East Pakistan, it is difficult to understand how its influence could have been as decisive as was claimed and the case rests on a fragile basis.[31] Certainly, in the northern districts of East Pakistan, there was a concentration of Hindus as they provided most of the tea-garden labour, and the poll there in favour of the Awami League was greater than in the southern districts where the Hindu population was smaller. But exactly the same thing was true of the Jama'at-i-Islami, the Muslim Leagues, and the Pakistan Democratic Party. Of course, it can be argued that the larger presence of Hindus in the northern districts stimulated voting on religious grounds and that in these districts Muslims tended to vote for the sectarian parties because they feared Hindu ascendancy, while Hindus voted for the Awami League because they feared the sectarian parties.[32] The weakness of this argument is that with both sides doing their best for the reasons stated, the Muslims must ultimately have the advantage. More important, however, are the obvious conclusions. These are:

[31] In West Pakistan much was made of the fact that in the eastern Province, schools and colleges were largely staffed by Hindus. It may well have been the case that, proportionate to their numbers, Hindus were unduly prominent in the teaching profession but whether they chose this poorly paid occupation from preference or because openings in more remunerative careers were not available to them is also open to question. Certainly, it can be conceded that some Hindu teachers tried to influence their pupils against the idea of Pakistan and against West Pakistan, but whether this contributed to the events which led to the creation of Bangladesh is doubtful. Nevertheless, in West Pakistan, many people, especially in official and military circles, held strongly to this theory of Hindu influence and, in 1971, Hindu intellectuals suffered accordingly.

[32] The statistical data used in these paragraphs is taken from the *Pakistan Economist*, Karachi, 20 and 27 March, 3 April, and 4 September 1971. It should be added, perhaps, that in all Provinces only 50 per cent of voters went to the poll. In West Pakistan this point was urged against Sheikh Mujib as showing he had not so overwhelmingly carried his Province as seats won might suggest. The strength of this argument depends on such questions as the number of women who voted, accessibility of voting stations, and similar material considerations.

(a) For the first time in its history Pakistan had experienced nationwide general elections based on universal adult suffrage and direct voting.

(b) The two victorious parties were clearly regional. The Awami League secured no seat in West Pakistan and the People's Party no seat in East Pakistan.

(c) Sheikh Mujib's party enjoyed an overall majority in the National Assembly.

(d) In the Provincial Assembly elections, held ten days later, Sheikh Mujib secured total control of the East Pakistan Assembly, whereas the Pakistan People's Party enjoyed majorities in Punjab and Sind. In Baluchistan and the North-West Frontier Province the National Awami Party of Mr. Wali Khan held majorities.

(e) The parties preaching Islamic orthodoxy were rejected.

(f) The Old Guard—familiar Muslim League leaders and so on—had lost their place.

(g) Both Sheikh Mujib and Mr. Bhutto had made extravagant promises, the fulfilment of which might prove difficult.

(h) There was ample room for a serious clash between Mujib and Bhutto especially over India where Mujib's attitude was accommodating and Bhutto's intransigent.

The overriding considerations of the time comprised one grave question and two towering facts. The question was whether Mujibur Rahman and Zulfikar Ali Bhutto had sense and moderation enough not to throw away this opportunity to frame an acceptable Constitution that would hold Pakistan together and get the armed forces out of politics. The two patent facts were, first, that Sheikh Mujib was in the most dangerous position that can overtake any popular leader. His supporters had put him in a situation where, by virtue of voting strength in the House, there was nothing to stand in the way of implementing the policy and programme he had been energetically and eloquently presenting. The second patent fact was that Yahya Khan and his advisers had blundered hopelessly in leaving to the National Assembly the determination of voting procedure. Had, as we have already suggested, there been provision for, say, a two-thirds majority, to which no one at the outset could have raised reasonable objection, the situation

which had come into existence could never have arisen. This
situation was that with his overall majority in the House and
with no voting procedure specified, Sheikh Mujib could carry
the day on voting procedure and, by consequence, on everything else. Assuming the familiar parliamentary procedures,
West Pakistan, politically speaking, lay prostrate before its
eastern brethren.

It was significant that on 14 December Major-General Sher
Ali Khan tendered his resignation as Minister of Information
and it was accepted next day. Rumour was strong that he had
in fact been dismissed, and it seems probable that Yahya Khan
felt himself ill-served by him. But if Yahya Khan had been
relying on the advice of Sher Ali Khan, that perhaps was unwise, for Sher Ali Khan was not trained in politics and his
views were certainly not free of bias in some respects.

Thus, amid much speculation and conflicting possibilities of
great import to the country, the year drew to its close.[33] It did
so on a note of anti-climax for, on 26 December, in Karachi,
took place the conference of Islamic Countries' Foreign Ministers.[34] It lasted for three days. The security arrangements were
extreme so that Karachi, or some parts of it, seemed belea-
guered. What benefit emerged from this gathering is not known
and the correct conclusion seemed to be that it was a very big
and very expensive non-event.

[33] On the outcome of the elections, the reader may wish to refer to Appendix A.
[34] This Conference appears to have been the brain-child of Major-General
Sher Ali Khan. There is nothing to suggest that either Sheikh Mujib or Mr.
Bhutto took the slightest interest in it. Having resigned twelve days earlier, Sher
Ali did not take part. An appreciation of the Conference in PO, 31 December 1970,
is a fair estimate. The Conference is said to have cost the Government of Pakistan
Rs. 67 lakhs. *

# IX

# Descent into the Maelstrom

It has been repeatedly remarked that after the elections Yahya Khan did not promptly summon the National Assembly, the oath was not administered in terms of Section 12 of the LFO, and the Assembly was not at once charged with its constitution-making task. Instead, Yahya Khan began a series of private *pourparlers* the object of which appeared to be to secure some prior measure of agreement between himself and the leaders of the two principal parties in the House. To many it was not clear why these negotiations *in camera* were necessary, because if there were to be some privately agreed settlement concerning the structure of the constitution and its main features, what duty would fall upon the National Assembly except to act, perhaps, as a rubber-stamp? Once the heads of agreement had been privately settled between the leaders, it would suffice to turn the job over to the parliamentary draftsmen. Something like this had been considered by Bhutto, if by no one else, as he later explained.[1] Mr. Bhutto has also tried to explain the reasons which, after the elections, led him to think some preliminary negotiations were necessary and he sought to clarify the dilemma in which, as he said, his Party found itself.[2]

It had been hoped that Mujib and Bhutto would seize the opportunity which, between them, they could wield in the national interest with the maximum degree of consensus. It was, therefore, with anxiety and regret that people witnessed a succession of events which belied any such hope. Mr. Bhutto adopted an angry mood, accusing the imperialist–capitalist press, both foreign and local, of misrepresenting him, and he directed threats of vengeance towards local newspapers and journalists who had vilified and calumniated his family and himself. Moreover, as the month passed, it was evident that

[1] *The Great Tragedy*, pp. 58–9.
[2] Ibid., p. 26 *et seq.*

far from any display of co-operation, sparring between Sheikh Mujib and Bhutto had started. It seemed that Mujib, content with his majority in the Assembly, was little interested in what Bhutto had to say, or offer.

Indeed, considering the divergence of opinion between the two leaders, perhaps it could hardly be otherwise. Apparently Bhutto sensed this for, on 20 December, in Lahore, he delivered a fulminating address in which he threatened to teach India a lesson and declared that his party had no intention of remaining out of office for the next five years.[3] The clash between the two men was clearly intensifying and the division of attitude was underlined in an important article entitled 'Coming to Terms with the Six Points' by Rehman Sobhan and published in Dacca.[4] Coming from the pen of one recognized as an intelligent and loyal adherent of the Awami League, the article possessed enhanced significance.

The contentions advanced by the author were:

(a) None of the political options open to West Pakistan's voters included the Six Points (except G. M. Syed's United Front in Sind). Consequently, those voters had no occasion to form any conclusion about them.

(b) The election results confronted West Pakistan with the reality of the Six Points as a unanimous demand of East Pakistan.

(c) The future of the country rested upon the willingness of West Pakistan to come to terms with the Six Points.

(d) East Pakistan's demand for autonomy grew out of two decades of economic injustice. If this were all, East Pakistan could now seriously consider a strong centre and, using its majority, exact due reparation. But the author dismissed this possibility as fantasy since East Pakistan did not exercise the power by which to enforce such rectifying legislation. 'For instance, if East Pakistan decides on a large expenditure programme for development, it would hardly be acceptable and just to extract heavy taxes from the Centre which would be largely

---

[3] *PT*, 21 and 22 December 1970. Why 'five years'? Presumably Mr. Bhutto thought that the new Constitution would provide for quinquennial Parliaments, subject, perhaps, to the possibility of earlier dissolution, on the British model.

[4] It was reprinted for the benefit of West Pakistani readers in the *Daily News*, Karachi, 24 December 1970.

realized, say, from the Punjab. This would be resisted
tooth and nail.'

The article went on to analyse the Six Points and argued
that there was ample ground for accepting them and that the
consequences would not be injurious. The author concluded
that the Six Points formed a package deal and that if all planning and development decisions became a provincial responsibility, practical necessity indicated that taxation, monetary,
trade, and foreign aid policy should move to the Provinces.
'There is no reason why they [i.e. Mr. Bhutto's party] should
not be able to come to terms with the Six Points which any
economist of even moderate competence will inform them is of
positive benefit to the richest regions of West Pakistan.'

The implications of this article were plain. Sheikh Mujib
and his party had no faith in their ability to make such adjust-
ments, through control at the Centre, as would do justice to
East Pakistan's claims on the economy—past, present, and
future. They regarded the past as done with and they did not
believe in any prospect of reparation for that past. But if the
future of the country rested upon the willingness of West Pakistan to come to terms with the Six Points, and if West Pakistan
did not do so, then that future was in peril. The option to
adopt the Six Points by any or all of West Pakistan's four Provinces was not open because the elections in West Pakistan had
not been fought on that issue. Mr. Sobhan was entitled to assert
this although it is difficult to understand how, if the new Constitution did confer the benefit of the Six Points on East Pakistan, they could be withheld from any Province in West Pakistan
that desired them. Moreover, from Mr. Sobhan's article it
could be inferred that since East Pakistan voted unanimously
for the Six Points, it would be a defiance of the people's will
not to make provision for the Points in the new Constitution,
at any rate so far as East Pakistan was concerned. Finally, there
was the claim—by no means trivial or invalid—that with the
adoption of the Six Points, West Pakistan would be better off.[5]

Apart from its importance, this article was fairly representative of the superior political talent being displayed in East Pakistan. There, political writing was cool, objective, and balanced.

[5] Which led, of course, to the inference that were East Pakistan to secede,
West Pakistan would be still better off.

The tactical moves were shrewd and the entire approach was, in its political *nous*, far more impressive than anything being demonstrated in the western wing. It appeared that the Awami League leaders, seeing victorious attainment of their aims ahead, could afford to be at confident ease, whereas in West Pakistan there was dismay and anger. They had been worsted in the elections and did not like it. One writer in West Pakistan actually went so far as to describe Rehman Sobhan as 'the Rosenberg of the Awami League'.[6] There will be occasion to speak of this again.

In Dacca, on 3 January, the New Year began with a speech by Sheikh Mujib in which he showed not the slightest spirit of accommodation. Indeed, all Awami League members of the National and Provincial Assemblies were required to take an oath that they would support the Party programme for provincial autonomy although the terms of the oath did not actually mention the Six Points. Likewise, his remarks on trade with India contrasted sharply with all that Bhutto had been saying, especially as regards any resumption, which Mujib clearly desired.[7]

The febrile atmosphere prevailing in West Pakistan was kept

[6] H. M. Abbasi in the *Daily News*, Karachi, 26 December 1970.

[7] There was material for angry controversy here. The trade embargo bore heavily on East Pakistan and one instance deserves mention as it had a curious corollary. Instead of being able to import Indian coal costing in Dacca about Rs. 60 per long ton, East Pakistan was obliged to use coal from China, Poland, Australia, and elsewhere costing from Rs. 130 to Rs. 180 a long ton. Coal is largely used in East Pakistan for brick-burning. Bricks are not only used as such, but—because the Province has inadequate supplies of stone—bricks are broken and used in cement-concrete construction. Thus, in East Pakistan, on this score alone, costs were unnecessarily high. West Pakistan has its own inferior coal for brick-burning and otherwise uses natural gas and oil fuel. However, West Pakistan requires about 30,000 tons of metallurgical coke a year for foundries and other industry and when in 1970, there was an acute world shortage West Pakistan foundries, etc., were threatened with closure. As India was the only available source, the Central Government sanctioned a surreptitious deal by which two cargoes of Indian coke were shipped to Karachi. The transaction was arranged through the firm of Ben and Company, of Singapore, through the instrumentality of a retired brigadier of the Pakistan army. The vessels were S. S. *Shunwing* and M. V. *Marian Elizabeth* which sailed from Calcutta on 3 and 13 June and reached Karachi on 22 June and 9 July respectively. Inevitably, the matter found its way into the newspapers (e.g., *PO*, 27 June 1970) and was used as an example of the unfairness with which East Pakistan was treated and of the hypocrisy of West Pakistan. Eventually, the Central Government was obliged to issue a statement which evaded the issue. The statement said that the coke had come from Singapore, which was true in a sense, since the purchase had been made in that city, but the coke itself was not manufactured there because Singapore has no coking coal and no cokeries. The source was India.

inflamed by incidents, trifling in themselves, but sufficient to promote violence or the threat of it. News was received of a book, which had just been published in the United Kingdom and entitled *The Turkish Art of Love*. It was illustrated; the author was one Dr. Pinhas ben Nahum, apparently a Jew of Indian nationality, and the contents were said to desecrate the name of the Holy Prophet. Clearly, a most incendiary combination, more than sufficient to bring the mobs on to the streets, smashing, burning, looting. Mr. Bhutto took advantage of the situation to state that if a people's government had been in power, it would have broken off relations with any country where such offensive books were published.[8]

In the same month of January, the Indian hockey team was due to visit Lahore to participate in the World Cup Hockey Tournament. In a speech at Peshawar, Mr. Bhutto said there could be absolutely no question of extending any goodwill to India until the Kashmir and other disputes were settled in a fair and just manner. He objected to the Indian team's visit and added that if the people's wishes were not respected, the organizers would be responsible for the consequences. Three days later, while condemning civic violence, Bhutto said he would not 'permit an Indian hockey team to land in West Pakistan'. As a matter of minor history, Yahya Khan's administration succumbed and the Pakistan Hockey Federation asked the International Federation for a postponement of the tournament 'in *unavoidable* circumstances' (my italics). The important point here is that, in condemning civic violence, Mr. Bhutto was unquestionably using the language of violence, well knowing that within the country a habit of civic violence had grown up and seemed to have become part of the national way of life.[9]

Even the press became infected and newspaper feuding was expressed in the airing of personal grievances and private vendettas to the accompaniment of all sorts of scurrilities, and this at a time when the country was about to face the gravest problems. An editorial entitled 'Lies as Truth, Filth as News'[10]

---

[8] *D*, 11 January 1971.
[9] 'What is totally incomprehensible is the perverted glee with which various segments of the political spectrum with hues ranging from deep blue to fiery red seem to opt for fratricidal conflict and eventual disintegration.' *Outlook*, Karachi, 19 August 1972.
[10] *Leader*, Karachi, 14 January 1971.

was a fair description of the press at the time and, notwithstanding its own contribution, another newspaper published a
severe warning in an editorial entitled 'Last Chance before We
Disintegrate'.[11]

It may be said that when measured against the salient facts
of Pakistan's political situation these are small matters. It may
be so, yet their significance is material. It has often seemed that
it was precisely these 'small matters' which helped to erode
what stability the country possessed and caused injury to such
thinking as has informed its public life.

A striking example of this occurred when, on 14 January,
while at Dacca Airport, preparatory to leaving for Karachi
after talks with Sheikh Mujib, Yahya Khan announced to
astonished journalists that 'Sheikh Mujibur Rahman is going
to be the future Prime Minister of the country'. This was an
unprecedented indiscretion. How did Yahya Khan know that
Sheikh Mujib was going to be the future Prime Minister or
even that he wanted to be? And what did 'future' mean?
Immediate or distant?[12] Had the Sheikh, in his talk with Yahya
Khan, expressed any desire or willingness? Had he come to
some settlement with Yahya Khan, leaving Bhutto out, or on
the assumption that Bhutto would be ready to serve in a Cabinet
formed by Sheikh Mujib? Did these words mean that Sheikh
Mujib would lead the National Assembly when it met to draft
the Constitution? And would Bhutto then find himself in opposition? The enigmas were insoluble. Matters were further complicated when Yahya Khan added, at the same gathering of
pressmen: 'I inherited a bad economy and I am going to hand
it over to Sheikh Mujib.'[13] But before or after acceptance of
the Constitution?

On return from Dacca, Yahya Khan and some of his advisers
visited Mr. Bhutto at his Larkana home. The substance of
what passed is, perhaps, best and, in the absence of other evidence, most reliably stated in Mr. Bhutto's own words: 'The
President informed us of his discussions at Dacca at which he
told Mujibur Rahman that three alternatives were open to the

[11] *Daily News*, Karachi, 13 January 1971.
[12] According to Mr. Bhutto, Yahya Khan said 'next Prime Minister of Pakistan' (*The Great Tragedy*, p. 20), but Mr. Bhutto was not present at the Airport and
Yahya Khan was reported by the press as having used the word 'future'.
[13] *D*, 15 January 1971.

Awami League, namely, to try to go it alone, to co-operate with
the People's Party, or to co-operate with the small and defeated
parties of the West Wing; and that, in his opinion, the best
course would be for the two majority parties to arrive at an
arrangement. For our part, we discussed with the President the
implications of the Six Points and expressed our serious misgivings about them. We nevertheless assured him that we were
determined to make every effort for a viable compromise and
said we were to visit Dacca in the near future to hold discussions
with the Awami League leaders.' For this purpose Mr. Bhutto
had already sent the General Secretary of his Party, Mr.
Ghulam Mustafa Khar, to Dacca to establish contact with
Sheikh Mujib and lay the groundwork for the visit. Mr. Bhutto
continued his narrative of events at Larkana with these words:
'The President informed us that the Awami League Leader was
most anxious for an immediate session of the National Assembly
and that he had asked the President to call the National Assembly to session on 15th. of February.'[14]

All this is of the utmost interest. Again we see the consequences of the failure of the LFO to specify voting procedure
and the kind of majority needed to pass the Constitution Bill.
Yahya Khan was right in suggesting that it would be best for
the two leading parties to agree on the terms of the Constitution, but why he should have referred to 'two majority
parties' as, according to Mr. Bhutto, he did, is incomprehensible. In that Assembly there could be only one majority party
and the Awami League had a majority over all the rest put
together. Hence, in the absence of any other specified majority,
Sheikh Mujib was as free to go it alone as he was to rely on
the votes of parties other than the People's Party. To describe
those other parties as 'small and defeated' was to argue nothing.
The vote of one member of the House was in every way equal
to the vote of another and Sheikh Mujib was obviously entitled
to look for such votes.

If one takes into account what, a few months previously, Mr.
Bhutto had said to Lieut.-General Peerzada concerning his (Mr.
Bhutto's) view of Sheikh Mujib's intentions, the nature of the
misgivings expressed at Larkana to Yahya Khan is clear. Probably Bhutto's misgivings reinforced those which Yahya Khan

[14] *The Great Tragedy*, pp. 20–1.

and his advisers were feeling, for although, on leaving Dacca,
Yahya Khan had expressed satisfaction with his talks with
Sheikh Mujib, it could not be denied that on the question of
the Six Points there had been no sign of yielding or compromise.

On the eve of Bhutto's departure for Dacca two interesting
events occurred. The first was a speech by Khondker Mushtaq
Ahmed, Vice-President of the Awami League, in which he said
that the time had come for the people of *West* Pakistan to prove
they were not secessionists.[15] The idea was as startling as it was
improbable, but the meaning was plain. Did West Pakistan
intend to play the parliamentary game according to the rules,
i.e. submission to the will of the successful majority, or did it
not? The second event was the expulsion, by India, of a First
Secretary of the Pakistan High Commission in New Delhi,
Zafar Iqbal Rathore, on the charge of involvement in subversive movements in Kashmir. Pakistan promptly responded by
declaring a member of the India High Commission in Pakistan,
B. L. Joshi, to be *persona non grata* on grounds of espionage and
subversive activities, and he was given forty-eight hours in
which to leave.

The arrival of Mr. Bhutto and his colleagues in Dacca on
27 January 1971 was attended by an unpropitious circumstance. In the welter of excited greeting six of them had their
pockets picked by nimble fingers and, between them, the unfortunate half-dozen lost some Rs. 11,000 in cash and two return
air-tickets. This occurrence was inauspicious but not crucial.
There were other attendant circumstances of greater weight.

*Vis-à-vis* Sheikh Mujib Mr. Bhutto was clearly at a disadvantage. This was one of the more unfortunate consequences
of the dissolution of West Pakistan. After the elections of 1970
Sheikh Mujib, in addition to being the leader of the majority
party in the National Assembly, could also claim to speak for
the eastern wing as a whole, but Mr. Bhutto could make no
such claim for West Pakistan. No doubt, Mr. Bhutto took the
view that his was the majority party in West Pakistan, but the
fact was that when negotiating with Sheikh Mujib, he had no
standing either in Baluchistan or the North-West Frontier
Province. Had there been no dissolution of West Pakistan,
Bhutto could have argued that just as Sheikh Mujib could

15 *PT*, 26 January 1971.

speak for the eastern wing so, he, Mr. Bhutto, could speak for the western, but in place of West Pakistan there existed four separate Provinces and no amount of dialectical subtlety could obscure the fact that Bhutto had a majority in only two of them. To what extent Sheikh Mujib took advantage of his position is not clear. From what is known of their private discussions, the impression is that Sheikh Mujib was content for Mr. Bhutto to regard himself as leader of the majority party of West Pakistan; the main reason for this attitude being that Sheikh Mujib was not interested in the western Provinces.[16] It is evident that Mr. Bhutto persisted in the view that Mujib's intentions were to secure complete independence for East Bengal. For Mr. Bhutto, the Six Points were 'a concealed formula for secession in two strokes rather than one',[17] and Mr. Bhutto later ingenuously explained: 'we wanted to avoid the application of the second stroke by arriving at an arrangement that would give the impression that Sheikh Mujibur Rahman's demands had basically been met without literally agreeing to them; and this could possibly be achieved by incorporating built-in constitutional and administrative safeguards that would act as brakes to the Awami League's runaway scheme. In this manner we wanted to arrest and reverse the harmful consequences of the Six Points.'[18]

Of the discussions held in January with Sheikh Mujib, Mr. Bhutto said he found the Sheikh intractable over the Six Points, since he claimed to have a mandate from the people and could not deviate one inch. Mr. Bhutto answered, with what significance he may not then have understood, 'that the People's Party had not received a mandate on the Six Points',[19] and that public opinion in West Pakistan was against the Points and considered that their adoption would mean the end of Pakistan. Mr. Bhutto recorded that he and his colleagues were 'prepared to go as far as possible to meet the essential demands of the Six Points on condition that nothing should jeopardize the unity of Pakistan. For this, we should have to assess and prepare public opinion in the West Wing; thus we requested a

[16] According to Mr. Bhutto, Sheikh Mujib's view was that West Pakistan problems 'were not his headache'. *The Great Tragedy*, p. 22.
[17] Ibid., p. 27.
[18] Ibid.
[19] Ibid., p. 21.

reasonable length of time before the convening of the National Assembly. Sheikh Mujibur Rahman was assured that in making this request we were not seeking any inordinate delay in the National Assembly session.'[20] It appears the Sheikh was unimpressed. He understood the difficulties of the People's Party[21] but was not prepared to accept them. He wanted a meeting of the National Assembly on 15 February since according to Bhutto, 'he sought to pressure the people of the country into submission, to leave no time for reflection. Mujibur Rahman was afraid of the consequences of any slackening of the momentum he had developed.'[22]

Mr. Bhutto is entitled to his point of view and doubtless he was right in saying that Sheikh Mujib was determined that the National Assembly should meet as soon as possible since, with his majority in the House, it was natural that he should aim at securing his objectives quickly. But the suggestion that Sheikh Mujib feared a 'slackening of momentum' is difficult to accept. Indeed, it was the Government that should have feared the consequences of postponement. With its overall majority the Awami League would become increasingly impatient as the convening of the Assembly appeared more and more elusive. Postponement simply sharpened hunger and eventually two things overtook the East Pakistani people—total disbelief in Yahya Khan and total desperation.

It was unfortunate that, by then, Mr. Bhutto was not only convinced of Sheikh Mujib's intention to secede but had also formed his interpretation of Mujib's tactics. 'Once the National Assembly came into session in his own territory[23] and under conditions completely within his control, Sheikh Mujibur Rahman proposed to convert the Assembly into a sovereign body and thus make the Legal Framework Order inoperative. This would have cleared the way for his majority under the stewardship of his Speaker to impose a Six Point Constitution in a short time, preferably before 23rd. of March. Having given the Six Points constitutional sanctity with himself as the legally constituted Prime Minister of Pakistan, with control over the

[20] Ibid.
[21] Ibid., p. 22.
[22] Ibid., p. 23.
[23] It was intended that the National Assembly, when convened, should meet in Dacca.

Armed Forces and general administration, and with East Pakistan under his command, the next step would have followed as night follows day.'[24]

Mr. Bhutto's meaning is clear although he was careful not to specify exactly what the next step would have been. Nor does he explain how armed forces, substantially composed of West Pakistanis, would have executed orders given by a Prime Minister whose purpose was to bring about separation of the two wings. Mr. Bhutto says that he and his Party 'were alive to these dangers';[25] but whether or not their assessment was right, it coloured their thinking when they returned to West Pakistan and met Yahya Khan, to whom Bhutto communicated the opinion that the Awami League had already dictated the Constitution.[26]

We have noted earlier that Mr. Bhutto more than once emphasized that there were then three major political elements —the armed forces represented by Yahya Khan, the Awami League led by Sheikh Mujib and the Pakistan People's Party led by himself. The soundness of reasoning, but want of prudence, in this statement became increasingly apparent as the private parleys continued. Moreover, it was growing plainer that, so far from clearing a way for the successful outcome of the Assembly's work, these conversations were promoting confusion and sowing mistrust. The confidence of those taking part was soon to wane, and there were other material portents. Indeed, the day was soon to come when whispered suggestions about collusion between Yahya Khan and Mr. Bhutto would be heard and Sheikh Mujib, without naming names, would refer to it.[27] Indeed, by the middle of March, these whispers became so audible that Mr. Bhutto felt it necessary to deny, by a mighty oath,[28] that there had been any consultations between the President and himself about the date on which the National Assembly would be summoned.

Before he left Dacca, Mr. Bhutto, at a press conference, made the following statements relative to the Six Points:

[24] *The Great Tragedy*, p. 23.
[25] Ibid.
[26] Ibid.
[27] Sheikh Mujib's earliest use of the word collusion in public that I can trace was 7 March 1971. The word 'conspiracy' was often on his lips, however.
[28] He swore by the Creed he holds sacred and by his children (*PT*, 15 March 1971).

(a) those Points relating to a federation and to a militia were acceptable;

(b) those relating to taxation and currency probably would be although there were problems to overcome;

(c) the question of handing over foreign trade and aid to the Province was the most difficult of all.

Again, in Rawalpindi, he urged the complexity of those problems to Yahya Khan and repeated to him 'the numerous hazards of going to the Assembly without making a final effort for a broad settlement and without sufficiently prepared public opinion for a basic compromise'.[29] According to Bhutto, he and his colleagues left Rawalpindi with the impression that the President appreciated their difficulties and 'would not announce a date for the National Assembly before the end of February.'[30] Bhutto concedes that Yahya Khan had made no final commitment, and on 13 February Yahya Khan announced he had summoned the Assembly to meet in Dacca on 3 March. Mr. Bhutto wrote later: 'This announcement took us aback. We were caught in mid-stream; we had not completed our consultations and we had not gone to the people of the West Wing for their approval for a Constitution based on far-reaching concessions. We thus found it impossible to attend the National Assembly session on 3rd. of March. We immediately contacted the President's Principal Staff Officer on the telephone and informed him of our inability to attend the . . . session on the 3rd. of March. . . .'[31] In Peshawar, on 15 February, Mr. Bhutto stated to the press that his party would not 'boycott' the Assembly, but that if there were to be no flexibility or compromise, particularly over the Six Points, he saw no purpose in his party's going there.

In assessing the line followed by Bhutto at this time, it has to be remembered that quite apart from what was being said in public by Sheikh Mujib and his colleagues, there were many in East Pakistan who uttered opinions in private which showed their determination that the Province should be master of its own affairs, whether in or out of a federation with West Pakistan. Moreover, these opinions were expressed not only by un-

---

[29] *The Great Tragedy*, p. 25.
[30] Ibid. What is meant by these words is not clear. Did 'the end of February' refer to the announcement or to the Assembly?
[31] *The Great Tragedy*, p. 25.

informed people, moved by the emotions of the hour, but also by men accustomed to handling affairs of great weight and from whom temperate views might be expected. Thus, A. Ahad, head of Dacca's leading firm of lawyers and a director of many important companies, at a lunch at Karachi in February 1971, informed some British businessmen that: East Pakistan must control all its internal affairs; East Pakistan must be free to buy in the cheapest markets, including India, irrespective of what West Pakistan could offer; East Pakistan must control its own commercial policy, etc.[32]

Of course, Mr. Bhutto was not alone in seeing the trend. As early as 1 February, immediately after his talks with Mujib, the *Pakistan Observer* published a very balanced editorial entitled 'Continue the Dialogue', and a few days later the *Pakistan Times*, in an editorial entitled 'A Dangerous Confrontation', stated that East Pakistan believed the hijacking of an Indian aircraft by Kashmiri freedom fighters had been expressly engineered so as to frustrate the transfer of power to the people.[33] However, Mr. Bhutto's statements were carrying him perilously close to breaking the rules of the parliamentary game. These rules do not allow a minority to absent itself from the House simply because it does not wish to be outvoted. Where the rule of the majority prevails the existence of a disappointed minority is inevitable, and there is no system so monolithic that no minorities exist in it. If the elected representatives of the minority do not enter the debate the views of that minority will not be heard. At any rate they will not be heard in the legislature. It is true that when Pakistan's Constitution of 1956 was passed the dissatisfied representatives of East Pakistan took no part in the final voting, but in the earlier debate their voice was frequently heard. Mr. Bhutto was not, of course, unaware of these things. He was also aware that the Awami League had a majority in the Assembly enabling them to pass a Constitution Bill drafted by them and, indeed, one had been drafted. Later, he was to say: '. . . a Constitution passed without the approval of the majority party of the West Wing would not have lasted, but it could have come into being and whatever its

---

[32] Ahad expressed similar views to foreign diplomats and, for a lawyer, seems to have been singularly indiscreet. He was arrested at the time of the army's crack-down and has never been seen since. There is little doubt he was shot.

[33] *PT*, 6 February 1971.

duration, would have played havoc with the country.'[34]

Mr. Bhutto has been much criticized for his stance, on two grounds. First, it gave room for suspicion in East Pakistan. Secondly, it was said that because of this stance Yahya Khan decided, on 1 March, to postpone the Assembly. There may well be substance in these criticisms and, certainly, Mr. Bhutto cannot be entirely exonerated, although he is but one of several who share the responsibility. Little notice has been taken of the implications of the simultaneous existence of the three major political elements pointed out by Bhutto—the Awami League, the Pakistan People's Party, and the armed forces. Of these, the first two were not in power but were answerable to the electorate, whereas the third wielded power but was answerable to no one.[35]

Perhaps this hybrid situation was the only possible one. This was substantially the view taken by the Martial Law administration and by Mr. Bhutto when Sheikh Mujib asked for a withdrawal of Martial Law. It was evident that the angularities of the situation—the supremacy of Martial Law; the prospect of Sheikh Mujib's command of the National Assembly; his want of representation in West Pakistan and the position of Bhutto's party as pre-eminent representative in two Provinces of West Pakistan but not in all four—created a bizarre game of three-way political chess in which, to be sure, each player manoeuvred his own pieces but with the complication that each was playing according to his own rules.

After Bhutto's press conference on 16 February events assumed a faster pace. On the very next day it was announced that the Lahore Horse Show had been cancelled. This annual event, of considerable social importance, normally took place in March and the army always figured prominently. Cancellation could only be interpreted as meaning that the armed forces wished no distractions. It also solved the problem of whether or not to invite Indian polo teams.

Three days later a very strange measure was adopted by Yahya Khan's government. It must be mentioned that, shortly before, Bhutto had taken from every elected member of his

---

[34] *The Great Tragedy*, p. 26. Yet again one sees the appalling blunder of not specifying voting procedure in the Legal Framework Order.

[35] Cf. Yahya Khan's broadcast on 3 December 1970 in which he said Martial Law was supreme.

Party an ante-dated resignation from the Assembly to which he had been elected. In addition, these persons bound themselves by oath[36] to follow him loyally. In fact, as matters stood at the time they were signed, these resignations had no value since, in terms of the LFO, resignation was possible only *after* the Assembly had met and a Speaker had been elected.[37] On 20 February the LFO was amended, with immediate effect, by which any member of the National or a Provincial Assembly could resign before the Assemblies met. The coincidence was too obvious not to provoke comment and an official explanation was given that this provision had been inserted merely as a technicality and to cure an omission.[38] The entire affair lent further weight to the suggestion of collusion, since Yahya Khan had, by this amendment, made it possible for Bhutto to force a postponement of the National Assembly by requiring all his men to resign prior to the summoning of the Assembly, thus making numerous by-elections necessary. This significant move was followed, on 22 February, by Yahya Khan's announcement that he had dissolved his Council of Ministers with immediate effect 'in view of the political situation'. Not surprisingly, this move was widely interpreted as a tightening of the military grip.

This interpretation was strengthened by military reinforcement in East Pakistan which, despite official secrecy, could not be concealed. At Chittagong Port a myriad suspicious eyes watched troops and their equipment disembark, and a thousand tongues reported.[39] The steady inflow of soldiers from West Pakistan strengthened apprehension. As the crisis intensified, more and more was heard of the army's role. The thesis was that the army was determined to hold the country together and allow nothing which might tend to any separation—political, economic, or other. Thus, even if Yahya Khan were ready to accept a constitution based on the Six Points, the army might not accept it. Of course, any such intervention, especially after a Constitution had been passed in the National Assembly,

[36] The terms of this oath will be found verbatim in *D*, 22 February 1971.
[37] Section 11.
[38] *D*, 21 February 1971.
[39] There was interference with these troop movements, particularly as the month of March wore on (Government of Pakistan's White Paper on *The Crisis in East Pakistan*, published by the Ministry of Information and National Affairs, Islamabad, 1971, p. 17).

might well lead to civic violence, but that did not dismay those in General Headquarters who belonged to the 'we'll-teach-the-bastards-a-lesson' school. Some scouted all this as fanciful but events were to prove that these ideas had more foundation than many supposed.

Against this backdrop, the rift between Bhutto and Mujib widened steadily. Sheikh Mujib made a further statement which contributed little or nothing to any amelioration of the deadlock, but which certainly underlined the margin of difference between Mr. Bhutto and himself.[40] His further remarks that the Six Points would not be forced on West Pakistan and that the Provinces of the western wing could, if they wished, provide additional funds for the Centre, were arid sarcasm. For his part, Bhutto, in a speech at Lahore on 28 February,[41] declared that either the LFO must be amended so as to remove the time limit of 120 days, or the convening of the National Assembly must be postponed. If neither proposal were accepted, he and his party members would not 'participate in the Assembly session on the 3rd. of March'.[42]

Two days later it was announced that the National Assembly meeting had been postponed to a day yet to be appointed. Certain other administrative changes were also made. All provincial governors were made Martial Law Administrators in their Provinces, except Admiral Ahsan who vacated his governorship. Lieut.-General Yaqub became Governor of East Pakistan as well as its Martial Law Administrator. Thus, among other developments, the army's political presence had become totally pervasive, to the exclusion of the navy and the air force.

---

[40] The statement is contained verbatim in *D*, 25 March 1971.

[41] The crowd was estimated at 500,000. Bhutto spoke with impassioned vehemence and some who heard him described the speech as a 'masterpiece of mob oratory'.

[42] *The Great Tragedy*, p. 29.

# X

# From Maelstrom to Holocaust

To no one's surprise, the announcement of the postponement of the National Assembly was received in East Pakistan with fierce resentment. The crowds surged on to the streets armed with sticks and cudgels; and Sheikh Mujib promptly called for a nationwide *hartal* on 3 March. The conclusions formed in East Pakistan were: (a) the army was determined to frustrate all effective moves towards a democratic transfer of power, and (b) there *was* collusion between Yahya Khan and Bhutto. It was also noted in both wings that the new decisions had not been broadcast by Yahya Khan himself but that a statement had simply been issued from the President's House and read to the nation by a radio announcer. It was asked whether these decisions had been forced on Yahya Khan and made in spite of him, or whether the method of delivery was simply cavalier. In West Pakistan reactions were mainly gloomy. It was said openly that each time the soldiers interfered in politics the result was worse.

In East Pakistan the strike called by Sheikh Mujib for 3 March was total and was described in the western provinces as having paralysed life in the eastern wing.[1] Throughout the Province everything was closed, including the airports and railways. The authorities responded by declaring a curfew from 7 p.m. to 7 a.m. on the night of 2/3 March, the apparent purpose being to safeguard important public installations and to show that it was not only Sheikh Mujib who wielded authority. Doubtless, these conclusions were sound but later it became clear that on 2 March there had been civil commotion with recourse to rifle fire, and a curfew had been imposed. Sheikh Mujib, whose writ alone was now running, declared that the *hartal* would continue daily for eight hours each day, the purpose being to cripple the administration and embarrass the Government by making life as difficult as possible for everyone.

[1] *D*, 4 March 1971.

Gangs armed with staves went round enforcing the *hartal* while, at nodal points, soldiers and police were posted. In West Pakistan, parties opposed to Bhutto called for a meeting of the National Assembly without delay and, in Karachi, organized a procession with the result that, on 4 March, Section 144 was imposed in the city for ten days.

Contemporaneously Yahya Khan invited twelve political leaders, including Sheikh Mujib, to meet him in Dacca at a Round Table Conference, an invitation which, predictably enough, Sheikh Mujib at once refused.[2] Instead, he called on East Pakistan to pursue peaceful *satyagraha* to ensure their rights, a Gandhian reference which could scarcely have been savoured by some in West Pakistan. He added, with grim significance, that on Sunday 7 March, he would address a public meeting in Dacca. That the crisis was mounting in intensity was not in doubt and many thought Sheikh Mujib would, at the meeting, declare East Pakistan's independence.[3] Meanwhile, stories of the despatch of troops from West Pakistan proliferated and spread widely.[4]

Bhutto's political opponents in West Pakistan, seeing a fine opportunity to discredit him as being a main contributor to the impasse, heaped criticism upon him. Clearly on the defensive, Bhutto emphatically denied any responsibility and described the reaction in East Pakistan to the postponement of the Assembly meeting as 'unwarranted'. This word seemed strangely equivocal and appeared to have been used by Bhutto to justify his silence on the question of summoning the Assembly at a time when his West Pakistan opponents were urging it.

To read the situation in East Pakistan was difficult as information was hard to come by, yet there could be no doubt that in Chittagong, on 2 March, trouble had been serious and, in Dacca, Sheikh Mujib claimed to have heard machine-gun fire. By 5 March Mujib was effectively running a parallel government and the life of the Province was ordered in compliance

[2] His statement containing the refusal will be found verbatim in *D*, 4 March 1971.
[3] Today, Bangladesh regards 1 March 1971 as the day on which the country became independent.
[4] It had become clear that West Pakistan and, more notably, the Punjab, had lost the political struggle, (a) by the dissolution of the One Unit; (b) by the errors in the LFO; and (c) by unnecessarily bullying East Pakistan.

with his directives.[5] According to these directives the banks
opened and operated. So, too, did the markets. All activity in
East Pakistan was organized in accordance with Mujib's orders.
He was firmly in the administrative saddle, since the army had
been withdrawn to barracks on the ground that there had been
'no incident of lawlessness since the lifting of the curfew'. It was
noteworthy that the Karachi newspaper, *Dawn*, on its front
page on 5 March used the word 'Bangladesh' for the first time
without the customary note of sarcasm.

Perhaps in anticipation of what Mujib might have to say on
7 March, Yahya Khan addressed the nation by radio on the
preceding day. He blamed Mujib, although not by name, referring to him as the leader of the Awami League. Specifically,
he claimed that the Sheikh had agreed to attend the Round
Table Conference and had afterwards withdrawn.[6] To a lesser
extent Yahya Khan also cast blame on Nurul Amin, the veteran
Muslim League leader and one of the two men who had been
able to secure a seat in the National Assembly against his Awami
League opponent. Mr. Amin's offence seemed to have been that
he described Yahya Khan's invitation to a Round Table Conference as 'another wrong step'. The use of the word 'another'
could only imply that there had been previous wrong steps and
that these were the work of Yahya Khan. Mr. Bhutto came in
for no criticism, express or implied, which was duly noted,
especially by his opponents and rivals. Yahya Khan's address
contained a lot about his 'moral duty' to preserve Pakistan, but
this was standard, familiar material and, at that moment, be-
side the point. He announced that the National Assembly would
meet on 25 March and affirmed that progress towards democracy would continue. Such satisfaction as might have been
derived from this was diminished when, next day, it was learned
that Lieut.-General Tikka Khan had been appointed Governor
of East Pakistan. It was a significant change for, in addition to
being a soldier who carried out orders, Tikka Khan was known
as a hard-liner and as representing the policy of 'firmness'.

[5] These directives will be found in the White Paper, *The Crisis in East Pakistan*,
1971, pp. 37–46.

[6] The explanation seems to be that before announcing these invitations Yahya
Khan had endeavoured to sound Sheikh Mujib through the East Pakistan Governor, Admiral Ahsan. Mujib allowed Admiral Ahsan to understand that he was
agreeable to such a conference and this understanding was conveyed to Yahya
Khan. Invitations were then announced.

To these announcements of 6 March, Sheikh Mujib replied next day in his eagerly awaited speech. As conditions for attending the National Assembly on 25 March, Sheikh Mujib demanded:

(a) Withdrawal of Martial Law.

(b) Return of troops to their barracks.

(c) An enquiry into recent shootings and killings, e.g. on 2 March.

(d) Immediate transfer of power to the elected representatives of the people (i.e. the National Assembly should become a sovereign institution).

He later added that after acceptance of these conditions the Awami League would consider whether to attend the National Assembly or not.

In addition, he proposed a ten-point programme to begin that very day and to last for a week. It amounted to a planned *hartal* affecting life in East Pakistan on as wide a scale as possible with such breaks as would cause the minimum inconvenience to the public. This programme provided for a prohibition on the transfer of funds from East to West Pakistan, in itself an indication of what some private and well-to-do people were thinking. In his speech Mujib denied that he had in any way indicated his readiness to attend the Round Table Conference and, more than once, he referred to the 'ruling clique in the Punjab'. There was no declaration of independence but it was plain that Sheikh Mujib was proceeding, step by step, to a planned situation in which such a declaration would seem amply justified and, therefore, have the full support of the people of East Pakistan. It was on this occasion that he made reference to collusion between the 'minority group' and others.

Three days later, an interesting official announcement became available to the public. It stated that during the recent disturbances in East Pakistan 172 persons had been killed and 358 injured. Of those killed, 23 were the victims of firing by the armed forces. In this extraordinary statement, many did not fail to notice that:

(a) the proportion of killed to wounded was extremely high;

(b) if, out of 172 killed, 23 were the victims of the armed forces, who was responsible for the rest? The police? Rioters killing each other? The figure of 23, quoted by

5

itself, looked suspiciously like a clumsy effort to exculpate the army as much as possible.

(c) If these figures were admitted officially, the actual casualties were probably a good deal higher.

(d) There was no indication that the Government intended any enquiry into these losses of life.

Meanwhile, non-co-operation continued and the civil administration was prostrate for the ninth day. In West Pakistan newspapers, to the ill-disguised pleasure of many, carried hints of 'sterner measures', and feelings were hardly sweetened when, on arrival at Dacca to assume his governorship, General Tikka Khan was offered a garland of shoes (a grave insult), and the Chief Justice of East Pakistan refused to administer the oath. The atmosphere then prevailing could be gauged by the evacuation, on 10 March, of 76 British women and children on the advice of the British Government.[7] Some United Nations personnel also left at the same time and Sheikh Mujib chided the Secretary-General adding that he had 'thus taken cognizance of the hazards to life and property to which the military forces are exposing those who are in Bangladesh.'[8] On 12 March, non-co-operation entered on its twelfth day and Martial Law Order No. 114 was promulgated specifying punishments for those who destroyed Government property or impeded the movement of the armed forces or their supplies. This Order was fair indication that there was interference with the movement of troops and that damage was being done to military installations.

On the day preceding, Bhutto had sent a long telegram to Sheikh Mujib offering to visit Dacca immediately so that they might meet and find a solution to the crisis. The telegram was ignored, except to the extent that Tajuddin Ahmed, General Secretary of the Awami League and one of the most militant among Sheikh Mujib's colleagues, said the League was not even prepared to consider it. In West Pakistan some of Mr. Bhutto's political rivals described the telegram as a 'smokescreen' and advised Mujib to take no notice. This and other moves have

---

[7] This appears to have been the first evacuation and was the object of criticism at the time. There were then about 1,000 British men, women, and children living in East Pakistan, but those evacuated were from the tea-gardens and living, therefore, in some measure of isolation.

[8] *D*, 12 March 1971.

been described by Bhutto as follows: 'The defeated leaders of West Pakistan tried to capitalize on the situation. They sought to blame the People's Party for everything. The press which was mainly in the hands of Big Business joined these attacks to confuse and confound public opinion. No gambit or stunt was spared to put blame on the People's Party. In their frenzied efforts to discredit the majority party of West Pakistan, the fate of Pakistan was forgotten.'[9] Certainly every effort was made to heap responsibility for the situation upon Bhutto's shoulders and his growing identification with the army was to increase further after his meeting in Karachi on 12 March with Yahya Khan, then on his way to Dacca. Indeed, talk of collusion between them had become so insistent that, as we have seen, Bhutto felt it necessary to publish a denial.[10]

Contemporaneously with Yahya Khan's visit to Dacca, an important change was made in the Central Government. The civil service head of the Ministry of Information and National Affairs, Syud Ahmed, an East Pakistani, was appointed Officer on Special Duty with the same rank as before, and replaced by Roedad Khan, a West Pakistani. This was much too significant an alteration not to be noticed. One newspaper commented as follows: 'Some people see this [the transfer of Syud Ahmed] in relation to the current East–West polarization, arguing it may have become embarrassing for an East Pakistani to work at the head of the Ministry when the policies laid down by him were being *disregarded in East* Pakistan' (my italics).[11] This interpretation may or may not have been correct, but the curious thing was that civil service heads of other Ministries, who also were East Pakistanis, remained in their posts. Was Syud Ahmed's allegiance in doubt, or did the Central Government desire to have the organs of propaganda firmly in its own control through West Pakistani personnel?

With the arrival of Yahya Khan in Dacca on 15 March,

---

[9] *The Great Tragedy*, p. 34.

[10] See Ch. IX, n. 28. His denial had special reference to postponement of the National Assembly on 1 March 1971. In its issue dated 6 March 1971, *The Economist*, London, stated, in an editorial entitled 'Does Pakistan Exist?', '. . . he [Yahya Khan] left it to Mr. Bhutto to try to get concessions out of [Sheikh Mujib]'. This could be interpreted as meaning that a collusive arrangement existed between Yahya Khan and Bhutto by which the former would hold the ring and the latter would handle Mujib. It does not follow that *The Economist* meant this or that it possessed information which would justify such a conclusion.

[11] *Punjab Punch*, Lahore, 21 March 1971.

events in East Pakistan entered upon their penultimate phase. The White Paper provides briefly stated notes of the day-by-day negotiations which, along with other events, can conveniently be subsumed under these headings: (a) the course of the negotiations; (b) the issues in dispute; (c) the final recourse to arms.

Yahya Khan reached Dacca (Sheikh Mujib had said earlier that he would be welcome as 'a guest of Bangladesh'), armed with the knowledge that Bhutto's party agreed in principle with the four demands made on 7 March by Sheikh Mujib but that any settlement, interim or final, must be with the consent of the People's Party.[12] This meant that Bhutto was agreeable to the lifting of Martial Law although he added that the 'modalities . . . of the withdrawal of Martial Law had to be worked out on the basis of common agreement'. After Yahya Khan reached Dacca he sent a message to Bhutto asking him to come to Dacca. Bhutto agreed to do so, provided Sheikh Mujib participated in the discussions. On 17 March a message reached Bhutto that he was required in Dacca for discussions with Yahya Khan since, according to the Principal Staff Officer, discussions were necessary as a result of Yahya Khan's talks with Sheikh Mujib. Mr. Bhutto writes: 'Having been informed that I was being summoned to Dacca to meet the President and not for the purpose of having discussions with Mujibur Rahman, we politely refused the invitation.'[13] On all counts, it is evident that Bhutto was right to refuse for, irrespective of whether his meeting with Mujib would help the situation, there was all the difference in the world between hearing from Mujib's own lips what he wanted and hearing Yahya Khan's version of it.[14]

The form of Yahya Khan's summons to Bhutto gives an important clue to his attitude. In this strange triangle of interests and determinations, the approach of Yahya Khan and those assisting him was authoritarian and imbued with a sense of their own rightness. In the main, a life spent in public administration does not fit a man for politics; a career in the

---

[12] *The Great Tragedy*, p. 36.
[13] Ibid., p. 37
[14] Long afterwards, Mr. Mazhar Ali Khan, a senior journalist who was in Dacca at this crucial time, wrote: 'We . . . soon realized that Yahya Khan and his spokesmen had been giving out incorrect versions of the draft agreement to the PPP [Pakistan People's Party]. The PPP's stand conveyed to the Awami League was also distorted.' *D*, 19 November 1972.

armed forces is an even worse preparation. In the present instance, the deficiencies were in no way compensated for by a
sense of patriotic devotion, however strong.[15]

Yahya Khan's insistence that Bhutto should visit Dacca indicated that Yahya Khan had assumed the role of umpire who,
after hearing what the two principal leaders had to say, would
proceed to give his award which would not necessarily be in
the form of a draft constitution. It might, perhaps, be in the
form of a decision on whether the National Assembly should
meet and, if so, how and for what purposes. Yahya Khan was
clinging to the idea that, in accordance with the LFO, he
would decide whether or not to authenticate the Constitution
Bill. If he did not, the Assembly would stand dissolved. It
seemed he had chosen to ignore Bhutto's opinion, sound as it
was, that the LFO had become a dead letter.[16] Indeed, according to the White Paper:[17] 'The President clearly indicated to
Sheikh Mujibur Rahman that the unequivocal agreement of
*all* political leaders was essential before he could consider agreeing in principle to any plan, in the interest of peaceful transfer
of power' (my italics).

It is easy to assess the reaction of the Awami League leaders.
They were intensely political and intensely suspicious and re-
sentful. Many of them possessed a strong intellectual bent of
mind and all were determined, come what might, that this
time they would not be thwarted in their purposes. Above all,
they did not like Martial Law, either in the abstract or in
practice. They considered that it had been abused by Ayub
Khan and was likely to be abused again, if only to frustrate
their electoral success in East Pakistan. For them, Martial Law
was nothing but a conspiracy of politically ambitious soldiers
to defeat the democratic aspirations of the country.

Mr. Bhutto's position was somewhat different. At that moment his was the more enigmatic figure for although he could
scarcely have *desired* to witness a truncated Pakistan, he must
have perceived the trend. Yahya Khan and his advisers may

---

[15] In most countries, the armed forces, the civil services, and the police regard
themselves, especially in the higher ranks, as the real repository of the patriotic
spirit. Hence, it comes about that any criticism of these services, and of the men
who run them, tends to be treated as unpatriotic criticism of the country itself.

[16] *The Great Tragedy*, p. 32.

[17] *The Crisis in East Pakistan*, p. 18.

have been foolish enough to suppose they could, with rifle and bayonet, withstand the current of opinion flowing fiercely against them—even disperse it—but could Mr. Bhutto suppose such a thing? Indeed, as we know from his own statement, Mr. Bhutto had concluded, some months before, that Sheikh Mujib desired a separation. Mr. Bhutto states that he had divined the Sheikh's intentions from his conversations with him. Moreover, Mr. Bhutto had advised Yahya Khan to have recourse to 'light military action'.[18] Thus, after Sheikh Mujib's sweeping electoral victory Mr. Bhutto must have realized that the future constitutional structure of the country would have to be very different from what had previously been intended. Why then did Mr. Bhutto compromise himself by having anything to do with military action, however light? Why not let Yahya Khan and his advisers bear the entire burden of that responsibility? Why was Mr. Bhutto not able to come to terms with Sheikh Mujib in such fashion as would make some continuing link possible, however tenuous?

Some explanation may be found in the fact that the character of the negotiations was entirely conditioned by circumstances and attitudes, and it may well be that Yahya Khan and his men had charted their course with no intention of deviating. So, too, Sheikh Mujib. Perhaps, also, Mr. Bhutto, but his navigation was a good deal more complex. He may have seen his purpose clearly enough, but he had to steer carefully between the Scylla of Yahya Khan and the Charybdis of Sheikh Mujib. In withstanding the determinations of the latter, it must not seem as if he had thrown in his lot with the military dictator; and in accommodating the Awami League, it should not appear that he was willing to see Pakistan broken up, much less be a party to its disruption.

The growing intransigence of the Awami League was soon demonstrated. On 17 March General Tikka Khan issued a Martial Law Order setting up an Enquiry Commission to investigate the circumstances of the army's being called in to aid the civil power on 1 March 1971. The Commission would have four members, one each from: the Civil Service of Pakistan,

---

[18] Interview with Mr. Kuldip Nayyar, *Statesman*, New Delhi, 23 March 1972. Addressing the Pakistan National Assembly on 14 April 1972 Mr. Bhutto said: 'Light military action was necessary as a last resort to counter secession . . .'.

the police, the army, and the East Pakistan Rifles. A Judge of the East Pakistan High Court would preside. Intended to meet Sheikh Mujib's third demand announced on 7 March, it is not surprising that he rejected the proposals out of hand. This rejection certainly reflected his state of mind, but it was clear that a Commission so constituted would attract no one in East Pakistan. It was improbable that an enquiry commission of five members of whom three were interested parties, i.e. those from the army, the police, and the East Pakistan Rifles[19] would form unbiased conclusions and, as Sheikh Mujib pertinently remarked, the Commission's 'very constitution by a Martial Law Order and ... submission of its report to the Martial Law authority are objectionable'. Perhaps the Commission was constituted so as to invite rejection, although this assumption credits Yahya Khan and his advisers with a subtlety they rarely demonstrated. The issues involved in this cut-and-thrust are of little importance now, but it is of interest to examine what occupied the minds of those who, everyone naturally supposed, were concerned to find solutions to the country's problems without breaking it up for ever.

On 19 March Mujibur Rahman asked Yahya Khan for a complete withdrawal of Martial Law; for the National and Provincial Assemblies to be invested with legislative powers; and for complete representative government at the Centre and in the Provinces. Yahya Khan replied with a draft Martial Law Regulation which provided for the setting up of Cabinets at the Centre and in the Provinces; the investment of the Assemblies with the legislative powers provided by Ayub Khan's Constitution of 1962; the abolition of Martial Law Administrators and Military Courts but retention of the Chief Martial Law Administrator's office. Clearly, this retention could nullify everything and it was founded upon the argument that if the Martial Law Proclamation of 1969 were revoked, or Martial Law otherwise withdrawn, the Central and Provincial Governments would have no legal validity.[20] To this argument Yahya Khan and his advisers clung unshakably. Upon it they raised all their objections and demurrers to all the Awami League's pro-

---

[19] It should be remembered that most of the officers of the East Pakistan Rifles were West Pakistanis.
[20] Cf. White Paper, *The Crisis in East Pakistan*, p. 17.

posals which called for the withdrawal or abrogation of Martial Law. In his address to the nation on 26 March Yahya Khan fell back on the same idea.

It is possible to theorize endlessly about such matters, but while it may be true that right lives by law, it is just as true that law by power subsists, and power is not a theoretical conception but a testable fact. Yahya Khan wielded power, but he did so without the people's concurrence and he seemed never to have realized how precarious his situation was. In resting upon the argument of legal basis, Yahya Khan made it clear he had no intention of abating the power he exercised *de facto* if not *de jure*.[21] Nor does it seem that he or any of the people round him ever considered the possibility of winning, by some adjustment, the concurrence of the nation. The arguments he advanced served only to convince Sheikh Mujib and his colleagues that Yahya Khan's government intended to retain all power and keep in their hands the decisive right to accept, to reject, to ignore, or to postpone constitutional change.

Yahya Khan made another attempt to meet the Sheikh's demands and a fresh draft Proclamation was prepared. It provided for the setting up of a Central Cabinet selected 'from the representatives of political parties of East and West Pakistan' and for the revocation of Martial Law on the day on which the provincial Cabinet Ministers took the oath of office. There were other proposals for political participation but the main point of interest is in the utter want of realism. Why should Sheikh Mujib, seeing that he had an overall majority in the National Assembly, agree to share office with other parties? And why should the abrogation of Martial Law await the day on which provincial Ministers took the oath?[22] It had never been suggested that there should be some sort of coalition and the LFO made no provision for it. Moreover, what would happen if the Ministers in *one* of the provincial Cabinets declined to take the oath? Doubt was reinforced when, on the evening of 23 March, Yahya Khan informed Sheikh Mujib that Martial Law, *if it was to be withdrawn*, would be removed on the day when the Ministers of *all* Provinces took the oath.[23]

[21] We have already noted that, years later, Pakistan's Supreme Court decided that Yahya Khan was a 'usurper'. See Ch. I, n. 10.
[22] Cf. White Paper, *The Crisis in East Pakistan*, p. 19.
[23] Cf. Ibid., p. 23. My emphasis.

Incessant negotiation, instead of satisfying the parties to these feverish dialogues, served only to underline their disagreements and, worse still, their antipathies. Their differences had been crystallized by the most revealing aspect of their discussions, namely, the proposal that *two* committees should be formed from the National Assembly, one for East Pakistan and one for the western Provinces. Yahya Khan agreed, provided the western leaders accepted it. Mr. Bhutto was agreeable provided that the Assembly met first as a single body and thereafter set up the two committees. How far was constitutional bifurcation, consistent with the notion of a single, sovereign state, to go?

Of course, activity in East Pakistan was not confined to the comings and goings at the President's House. Continuous inflow of troops from West Pakistan bred the conviction that sooner, rather than later, all discussion would be summarily terminated by the armed forces. Yahya Khan and western political leaders found that there was ample evidence of East Pakistan's intractable hostility. Violence throughout the eastern Province was spreading: the armed forces were subjected to much provocation in the form of contemptuous insult and violence. Information about murderous attacks on West Pakistanis increased. Mr. Bhutto, for his part, was convinced of Mujib's secessionist plans and made the point, at a meeting with Yahya Khan, that the redrafted Proclamation would not 'even be a legal bar to a unilateral declaration of independence by the Awami League',[24] a fair indication of his apprehensions.

Then came 23 March, a day till then known as 'Pakistan Day' and celebrated as the anniversary of the day on which the country adopted its own republican constitution and finally broke the constitutional link with the British Crown. In 1971 rallies were held throughout East Pakistan but with very different purposes, and the occasion was renamed 'Resistance Day'. The Bangladesh flag was unfurled amid scenes of enthusiasm. Sheikh Mujib took the salute at a march past of his partymen, some of them bearing arms. Civil violence became more intense, as did the propaganda favouring secession. Next day Mr. Bhutto met the President and, at 6 p.m., Awami League leaders met the presidential advisers. Mr. Tajuddin Ahmed later said his party had expressed its entire point of view at the meeting and

[24] Ibid., p. 21.

added: 'From our side, there is no need of further meeting.'[25]
Describing these events, the White Paper vaguely adds: 'In the
meantime, reports had become available of Awami League
plans to launch an armed rebellion in the early hours of 26
March.'[26]

So it was that on the night of 25/26 March, the armed forces,
acting on the orders of President Yahya Khan, entered upon
'their duty' to 'restore the authority of Government.'[27] Two
years to the very day after proclaiming Martial Law and pledg-
ing himself, as he expressed it, 'to strive to restore democratic
institutions in the country', General Yahya Khan found it
necessary to employ the armed forces against the people of one
Province and to ban the political party which had secured an
overall majority in the National Assembly following Pakistan's
first direct general elections—elections organized by himself
and based on universal adult suffrage.

[25] *The People*, Dacca, 25 March 1971, quoted in the White Paper, p. 27.
[26] The White Paper, p. 27.
[27] Yahya Khan's radio address to the nation on 26 March 1971.

# XI

# Holocaust—Phase One

We come now to what is, perhaps, the most controversial chapter in the entire history of the old Pakistan. As with many similar controversies, the issues, the merits, the blame, and the facts have become obscured by ignorance, by gratuitous interference, and by extraordinary emotional involvement by people who know nothing about Pakistan. Everything has been further complicated by the circumstances, and Sheikh Mujibur Rahman can no more adduce solid grounds for his figure of three million lost lives than can General Tikka Khan for his figure of 30,000. That there was widespread loss of life, injury to persons, and damage to property is indisputable. The difficulty is to reach a fair assessment and trace the supporting evidence.

Justifying his decision, later, Yahya Khan claimed that plans to launch armed insurrection in East Pakistan on the night of 25/26 March had been discovered. The White Paper states (page 40) that an operational plan had been worked out and that the uprising would begin on the Awami League's signal. Describing the plan, the White Paper explains:

(a) EBR [the East Bengal Regiment] troops would occupy Dacca and Chittagong to prevent the landing of Pakistan Army by sea or by air;

(b) the remaining EBR troops with the help of EPR [East Pakistan Rifles], police, and armed razakars [the word *razakar* means 'social worker' and the term has served on various occasions as a guise for private armies as well as officially armed bodies of men] would move to eliminate the armed forces at various cantonments and stations;

(c) EPR would occupy all key posts of the border and keep it open for aid from outside;

(d) requirements of further arms and ammunition would be met from India; and

(e) Indian troops would come to the assistance of the Awami League rebel force once the latter succeeded in the first phase of occupying key centres and paralysing the Pakistan Army.[1]

The White Paper goes to on say that 'the early hours of Friday morning [presumably, Friday 26 March 1971] were fixed as the zero hour for the armed uprising'.

There are four points to make concerning this explanation. First, it is reasonable to suppose that the stage had indeed come when the Awami League and others recognized that recourse to arms might be necessary, and that plans had accordingly been made. Secondly, Bengalis in the army were deeply infected with discontent and secessionist ideas. This stemmed, in part, from the fact that the majority of their officers were from West Pakistan. The explanation given was that adequate officer material had not so far come forward in East Pakistan. Thirdly, the people of East Pakistan had become used to the idea of the army's employment as an instrument of political suppression and had learned to defy it.[2] Fourthly, at all times Yahya Khan and his men were well informed as to what was going on in the Province.

There is little doubt that each side was aware of what was being said or planned even in the innermost councils of its adversary. Mr. Bhutto expressed himself most critically of Pakistan's intelligence services[3] and, certainly, there was substantial ground for such criticism although whether the criticism best applies to the gathering of information or to the proper use of it is a separate question. The fact is that each side was fully exposed to the other.[4]

---

[1] It should be borne in mind that the White Paper is dated 5 August 1971, i.e. rather more than four months after Yahya Khan began his pre-emptive action.

[2] Cf. *FCTC*, p. 254, referring to events in 1968: '. . . the continued use of the armed forces could lead to a situation in which familiarity bred contempt. In other words, men would learn to dislike soldiers and then to defy them as they had the police.'

[3] *The Great Tragedy*, p. 79.

[4] As evidence of the extent of the Awami League's intelligence apparatus, I can cite the following instance. Some days prior to 25 March, Mr. Arnold Zeitlin, correspondent of the Associated Press of America, interviewed Sheikh Mujib at about noon. Afterwards, Mr. Zeitlin returned to his hotel, prepared his despatch and took it personally to the telegraph office. At about 8.30 that evening, a local journalist (afterwards shot by the army) telephoned to say that Sheikh Mujib had seen the contents of the despatch which he desired to be cancelled as he considered some of it injurious to himself. The point here is not whether it was injurious or whether Sheikh Mujib was entitled to ask for its recall, but that persons in the telegraph office were keeping Sheikh Mujib informed as to what was being sent out. I am indebted to Mr. Zeitlin for this information.

The White Paper also had a good deal to say about atrocities inflicted upon civilians who were not Bengalis or who did not agree with, or had opposed, the Awami League. Stories are narrated, in some detail, of the cruel vileness committed upon children, women, and men. No doubt, there was some truth in them but their repetition here is unnecessary. More important is to ascertain the moment when Yahya Khan concluded that Sheikh Mujib intended no settlement but, instead, had planned an armed uprising. In the absence of documentary evidence an answer can only be conjectural. Still, we do know that:

(a) in mid-1970 Mr. Bhutto had given his opinion to General Peerzada that Sheikh Mujib desired separation;

(b) on 17 February 1971 the Lahore Horse Show was cancelled;

(c) after 1 March 1971 carriage of mails between East and West appeared to have been suspended in order to limit private communication about the state of affairs in East Pakistan;

(d) after 3 March the movement of troops to East Pakistan was intensified;

(e) on 7 March General Tikka Khan, a recognized hardliner, became Governor of East Pakistan;

(f) on 14 March Syud Ahmed, an East Pakistani, was removed from his post as civil service head of the Ministry of Information and National Affairs;

(g) on 24 March Tajuddin Ahmed, the Awami League's General Secretary, gave an ultimatum by informing Yahya Khan that he had twenty-four hours in which to secure Bhutto's agreement to a plan for *two* National Assembly drafting committees, failing which independence would be declared. He also said his party saw no need for further meetings.

(h) Yahya Khan's government was informed of a plan for insurrection.

It is reasonable to suppose that General Headquarters had long studied questions of internal security in the country as a whole. Apart from subversive movements, there were problems of the veiled or explicit support by such countries as India or Afghanistan. Further, as the East Pakistan situation deteriorated, military plans would have taken specific shape involv-

ing a military build-up. This would require time, and therefore
would affect the moment of decision. These staff appreciations
would be coloured by the important issue of the political involvement of the armed forces.

By March 1971 Yahya Khan had ample reason to foresee
some kind of violent show-down and, depending upon the intelligence appreciations, three options were open. He could: (a)
allow the East Pakistan secessionists to strike first; (b) pre-empt
the situation by taking the initiative; or (c) frustrate the secessionists by coming to terms with Sheikh Mujib if he could. To
adopt option (a) or (b) would imply an intention to preserve
the old Pakistan come what might. This would mean that
Yahya Khan thought his troops could control the situation and
liquidate the insurrectionists and centres of Bengali nationalists.
Option (c) involved very different considerations.

Any bargain with Sheikh Mujib would mean going far towards meeting the Six Point programme and the Awami League's draft proclamation, with the concomitant possibility of a
declaration of independence then or later. If that happened
what attitude would Bhutto and his party adopt, and what
would be the attitude of West Pakistan generally? Even if there
were no risk of a declaration of independence, the nature of
the settlement would certainly mean that the line distinguish-
ing it from autonomy would be very obscure. Speaking of the
Six Point formula, Mr. Bhutto wrote later: '. . . the formula,
taken as a whole, was a veiled charter for confederation which
contained the genesis of constitutional secession'.[5] The risk of
secession was clearly there, especially after the demonstration
on 7 March of a fierce Bengali nationalism.

It was possible, in the interests of peace, in order that Muslim
should not kill Muslim, and in the spirit of democracy that
Yahya Khan might still have sought a peaceful settlement. But,
had he done so, would he have been able to implement it?
Would his military colleagues have permitted it? Would not
they and the West Pakistani people have said that rather than
accept such a settlement, it would be better to fight it out?
After all, the soldiers of West Pakistan had no high opinion of
the military prowess of their East Pakistani brethren-in-arms.
And if it were suggested that India might intervene, their

[5] *The Great Tragedy*, p. 11.

answer would be that they had given the Indians a sound thrashing in 1965 and could do so again. But if East Pakistan had seized the opportunity to declare independence, could Yahya Khan have extricated his troops and West Pakistani civilians? Would East Pakistan have allowed him to ship away his arms and ordnance? At that ominous stage, would not the forces of East Pakistan have fallen upon them like predators upon some hapless, stricken creature? On the other hand, if West Pakistan had accepted East Pakistan's constitutional demands and East Pakistan had proceeded to impose its will in the National Assembly, the outcome for West Pakistan would surely have meant political subservience and every economic disadvantage, including the loss of a tied market for the products of West Pakistan industry.

However, it was widely suspected in some circles that Yahya Khan was totally insincere and had not the least intention of coming to any settlement.[6] It has been said that the postponement of the Assembly from February onwards was to provide time in which to reinforce the troops, and that postponement on 1 March was to provoke a fevered crisis which would make it possible to crush Sheikh Mujib, the Awami League, and Bengali nationalism in one swift, decisive blow.

Why was 25/26 March the date on which Yahya Khan decided to strike? Could he not have had recourse to something else, in the hope that better counsels would prevail? Was it not possible that each side was playing a game of bluff, hoping the other would be the first to throw in the cards? Assuming the accuracy of Yahya Khan's intelligence and assuming the timing to have been sound with respect to his own military position and the scope of the enemy threat, how was it that the pre-emptive action, instead of achieving its purpose, was transformed into a long-continued tragedy bringing death, dishonour, and misery to millions? Yahya Khan later said: 'I should have taken action against Sheikh Mujibur Rahman and his colleagues weeks ago, but I had to try my utmost to handle the situation in such a manner as not to jeopardize my plan of peaceful transfer of power. In my keenness to achieve this

[6] Had not Sheikh Mujib advised Mr. Bhutto not to trust the military? Had he not said that if they destroyed him, Sheikh Mujib, they would destroy Mr. Bhutto also? Ibid., p. 43.

aim, I kept on tolerating one illegal act after another.'[7] Yahya Khan did not say what sort of action he ought to have taken, but one assumes he meant the arrest and detention of Sheikh Mujib and his colleagues, after the elections. Was he in any position to take such action? Were his troops already there, 'weeks ago'? The explanation that Yahya Khan was deterred from taking action by his keenness for the peaceful transfer of power is not convincing.

It is said that when taking leave of General Tikka Khan at Dacca Airport on 25 March, Yahya Khan's last order was laconically expressed: 'Sort them out!'[8] In the ensuing weeks this phrase was on the lips of many an army officer, whether or not Yahya Khan actually used it. There is a widely held but unsubstantiated belief that on the night of 25/26 March the army went berserk, careering madly through the streets of Dacca, bent upon indiscriminate massacre. It is very doubtful indeed, however, that the pre-emptive action was executed that night other than in accordance with a carefully prepared plan and well defined objectives. There is ample reason to suppose it was only later that the troops could be said to have misconducted themselves.

The objectives were plainly threefold: to pre-empt the reported intentions of the Awami League; to crush Bengali nationalism; to destroy those who favoured separation from West Pakistan or were suspected of it. As thus conceived, the plan, in the minds of the planners, therefore required:

(a) destruction or capture of 'mutinous' army and police units;[9]

(b) elimination of subversives, left-wing intellectuals, suspect educationalists, and students; politicals and professionals known for separationist tendencies or other uncongenial notions; trade-union leaders; and Hindus, the last-named, as a class, being considered traitorous;

(c) destruction of symbols of resistance such as the Shaheed

----

[7] Address to the nation on 26 March 1971.

[8] According to an Indian source, Major-General D. K. Palit, *The Lightning Campaign*, Thomson Press, New Delhi, 1972, p. 25. If true, this information may have reached General Palit from journalists who fled to India from East Pakistan.

[9] I use the word 'mutiny' because, after 25 March, West Pakistanis, especially in Government service, were fond of drawing comparisons with the Indian Mutiny of 1857.

Minar and centres of propaganda such as opposition newspaper presses

All that is known of the operation confirms that the action was limited to carrying out these objectives. Any person foolish enough to be on the streets after the curfew was broadcast was likely to be shot, but the suggestion that there was widespread indiscriminate slaughter of civilians that night,[10] the bodies being collected and thrown into the two rivers of Dacca, cannot be supported. It is true that secrecy measures were adopted and that persons living in hotels were warned to draw their curtains and not peer through windows, but there are sound reasons for supposing that the shooting that night was confined to marked men and listed groups. These reasons are as follows. To begin with, myths about the army massacring civilians in Dacca under cover of night and disposing of the bodies before daybreak were already familiar.[11] To slaughter civilians in their thousands, collect the bodies, and throw them into the rivers, all after 10 p.m., would involve a logistical problem the army would be likely to shun when graver questions of mutiny were at hand. If there had been indiscriminate firing, the proportion of wounded to killed would have been about three to one. Moreover, the evidence of wounded either going to hospital or dying later is remarkably sparse. This night action was evidently entrusted mainly to Special Force personnel said to have been trained on the lines of American Green Berets. It is true that armour was on the streets but it was used to bulldoze barricades and batter down printing-press buildings. It is also the case that mortars were in action against specified targets, e.g. the Rajabagh Police Barracks. All the reliable eye-witness evidence that exists indicates that the number of corpses was small. This evidence is necessarily limited, since no Dacca resident would have gone out counting them, and foreign journalists were confined to their hotels, to be expelled from Dacca later. Mr. Arnold Zeitlin, correspondent of the Associated Press of America, saw about a dozen bodies lying on the grass outside the Iqbal Hall at Dacca University. This, and Jagnanath Halls,

[10] Cf. *Paris Match*, 10 July 1971, p. 70: 'At Dacca, more than 700,000 inhabitants have fled or are dead.' That there were thousands of deaths on 25/26 March is not explicit here, but the innuendo seems plain.

[11] See *FCTC*, p. 246.

were centres of dissidence and both were targets on 25/26 March. On 19 April the German newsweekly, *Der Spiegel*, published a photograph showing seven civilians who had been shot, their bodies guarded by a soldier. Casualty figures of this size bear no relation to tales of indiscriminate slaughter, and even seem low to those who, like the present writer, witnessed the Great Calcutta Killing, in 1946, when main thoroughfares, such as Central Avenue, were littered with corpses.

It is probable that troops sent from West to East Pakistan were possessed by the idea that Hindus were at the bottom of all the trouble, and that if they were called upon to fire on civilians it would not be on their Muslim co-religionists but on the Hindu troublemakers. Mention has been made of Sheikh Mujib's reference to *satyagraha* and to West Pakistan's aversion for the writings of Rabindranath Tagore whose song, *Amar Sonar Bangla*, had been suggested as a national anthem for Bangladesh. During the electioneering period it was reported that slogans had been raised mentioning deities of the Hindu pantheon, and in mid-1970 the prominence of Hindus among labour-leaders had become noteworthy. In that year, also, opportunity was taken to form a committee of twelve, of whom at least six were Bengali Muslims, to preserve the memory of Trilokya Nath Chakrabarti Maharaj, an East Pakistani Hindu writer and scholar, whose books had been banned by the Government.[12] This act appeared not only to be defiant in itself but was interpreted by many, especially in the army, as evidence of a rising Hindu penetration, and of increasing attachment to India.

Lists had been prepared of persons suspected of holding Bengali nationalist or separationist views, and guilt by association was not unknown. Yahya Khan had with him, in Dacca, a formidable intelligence organization led by the Director of Military Intelligence and the Director of the Intelligence Bureau. The Special Force teams were mainly from West Pakistan and worked in collaboration with East Pakistanis who were better informed, but such collaboration has its obvious dangers and many East Pakistani informers worked for both sides. For this reason many were able to escape the army's wrath, having been warned in time, and it helps to explain the intelligence leaks

[12] *PO* 16 August 1970.

which occurred.[13] A good deal that happened remains shrouded in mystery, although time may reveal much. Those unwise enough to make enquiries about missing persons were usually met with the bland reply that the person in question, conscious of his wicked treachery, had probably taken refuge with his Indian friends.

The mutinous army and police units turned on their West Pakistani officers and killed them virtually to a man. They also engaged the army, notably in and around Chittagong, and some of them continued to operate into the month of April.[14] However, with its superiority in weapons, the army was able to overcome them in the end, and any who resisted were mercilessly dealt with.[15] The East Pakistan Rifles were renamed East Pakistan Civil Armed Force, as if to exorcise the memory of a unit which had taken up mutinous arms.

Precise detail is wanting about centres of political opposition and symbols of resistance, but Mr. Bhutto has described how, at about 11.30 p.m. on 25 March, he and his friends were awakened by gun-fire. 'A number of places were ablaze and we saw the demolition of the office of the newspaper, *The People.*'[16] Not only were the premises demolished, but the presses were smashed and persons on the premises killed. The Shaheed Minar at the University was damaged and later broken up completely; the site was then levelled and tidied. To prevent any attempt at reviving memories of the place, the word *masjid*, meaning 'mosque', was placed there so that any counter-action in the form of surreptitious slogan-writing would have had the aspect of sacrilege. On the wall, the *Kalima* (the Sacred Creed of Islam) was inscribed in Arabic characters, but so distorted and misshapen as to give the appearance of Bengali script, an interesting example of self-deception.

I have pointed out earlier that Yahya Khan's decisions were largely the product of forces he never put in train. Bhutto claimed that had things been managed differently during Yahya

---

[13] Later Mr. Bhutto said that the progressive forces had been singled out for liquidation. Address to the National Assembly, 14 April 1972.

[14] All this is explicit in General Tikka Khan's broadcast on 18 April 1971.

[15] For example, the police at Rajabagh Police Barracks, Outer Circular Road, Dacca, refused to surrender. They were bombarded with mortars and the buildings reduced to ruins. When I saw the place, in November 1971, it had been re-built with only doors and windows to be fitted. The rubble of the old buildings still lay on the kerbside.     [16] *The Great Tragedy*, p. 50.

Khan's dispensation, the situation in East Pakistan would not have deteriorated as it did,[17] yet it was probably too late for a simple cure. By the time Yahya Khan became responsible for the nation's affairs, the involvement of the armed forces had become customary and, it seemed, irresistible and there was nothing that apolitical soldiers, conscious of the inherent dangers, could do about it.

Having returned to Karachi, Yahya Khan addressed the nation by radio on 26 March. After touching on the course of events which followed his announcement that the National Assembly would be summoned on 25 March, he said:

(a) He had been prepared to agree to Sheikh Mujib's scheme whereby Martial Law would be withdrawn, provincial governments set up, and the National Assembly sit *ab initio* as two committees, provided he had the unequivocal agreement of *all* political leaders.[18]

(b) His discussion with 'other political leaders' showed they were much disturbed by these proposals.

(c) Sheikh Mujib's action of starting his non-co-operation movement was 'an act of treason'. 'He and his party . . . have created turmoil, terror and insecurity.'

(d) 'The armed forces . . . have been subjected to taunts and insults . . . I am proud of them.'

(e) Sheikh Mujib 'failed to respond in any constructive manner . . . he . . . kept on flouting the authority of Government even during my presence in Dacca. The proclamation that he proposed was nothing but a trap . . . he has attacked the solidarity and integrity of the country —this crime will not go unpunished.'

(f) He announced a complete ban on the Awami League as a political party, a ban shortly afterwards made effective by Martial Law Order No. 18 which prohibited the propagation of the manifesto of the Awami League.

(g) He also announced a re-imposition of censorship throughout the country, and all political activity was suspended but this did not prevent Mr. Bhutto and Abdul Qayum Khan from holding press conferences a few days later which were intensely political in character.

---

[17] *The Great Tragedy*, p. 57 et seq.
[18] My emphasis. The vagueness is plainly deliberate.

When Mr. Bhutto returned to Karachi from Dacca he thanked God Pakistan had been saved. But to many people it seemed plain that much time must pass, much effort be expended, and a wealth of political tact displayed before the country could achieve political stability.

# XII

# Holocaust—Phase Two

The immediate consequence of the pre-emptive action was a swift and voluntary evacuation by the terror-stricken population of Dacca. Hundreds of thousands fled the city, particularly among the poorer classes, many of whom were not Dacca-born but had come from their villages for work. With all speed they repaired to safe refuge, on their way broadcasting tales of atrocity and destruction brought by the soldiery. The result was predictable. Enraged townsfolk and villagers turned on any of their countrymen who were not of Bengali race and the carnage among Biharis and West Pakistanis began. One reason Yahya Khan had given for adopting armed measures was that, prior to 25 March, murderous assaults had been inflicted by Awami League men on those that had opposed them. However, according to the details given in Yahya Khan's White Paper, the total number of persons killed before 25 March was 348, whereas the number killed after 25 March was at least 75,000 and may have been as many as 100,000. In short, the pre-emption, far from putting an end to such murders, actually multiplied them.

In Dacca, Chittagong, and other industrial centres all work came to a standstill. Workers remained absent for weeks and, as late as June 1971, notices still appeared in newspapers calling upon employees to return to mill and factory. Chittagong Port was deserted and vessels were sunk in the Karnaphulli River by frogmen using limpet mines. The accumulation of unhandled cargo rose to about 200,000 tons as compared with Chittagong's normal capacity of 80,000 tons.[1] Ships en route to the port were inevitably diverted by their owners, along with their cargoes—some to Calcutta, much to Pakistan's chagrin. Absence of dock labour made discharge of military stores difficult and dock-workers were sent from West Pakistan. Of course, these were but the lesser aspects of the destructive impact of events

[1] As reported by the Insurance Association of Pakistan to its members.

upon the country's economy. It became necessary for the Government to provide various forms of taxation relief, but perhaps the biggest single financial problem, calling for swift remedy, was the looting of paper currency from banks, in which crime bank officials lent willing hands. The amounts involved were considerable and called for drastic measures.

Not surprisingly, the Government sought to suppress as much information as it could about these untoward happenings and, indeed, all communication between East and West Pakistan was closed. So complete was this suppression that one journalist, whose sympathies towards East Pakistan were not markedly strong, wrote: 'The East Pakistan situation is not available to West Pakistan.'[2] All air traffic for private passengers to East Pakistan was suspended and when re-opened on 12 April. foreigners still required official clearance before proceeding to Dacca.[3]

The efforts of the Government to control information at so critical a time were understandable but, because of mismanagement, damaging to the country. First, all foreign correspondents were confined to their hotels, and then, on 29 March, they were deported by air from Dacca to Karachi. It was a mistaken decision and Yahya Khan tried to explain it away by saying that it was in the best interests of the journalists themselves.[4] The matter continued to be pressed and, as late as August 1971, in an interview given to the French newspaper, *Figaro*, Yahya Khan again tried to justify the decision but added: 'Finally, I regret it.' But he seems never to have touched on the factors which made this decision weigh so heavily against Pakistan at the time. At the hotel where the journalists were confined there was a great display of military authority and a general atmosphere of hostility. At Dacca Airport, prior to embarkation, all luggage was minutely searched and every scrap of paper—notebooks, draft despatches, letters from home, hotel bills, expense vouchers, blank stationery—was held back and, on arrival at Karachi, the journalists were obliged to submit to a similar search. If, therefore, later reporting was sometimes tinctured with ill-will there was little cause for surprise, especially

[2] Z. A. Suleri, 'Problems are Foundational', *PT*, 2 May 1971.
[3] This requirement was finally removed on 4 June 1971.
[4] Press conference reported in *D*, 25 May 1971.

as the Government of Pakistan had already acquired an adverse reputation for its treatment of foreign correspondents.[5]

Some of the reporting aroused much anger in Pakistan's western Provinces, particularly against British and American newspapers and radio. Mr. Bhutto said afterwards: 'the attitude of the British and American press has been, to say the least, deplorable',[6] but this language, by comparison with what was said elsewhere, is remarkable for its mildness—compare the editorial on the subject which appeared in the *Daily News*, Karachi, with the title 'They Spread Lies and Lies Only'.[7] No doubt, British and American reporting was prolific and vigorous but whether it exceeded anything appearing elsewhere is doubtful. *Der Spiegel*, for example, published a description of attacks by Pakistan's armed forces on East Bengal villages including the use of napalm by the Pakistan Air Force;[8] and, three months later, the French magazine *Paris Match*[9] carried an article on events in East Pakistan with the heading: 'The truth at last on repression in Pakistan. It has been atrocious.' It appears that these German and French comments did not arouse the least murmur, and the reason is plain. In Pakistan about five or six per cent of the people understand and read English, i.e. at that time some six million persons, and they had fair access to British and American journals. The numbers who understand other European languages are negligible, and magazines and newspapers in those languages are not easily available.

A classical situation had developed in East Pakistan—the situation in which terror-stricken refugees spread through the land carrying their tales, often exaggerated, of horror and violence. Falling on ready ears, these stories exercised their predictable effect and atrocity repeated itself except that, for the time being, the weapon was in another hand. It was then that the crimes against non-Bengalis, described in the White Paper, began on a fearful scale. This, in turn, was to be followed by those Province-wide operations which—whatever be the truth

---

[5] Notably, in the case of Mr. Jacques Nevard, of the *New York Times*, during the Ayub Khan era, who was charged, in very peculiar circumstances, with contempt of court in Pakistan. The incident is narrated in *FCTC*, p. 83.

[6] *The Great Tragedy*, p. 53.

[7] 9 April 1971. Three British journals were named: *The Times*, *Guardian*, and *The Economist*; and three American: the *New York Times*, *Newsweek*, and *Time*.

[8] *Der Spiegel*, 19 April 1971.

[9] Issue dated 1 July 1971, p. 24.

and much must ever remain obscure—brought the armed forces into total disrepute. Every Bengali became convinced that all of which the West Pakistani soldier was accused was indeed true and it was by reason of this belief that the soldiers of West Pakistan found themselves fighting, afterwards, in a land where every man's hand was against them.

The Province-wide action of the army led to a vast evacuation from East Pakistan into India. The Hindu population in the northern districts fled in particularly large numbers. They had heard much of spreading military terror and of the attacks on Hindus in Dacca. The number of persons—Muslim and Hindu —who fled across the border is still uncertain but no one has ever denied that it ran into seven figures. Yahya Khan ordered a census of persons who left East Pakistan in this way and the result was a figure in the order of 2·25 million.[10] The Indian Government claimed a figure exceeding nine million and the United Nations High Commissioner for Refugees stated that at the beginning of August 1971, 7,144,300 Pakistani refugees had entered India and that more were still crossing the border into that country. It is clear that millions of people do not leave hearth and home, goods and chattels, to face all kinds of privation and want except for some compelling reason which, in the present instance, seems to have been fear, presumably of the conduct of the army, as it passed from village to village. The army succeeded not only in making its name hateful throughout the Province. It succeeded also in creating grounds for India to build up a *casus belli*, since India could not remain indifferent to fighting on its borders between Pakistan troops and insurgents or to an invasion of millions of unarmed but starving, moneyless men, women, and children, an invasion that could be neither resisted nor digested.

Meanwhile, the resistance offered by the Mukti Bahini and other so-called freedom fighters continued, along with acts of sabotage such as damage to electric transmission, railways, and communications generally, but it was evident that the insurgents could not hope to engage the army in pitched battle, and furtive acts of isolated destruction, while troublesome, could not expel the detested Government. But the temper of the people

[10] *PT*, 11 August 1971. According to the official count of the Government of Pakistan the figure at the end of August was 2,002,623. *D*, 2 September 1971.

was such that, to hold East Pakistan, a formal occupation was necessary. In addition to troop reinforcements some 5,000 policemen were sent from West Pakistan. Local levies were recruited known as Razakars and Badars, largely from the Bihari community. These men, armed with rifles, helped to patrol streets, guard railway bridges and other nodal points, especially at night. The prominence of the Bihari community in these paramilitary formations did that community little good but, in general, these levies were not considered important. People regarded them as little more than a trigger-happy nuisance. On 12 June 1971 the curfew was finally withdrawn in Dacca but after dark the city remained lifeless. Oppressed by the sense of all that had happened few people left their homes when dusk had fallen. Those who did, whether pedestrians or motorists, were invariably stopped and usually searched.[11] The atmosphere of military occupation was pervasive.

Everything was provoking undying resentment. Defections among civil servants, whether employed at home or abroad, began at a very early stage. On 6 April a team of civil servants was sent from West Pakistan to shore up the administration and provide 'patriotic' stiffening. By August it was publicly known that Bengali members of Pakistan's Foreign Service, posted to embassies in various foreign countries, had declared their allegiance to Bangladesh. Bengali officers in the Pakistan Navy had refused duty and all Bengali flying personnel, in the Air Force or in civil aviation, were grounded. Thus while on the one hand Yahya Khan's government was making much play with the argument that the people of East Pakistan, in voting for the Six Points, had not voted for secession, all action showed no confidence in the alleged attachment of Bengalis to Pakistan.

In June an amnesty was offered, in general terms, to all who

[11] Personal observation. On 1 November 1971, at about 10.30 a.m., I was at Demra Ferry, on the Sitalakha River, half way between Dacca and Narayanganj. This ferry is important, being the first on the road to Chittagong and is capable of carrying motor-vehicles. The ferry office was then occupied by a small *posse* of West Pakistan policemen, noticeable for their poor turnout and slovenly manner. They had been in East Pakistan for about six months and were not happy as was clear from conversation with them. When the ferry boat arrived, about thirty Bengali civilians disembarked and were lined up by the police who searched their belongings. One man was taken into the office and reappeared much shaken. He said he had been relieved of the contents of his wallet but I did not see it myself. Still, true or not, peculation and stealing of this sort was what East Pakistan civilians said and believed of police and soldiers from West Pakistan.

had left their homes and it was reported that some 2,000 officers and men of the East Bengal Regiment and the East Pakistan Rifles had surrendered. Indeed, on 5 September Yahya Khan announced a general amnesty to all who had 'committed offences during the disturbances in East Pakistan on 1 March and ending on 5 September'. The amnesty extended to the armed forces, para-military bodies, and to the police. Later, it was made clear that it did not apply to those members of the National and Provincial Assemblies (and some other persons), against whom proceedings had been started and who had been given a chance to clear themselves. More specifically, it did not apply to Sheikh Mujibur Rahman who had already been taken into custody and flown to a jail in West Pakistan, there to stand trial *in camera* before a special tribunal set up for the purpose.[12]

The grant of amnesty would have been more encouraging had it not been for Martial Law Regulation No. 88 which had been issued a short while before. This Regulation empowered zonal Martial Law Administrators to convene special criminal courts with the prior approval of the Chief Martial Law Administrator. To these courts the Evidence Act of 1872 did not apply except for Sections 121-6, 133, and 134. Most of the safeguards ensuring validity and relevance were therefore excluded. The evidence of accomplices was made admissible and also the statements, made in writing or 'verbally',[13] of persons who were dead or whose presence could not be secured without unreasonable delay or expense. Once convened, these courts could not adjourn. They could make their own 'secret enquiries' relating to the charges against an accused and it was not necessary to record anything more than a memorandum of the evidence. The nature of the trials conducted in circumstances such as these requires no discussion or analysis and the only redeeming feature about this Martial Law Regulation was the fact that

[12] The grant of amnesty was related to the visit of David M. Abshire, Assistant Secretary of State for Congressional Relations, and of S. M. Khan, civil service head of the Pakistan Foreign Ministry, to the Soviet Union. It was stated that in response to the amnesty, 2,620 persons surrendered, of whom 50 per cent were Awami League workers and 35 per cent East Bengal Regiment and East Pakistan Rifles personnel (*PO*, 30 September 1971). The figures appeared significantly large, but how many did not surrender has never been estimated or, at any rate, has not been disclosed.

[13] Presumably 'orally' was meant.

no death sentence could be awarded. The possibility of judicial murder was ruled out.

Before turning to Yahya Khan's next moves, the major consequences of the events discussed above may be summarized. They were:

(a) A total rift between the two wings of the country, laying the foundation for ultimate division.

(b) A mass migration to India creating an involvement of the gravest import.

(c) Incalculable blows to the economy.

(d) An alienation of world opinion and world confidence.

(e) A firmer grasp of power by the army and the bureaucracy.

# XIII

# Political Measures after
# March 1971

It was plain that after the pre-emptive action on 25/26 March, and contemporaneously with the neutralization of the insurgents and the pacification of the countryside, Yahya Khan's immediate tasks were to: (a) win back the confidence of East Pakistan; (b) revitalize belief in the prospect of an acceptable constitution; (c) counter Indian propaganda and restore Pakistan's world-image; (d) repair the damaged economy. To embark on these tasks implied, of course, that the old Pakistan could be held together, a belief itself flowing from the decision to pre-empt. Moreover, the doctrine that the Awami League (as distinguished from the people of East Pakistan) and India were in conspiracy[1] was based on the idea that the people of East Pakistan as a whole desired unity despite all that had happened and was still happening. Criticism of India as a base for insurgents and rebels justified the doctrine that once these marauders had been killed or captured tranquillity would return.[2]

Some people considered the pre-emptive strike unwise and the *coup* itself a failure which had left the two wings irretrievably sundered. It is doubtful whether East and West Pakistan were indeed irretrievably sundered, but the difficulty was to resolve the visible contradictions. Was it possible to win back East Pakistan's confidence when the army was roving the countryside seeking to destroy the self-styled liberation forces, challenging the loyalty of any person it suspected, and making use of courts organized in terms of Martial Law Regulation No. 88?[3] Was not the very scope of these military operations a measure of the prevailing disaffection? Could confidence be restored

---

[1] See the rambling statement issued by the Pakistan Government in which this suggestion is made. Quoted verbatim in *D*, 7 May 1971.

[2] The discussion of India's role is reserved for the next chapter.

[3] The actual number of these courts does not seem to be on public record.

among people who, apart from the millions in India living in misery and destitution, had scarcely a family with no loss of some sort to record? Had not Sheikh Mujib, East Pakistan's hero, been removed to West Pakistan, there to stand trial in secret (but only *after* he had been declared a traitor and rebel)[4] by the same President who was now appealing for faith and goodwill?

Judged by any standards the task of reconciliation was formidable, but Yahya Khan believed it could be accomplished. To understand his confidence it is necessary to know more about the man and the apparatus he had fashioned. As Commander-in-Chief of the army in Ayub Khan's time, he had gathered round himself officers on whom he could personally rely, believing, as there is some evidence to suggest, that he might one day become President.[5] It must be noticed that out of this situation there developed an army caucus for, as has been said earlier, with the departure of the Navy and Air Force Chiefs from their positions in the Central Secretariat as advisers and controllers of various ministries, and after the departure of Admiral Ahsan from East Pakistan, the presence of the Navy and Air Force in the nation's political management had disappeared.

Among the officers whom Yahya Khan had drawn around himself were General Abdul Hamid Khan—an old regimental comrade who, in Yahya Khan's administration, took care of the army on the service side; Lieut.-General S. G. M. M. Peerzada; Major-Generals Gul Hasan, A. O. Mitha, M. Akbar, and Ghulam Umer. Lieut.-General Akhtar Hussain Malik[6] may have once been a member of this coterie but, in 1967, he had been sent to CENTO while other senior generals, with whom the personal equation was not so intimate, were appointed governors of the newly re-established Provinces of West Pakistan. Yahya Khan's close association with Peerzada dated from the time when the latter was appointed Director of Military Operations under Yahya Khan, then Chief of the

[4] Yahya Khan was guilty of this on at least four occasions.

[5] At the time of Ayub Khan's illness in January 1968 there was much talk of a praetorian succession with Yahya Khan's name prominent, since he was Commander-in-Chief. This prospect the Air Force did not like, a fact much underlined by Yahya Khan's burst of fervent praise for that service in April 1968. All this led to misunderstanding between Ayub Khan and Yahya Khan.

[6] Killed in a road accident in August 1969.

General Staff, and when Yahya Khan became Commander-in-Chief, the association became closer still when Peerzada was appointed Adjutant-General. It was the Adjutant-General's Branch which processed the first Martial Law declaration upon Ayub Khan's departure and it is possible that some preparation in this respect had been in train even when Ayub Khan's exit was not certain. It seems that Yahya Khan developed a deep trust in Peerzada and found it convenient to take him to the Secretariat of the Chief Martial Law Administrator where, as Principal Staff Officer to the President, he was sometimes referred to in private conversation as the 'Prime Minister'.

Gul Hasan was one of Yahya Khan's 'discoveries' and served, first, as Director of Military Operations and, later, as Yahya Khan's successor in all important appointments on the General Staff from 1966 onwards. While Gul Hasan was long regarded as a member of the group that Yahya Khan had formed round himself, his principal devotion was clearly to his profession; his reputation stood high and he was generally regarded as a prospective Commander-in-Chief. Such rift as may have developed, a good deal later, between him and Yahya Khan was probably influenced by the antipathy that existed between Gul Hasan and Peerzada and, in the last year or so of Yahya Khan's administration, they were scarcely on speaking terms. Such, however, was the ascendancy of Peerzada over Yahya Khan that some found Gul Hasan's survival extraordinary. This may well have been a tribute to Gul Hasan's high reputation in the army. After 25 March 1971, the caucus comprised:

(a) General Abdul Hamid Khan and Major-General Gul Hasan, handling the army.

(b) Lieut.-General S. G. M. M. Peerzada whose political responsibilities had special reference to the Pakistan People's Party and the National Awami Party, both groups.[7]

(c) Major-General Ghulam Umer whose political responsibilities had special reference to the Jama'at-i-Islami and the three Muslim Leagues whose unification he laboured to bring about. This concern with rightist parties showed itself particularly in East Pakistan, after 25 March, and

---

[7] Holding a B.A. Honours degree from St. Xavier's College, Bombay, Peerzada was considered qualified to deal with leftist-inclined politicians. The town wits sometimes referred to him as holding the 'socialist' portfolio in the Martial Law administration.

 it brought him into collision with the People's Party, which served him ill when Mr. Bhutto became President.[8]

(d) Lieut.-General A. O. Mitha, an old regimental comrade, dealing with the civil service.[9]

(e) Major-General M. Akbar, Director of Military Intelligence, who supervised intelligence affairs generally.

(f) Brigadier Karim, an East Pakistani, on the staff of the Chief Martial Law Administrator, to supervise and advise on East Pakistan affairs.

(g) Brigadier Abdul Karim, on the staff of the Chief Martial Law Administrator, to supervise civil affairs. He later became Chief of the General Staff in Mr. Bhutto's administration.

(h) Lieut.-Colonel M. A. Hasan, legal and constitutional adviser. He was a prominent member of the prosecution in the Agartala Trial.

In addition, mention should be made of the Commander-in-Chief of the Air Force, Air-Marshal Rahim Khan, who, although not a soldier, enjoyed a good personal equation with Yahya Khan and was in constant touch with him on general military matters, by contrast with the Commander-in-Chief of the Navy who was completely neglected.

This background, briefly stated as it is, clearly indicates that Yahya Khan was not a lonely man, making his own decisions, right or wrong. On the contrary, this well-knit group was jointly committed to the political tasks which the events of March 1971 had made necessary, for, whether or not this group understood that the battle for East Pakistan had been lost in a few hours of darkness, these men had no option but to proceed. And those who stood around Yahya Khan well knew that the alternative was to court dismissal by a chief who expected complete obedience and was capable of peremptorily ending the career of any man who did not render it.

For some three months the position after 25 March was studied by these men and, on 28 June, Yahya Khan addressed

---

[8] A product of Aligarh University, Ghulam Umer claimed to have been a pre-partition student leader which seems improbable as he was commissioned into the old British-Indian Army in 1942.

[9] It will be recalled that this officer did not get along well with the civil legal administration.

the nation, stating what was, in fact, the outcome of their study. He said that:

(a) he re-affirmed his aim to restore democratic government;

(b) he declared that East Pakistan had voted for provincial autonomy and not for secession;

(c) he accused Sheikh Mujib and the Awami League of defiance, obduracy, and of seeking secession;

(d) he declared his conclusion that the framing of a constitution by an Assembly was not feasible;

(e) he considered there was no alternative but to have a constitution prepared by a 'group of experts' (afterwards spoken of as the 'Constitution Committee') whom he had, as it appeared, already selected;

(f) 'Martial Law cover' would remain 'for some time';

(g) political parties must be 'national' and he had already recommended to the Constitution Committee that 'it would be a good thing if we ban any party which is not national in the practical sense' and that 'we must eschew the habit of sub-parties';

(h) his proposed constitution could be amended by the National Assembly by means of machinery to be provided by the constitution itself;

(i) the Legal Framework Order would be amended to suit the new arrangements;

(j) by-elections would be held to fill vacant seats in the Assemblies.

This address raised a host of questions and doubts. Quite apart from the hostility or indifference with which these proposals might be greeted in East Pakistan, there was much to provoke disapproval in West Pakistan too. It was noted with bitterness that Yahya Khan had discovered, but only after much bloodshed and at the risk of losing East Pakistan, that it would have been wiser for him in the first place to have offered a draft to the National Assembly for its consideration. It was noted that the names of the constitutional experts were not disclosed, but that they had already been appointed. It was noted that amendments to the proposed constitution would depend on the mechanics provided in the constitution itself and on that point no one had the least information. Further, what was meant by 'national parties'? A party with a trifling repre-

6

sentation in both wings of the country might claim to be 'national' whereas a party such as Mr. Bhutto's with a large representation in the National Assembly, but from one wing only, might be termed 'regional'. In short, it appeared that in creating these stipulations Yahya Khan's administration was trying to reserve powers of manipulation comparable with those which had made the Legal Framework Order suspect and which would make the transfer of power, when it came, illusory.

These possibilities seemed to acquire further weight when, on 27 July, Yahya Khan gave an interview to the Iranian newspaper, *Kayhan*, in which he said that during the elections in December 1970 the Awami League had practised 'intimidation, terror and malpractice'. Shortly afterwards, this statement was repeated, with illustrative detail, in the White Paper,[10] where it was explained that the Government 'did not interfere lest this be interpreted as official interference in the election campaign'.[11] It followed that:

(a) The elections had not been as free and as fair as had been claimed.

(b) Whatever had happened during the elections in East Pakistan had taken place under the nose of the Martial Law administration which was either powerless to prevent it or did not wish to try.

(c) Condemnation of the Awami League's conduct had only become necessary four months after 25 March 1971.

Moreover, if there had been malpractice in East Pakistan, could it not happen in West Pakistan, also? And, if there should be malpractice in the forthcoming by-elections, would the Government interfere this time? If so, how?

On one important point the public was not kept in the dark for long. In September Yahya Khan made it known that the National Assembly would have ninety days after receiving the draft constitution, in which to propose amendments. These amendments would, however, require his assent. Moreover, before the Assembly could meet, by-elections would be necessary. In August a list of 88 East Pakistan Assembly members was issued stating that they were clear of all adverse allegations and that they retained their seats. This left 79 East Pakistani mem-

[10] *The Crisis in East Pakistan*, p. 5 et seq.
[11] Ibid., p. 6.

bers who were called upon to answer charges, failing which they would vacate. In particular, the seats held by Sheikh Mujib and Dr. Kamal Hossain were declared vacant although, so far as anyone knew, Sheikh Mujib's trial, which began in August,[12] had not yet concluded and his guilt or innocence was still unpronounced.[13] Shortly afterwards, the public was informed that by-elections would be held during the period 25 November–9 December 1971.

All this is closely relevant to the political involvement of some senior officers who, whatever the protestations to the contrary, desired power even if concealed behind a civilian façade. Yahya Khan said he did not believe it was the function of a soldier to 'rule' the country,[14] but everything turns on what is meant by 'rule'. The praetorian role probably suited these generals very well, being content with the reality rather than the appearance of power and it is likely they expected to achieve their purposes through the amalgamation of the three Muslim Leagues, a task assigned to Major-General Umer. The merits of this plan were obvious—links with Jinnah's memory and the foundation of Pakistan, as well as the claim to being a 'national' party.[15]

It is relevant also to Bhutto's involvement with Yahya Khan and the former's alleged opportunism. From Bhutto's own testimony, we know there had been consultations between him and Yahya Khan, and a moment came when Bhutto was roundly accused of collusion, which he most vehemently denied. We have only Bhutto's account of the nature of their discussions and of the advice Bhutto is supposed to have given, but what-

[12] The Special Tribunal to try Sheikh Mujib was established by Martial Law Regulations Nos. 84 (dated 24 July 1971) and 92 (dated 26 September 1971). Both were later repealed by Mr. Bhutto who also annulled the Tribunal's proceedings. Sheikh Mujib continued the hero and Mr. Bhutto, seeking at that time to embarrass Yahya Khan (the reasons will soon appear), was reported as having asked whether Yahya Khan's amnesty applied to the Sheikh. In other circles there was much doubt as to the wisdom of keeping Sheikh Mujib in prison and under trial. In West Pakistan, a 'Mujib lobby' became sufficiently noticeable to achieve newspaper mention (*Daily News*, Karachi, 27 September 1971). At that time, a current of opinion favourable to Sheikh Mujib developed to the extent that Yahya Khan was reported as having said that he would 'consider freeing Sheikh Mujib if the nation demands his release'. *PO*, 3 November 1971.

[13] Except, of course, by President Yahya Khan.

[14] TV interview given in Islamabad to the international networks.

[15] Not to mention the immense funds accumulated, in Ayub Khan's time, by the (Convention) Muslim League. These funds were the subject of Martial Law enquiry, but the results of that enquiry seem to be unknown. The successful amalgamation of the Muslim Leagues, had it come about, might well have succeeded in thwarting Bhutto's People's Party.

ever happened before March 1971, there is little reason to suppose the two men drew closer afterwards.[16]

For Mr. Bhutto the position after December 1970 was simple. So long as Sheikh Mujib was there, wielding an overall majority in the National Assembly, he, Bhutto, could, at best, play second fiddle and, at worst, be in impotent opposition. But, as it happened, with or without Bhutto's advice, Yahya Khan took the decision which sealed the fate of the old Pakistan and an entirely new situation was created which opened up clearer vistas for Bhutto. He began to play his cards accordingly.

Whatever the fluctuations in the relationship between Yahya Khan and Bhutto, it is evident that the correct interpretation to be placed upon it is a familiar one—especially in politics. Each was using the other, or thought he was. For neither Yahya Khan nor his advisers liked Bhutto. They did not trust him, and Yahya Khan is credited with having said that he would transfer power to Bhutto only over his, Yahya Khan's, dead body.[17] However, after March 1971, Yahya Khan and his generals had the upper hand and it seemed to them that, with the exercise of some skill, especially in organizing the miniature general election in prospect in East Pakistan, they could dispense with Mr. Bhutto and his seats in the National Assembly, or at least they should be able to neutralize him.

One reason for the army's dislike of Bhutto was his approach to constitutional and other political questions which, in several respects, ran counter to what the political generals treated as articles of faith. After March 1971 Bhutto gave frequent and emphatic expression to these views, especially on constitutional matters which, at that time, were paramount. Thus, he did not want a return to parity in the National Assembly as between East and West Pakistan. He did not want separate electorates based on religion, nor did he want fresh elections. He considered that the number of seats to be deemed vacated in East Pakistan should be kept to the minimum and he called for an early summoning of the National Assembly, saying he was

[16] Indeed, there is reason to suppose that during the political discussions, between March and December 1971, with Yahya Khan and his advisers on one side, and Bhutto and his party colleagues on the other, acrimony was not wanting. Later, Bhutto was to show he had not forgotten this.

[17] In addition to being indiscreet, Yahya Khan was addicted to strong language. Thus, on one occasion, he said that if anyone offered him aid with strings, he would 'throw it in his face'. *Kayhan*, 27 July 1971.

ready to attend it, if necessary with Sheikh Mujib as Prime Minister and himself in opposition. The inference here was that Sheikh Mujib ought to be released and allowed to re-enter the country's political life. For this reason, and because the word *awami* (it means 'people's') was frequently on his lips, he was accused of wooing East Pakistan's Assembly members and he made frequent mention of reconciliation between East and West Pakistan. He further said he did not believe in any military settlement of the country's problems and that he did not want 'unknown experts' drafting the constitution.[18] He persisted in calling himself 'leader of the majority party' and 'therefore, next to the President',[19] self-descriptions which appealed little to the political generals. As a result of such statements he was accused of seeking power for its own sake[20] and he became the object of sustained attack in Government-controlled newspapers. His rising sense of frustration was revealed in his own words: 'By November, I will either have effective control or I will go to jail',[21] but newspaper attacks were not enough. Other methods were also at work and acute dissensions arose inside Bhutto's party, fostered, it appeared, by the Government through surreptitious channels. It was beginning to seem as if Mujib's words might yet come true: 'If they destroyed him [Mujib] first, they would also destroy me.'[22]

Later in 1971 the political intentions of Yahya Khan and his group with respect to Bhutto became plainer. It was said that the miniature general election in East Pakistan would afford excellent opportunities to create a National Assembly which would fit in well with the policies that Yahya Khan and his group desired to promote, and evidence of a plan to that end soon emerged. As early as 15 October, out of 79 seats declared vacant in East Pakistan, fifteen had already acquired National Assembly representation because the candidates were declared to have been elected unopposed, although elections were not due until the fortnight 25 November–9 December. The political complexion of these successful members was unmistakable, comprising, as they did:

18 Interview reported in *Kayhan*, 17 July 1971.
19 *PT*, 25 June 1971.
20 'Of Men and Matters', *PT*, 8 August 1971.
21 Quoted in an editorial entitled 'Power or Prison', *PT*, 7 July 1971.
22 *The Great Tragedy*, p. 43.

| | |
|---|---|
| Pakistan Democratic Front | 5 |
| Jama'at-i-Islami | 5 |
| (Convention) Muslim League | 2 |
| Qayum Muslim League | 1 |
| Nizam-i-Islam Party | 2 |

These unopposed results disclosed several things. First of all, on the basis of what thus appeared, there would again be a confusing multiplicity of parties in the House, creating plenty of room for party contention although with a general drift as to outlook. Much more important was the fact that this number of unopposed returns so early in the day spoke of an indifference in East Pakistan to the by-elections, and it was also noteworthy that the unopposed candidates did not include a single man from Bhutto's party.

It was said in Dacca that some intending candidates were being warned by District Magistrates, acting on the instructions of the Martial Law Authorities, not to oppose certain candidates already nominated in some constituencies.[23] A People's Party leader, Abdul Hafeez Pirzada, then in Dacca, sent a telegram to Yahya Khan stating that some candidates nominated by his party for the by-elections were being pressed not to oppose candidates already nominated by certain rightist parties.[24] It was further reported that others were being dissuaded from standing for election either by physical force at the hands of the military or by the threat of it, and it was significant that the Governor of East Pakistan, Dr. A. M. Malik, made reference to 'not entirely satisfactory elections'.

This was a bold statement for Dr. Malik to make seeing that he was the appointee of the Martial Law administration. His appointment was clearly intended to placate sentiment in East Pakistan by giving to that Province a civilian governor born on its own soil, but the idea was a nullity at the outset. Not only was the purpose as transparent as it was disingenuous but Dr. Malik's past associations with the Central Government over the years robbed him of whatever credibility he might otherwise have had. Moreover, a Martial Law Administrator remained, the only change being that General Tikka Khan returned to military duty and was replaced by Lieut.-General

---

[23] Notably in the case of the Jama'at-i-Islam leader, Choudhury Ghulam Azam.
[24] *PO*, 5 November 1971.

A. A. K. Niazi. But this was not all. If the eastern Province was deserving of a civilian governor after everything that had happened there, why not the western Provinces where there had been no rebellion and no secessionist moves? This discrimination simply underlined the truth of Dr. Malik's appointment —a sop to East Pakistan without sacrificing an iota of control. To make matters even worse, Monem Khan, Ayub Khan's ex-Governor of East Pakistan, a heartily detested figure, was actually invited to Malik's installation ceremony.

It has been suggested, particularly by Bhutto's political opponents in Pakistan, that the entire business, from the time Sheikh Mujib's sweeping victory upset all earlier calculations, was a gigantic charade in which Bhutto emerged as the Machiavellian figure pulling all the strings and manipulating all the puppets, including Yahya Khan and his generals. The suggestion is altogether too extreme, except, perhaps, for those content to avail themselves of the convenient benefit of hindsight. There is no doubt that Bhutto and Yahya Khan consulted together at various times when Bhutto was asked his opinion and gave it. It is reasonable to suppose that Bhutto had made up his mind that if, in the face of events in East Pakistan, the worst were to happen; if, indeed, the country had to divide, he would not let it seem that he bore any responsibility for it. Probably, he did not find such manoeuvres difficult for he already had the political measure of Yahya Khan which is one reason for his insistence, when he visited Dacca in March 1971, that the meetings should be held with all three major figures present— Yahya Khan, Sheikh Mujib, and himself. Some of his dealings with Yahya Khan—notably the amendment to the Legal Framework Order by which resignations from the Assemblies, even before they were convened, were made possible and, hence, a plethora of by-elections on the eve of summoning the National Assembly—suggested a degree of collaboration which did not in fact exist. Indeed, as we have seen, Bhutto once found himself obliged to deny, on oath, the suggestion of collusion. But to place on his shoulders responsibility for all that happened is too heavy a strain on credulity and the correct conclusion, from all that happened after the elections, indicates that each man was using the other, or hoped he was.

The military undertakings of the political generals in East

Pakistan culminated in disaster. The three Muslim Leagues were never persuaded to come together. Qayum Khan and his latter-day Muslim League made little impression and no other party had the least prospect of securing a majority in the National Assembly or even of adequate representation in the House. Thus, although there can be no doubt of the generals' determination to retain an untrammelled upper hand,[25] with or without a civilian façade, they found it more difficult than they had supposed. Had there been no war with India, it is not easy to say what would have happened but it is probable that conflict with India saved the country from continuing violence in East Pakistan and from civic unrest in the western wing.

[25] This determination is lucidly traced in a letter dated 17 March 1971, written by a Mr. Rezaur Rahman from Dacca, himself a Bengali, to a friend in West Pakistan. The authenticity of this letter is not in doubt and it is generally regarded, by those familiar with the events of those times, as a remarkably accurate analysis of what was happening and of what was being thought and planned. See Appendix A.

# XIV

# The Indian Involvement

It is said that soon after partition, a paper prepared by the Indian Ministry for External Affairs for the benefit of the Indian Cabinet advised: 'The first object of India's foreign policy must be the liquidation of Pakistan, by fair means if possible, by other means if necessary.'[1] The report of this statement may, or may not, have been well-founded, but such information helped to bolster the oft-stated Pakistani view that India had never reconciled itself to the partition. Indian political leaders had often spoken to the contrary and years later Mrs. Indira Gandhi reiterated that, for India, the partition was a settled fact.[2] Nevertheless, the fifth chapter of the Pakistan Government's White Paper begins: 'The reasons for India's interference in Pakistan's internal affairs are manifold. . . . The root cause . . . is that India never really accepted the establishment of Pakistan . . . .'

In using the word 'manifold' the authors said more than they perhaps intended. Whatever may have been India's secret reservations in 1947, there is little doubt that after Ayub Khan's Kashmir adventure in 1965 the Indian Government resolved to take every opportunity of reducing Pakistan's ability to create trouble and impose upon India unwelcome military expenditure. The documentation supporting this suggestion is necessarily sparse but the idea is certainly implicit in Mrs. Gandhi's elaboration of India's attitude to Pakistan in the course of a newspaper interview,[3] and it is the thesis of this chapter that India's role in the events of 1971 was the outcome of such a determination. This is not, of course, the same thing as saying that India was the begetter of those events, nor does it exonerate those in Pakistan who helped to provoke them.[4]

---

[1] Information from a former senior official of Pakistan's Foreign Ministry.

[2] D, 16 November 1972. See also FCTC, Ch. VII, p. 118 et seq. discussing India's designs towards Pakistan. [3] D, 16 November 1972.

[4] Of course, much is obscure and likely to remain so. In this chapter, I have taken Major-General D. K. Palit's book, The Lightning Campaign, to be fairly representative of the Indian military point of view.

In the implementation of a post-1965 policy such as is suggested here, it is reasonable to suppose that India did not overlook the potentiality in East Pakistan. The accusations directed towards India at various times had mostly to do with subversion in East Pakistan, and indeed, the first specific charges against India concerned the eastern Province, when Mr. P. N. Ojha of the Indian High Commission was named in relation to the Agartala Trial. When those proceedings were abated, however, nothing was said about Mr. Ojha.[5] Chapter IV of the White Paper begins with these words: 'Direct evidence of India's collusion with anti-State elements in East Pakistan came to light when the Agartala Conspiracy was unearthed in 1967', and at one moment it seemed as if Yahya Khan's government was toying with the idea of reviving the Agartala Case.[6] In 1970 Mr. S. M. Zafar, Law Minister at the time of the Agartala Trial in 1968, said that the Case had never been withdrawn. It was only the Act setting up the Tribunal for the purpose of the trial that had been repealed. With crucial electioneering in progress, with the Six Point Programme and provincial autonomy as the principal issues, one can only wonder how East Pakistan viewed that statement particularly as it came from the lips of a Punjabi.

The background to India's moves in 1971 is conjectural, and the best one can do is to consider what is known of events both before and after 25 March. The first event in the chain was the hijacking, by two Kashmiri Muslims, of an India Airlines Fokker Friendship aircraft which was then ordered to land at Lahore. The incident seemed to have a background for, about five days earlier, Zafar Iqbal Rathore, a First Secretary in the Pakistan High Commission in Delhi, had been expelled by the Indian Government on the ground of involvement in subversive operations in Kashmir. The Pakistan Government said this expulsion was intended to divert attention from Indian repression in Kashmir and it responded by ordering B. L. Joshi, of the India High Commission, to leave Pakistan, alleging espionage and subversion. On 30 January the hijacking occurred[7] and the aircraft landed at Lahore.

[5] See *FCTC*, pp. 184–5 and 189.
[6] Official statement, see *D*, 7 May 1971.
[7] The White Paper says 'In February'.

The Pakistan Government's attitude seems to have been perfectly correct. The Indian civilian passengers were cared for and promptly returned safely to their country and the Government seemed also to have in mind the quick return of the aircraft, but this sensible idea was frustrated by the Lahore mob as soon as rumour of the intention circulated. There was rioting and stone-throwing, and police had to have recourse to tear-gas. On 3 February the matter was settled finally when the hijackers destroyed the aircraft and the damage to Pakistan was irretrievably done. Sheikh Mujib publicly deplored this action and called for an official enquiry. Bhutto expressed sympathy with the affair and it was believed that when he spoke to the hijackers on 2 February, he congratulated them. The truth seems to be, however, that he expressed disapproval and said they should not have brought the aircraft to Lahore. If this be so, it does credit to his perspicacity.

The Pakistan Government's hand was forced and if, as Pakistan has claimed, the entire business was a cunning Indian plot, it can only be said that it was the ignorant in Pakistan who contributed to its successful consummation. The destruction of the aircraft clinched everything and, on 5 February, the Indian Government announced that until the question of compensation was satisfactorily settled, flights over India by Pakistan would be prohibited, thus making it necessary for Pakistani aircraft to fly via Ceylon or north of India's Himalayan boundary, if air communication between the two wings was to be maintained. The truth of the matter may never be revealed, but India's note to Pakistan[8] indicates an association with Rathore's expulsion which, in turn, does suggest a plot to justify sealing off Pakistan's over-flights. The Pakistan White Paper states that in 1967 the Indian Government had assured East Pakistani subversives that on 'D-day India would block air and sea routes' linking East and West Pakistan.

Although the hijacking and its consequences fitted well with India's later operations, there are some solid objections to the suggestion of an Indian plot. Was it necessary to adopt so elaborate a plan, which was not certain of success? Would it not have been possible, at any desired moment, to close the over-India route on some less dangerous pretext? How, in January,

[8] Printed verbatim in *D*, 15 February 1971.

could India have known what Yahya Khan intended in March, assuming Yahya Khan himself knew? Was not the Indian Government playing with the lives and safety of some forty innocent Indian civilians including children? How could the Indian Government be sure the hijackers would faithfully play their part, bearing in mind that these men had no hope of escape? Suppose the hijackers were lured, say by money, from the aircraft which the Pakistan Government then promptly returned, the plot would not only have failed, but Pakistan would have earned much credit. There was even the risk of losing an aircraft with no prospect of compensation although, assuming the plot, that might be a small price to pay.

The mystery thickened and the attitude of the Pakistan Government towards the hijackers changed abruptly. From being heroes, they were taken into custody for interrogation and, later, put on trial. Early in March the Pakistan Government instituted an enquiry presided over by a High Court Judge. The report, completed in April, concluded that the entire affair had been organized by the Indian Government,[9] but as the report has never been published, the grounds for this conclusion are unknown. Still, the result was that air-communication between the two wings had been crippled. If Pakistan's central Government believed that India intended material injury to Pakistan, it is strange that the gravity of the situation was not better grasped. If it were concluded that India had struck, with serious intent, at the links between the eastern and the western Provinces, would it not have been wiser to placate the people of the eastern wing instead of driving them to desperate measures? And to create a situation which provided India with tangible grounds[10] for interference was surely the plainest folly.

[9] A summary was published in Pakistan's newspapers of 21 April 1971. The two hijackers and four accomplices were tried before Mr. Justice Yaqub Ali of the Supreme Court and Mr. Justice Abdul Kader Sheikh of the Sind and Baluchistan High Court, the latter having conducted the enquiry referred to in the text. See also Appendix C.

[10] We shall come to these grounds shortly. General Palit wrote that the hijacking appeared to be a 'put-up' job, i.e. by the Pakistan Government because Pakistan was beginning to mobilize. If that were the correct interpretation, then Pakistan paid an astoundingly high price for its Government's ingenuity and it seems very strange that, at such a critical political juncture, Pakistan should be seeking a confrontation. In any case, Palit was careful not to suggest *general mobilization* and there is a considerable difference (*The Lightning Campaign*, p. 30).

The propagandist note which prevails throughout the White Paper moderates its value, but the Pakistan Government has provided no other means of determining how it was then reading India's intentions. The general proposition that India meant injury to Pakistan was one thing, but the accurate appreciation of how and when that injury would be wrought was quite another. It may well have been that early in 1971 there was a concentration of Indian troops in West Bengal 'ostensibly for internal security in connection with the elections. Instead of normalizing the position after the Indian elections were over, additional Indian army formations were moved towards the East Pakistan border in the latter half of March 1971. . . .'[11] Yet this was scarcely surprising, for India had shown itself to be in full sympathy with the Bangladesh movement at an early stage and, on 30 March, both Houses of the Indian Parliament passed a resolution, moved by Mrs. Gandhi, expressing 'profound sympathy and solidarity with the people of East Bengal and assured them[12] that their struggle will receive the wholehearted sympathies and support of the people of India'. In addition, funds were raised to help Sheikh Mujib. Later, of course, armed help was much more explicit and the White Paper has much to say about India's provision of training facilities, of arms and other supplies, for the Bangladesh army, as well as for a Free Bangladesh radio.

General Palit has provided a satisfactory interpretation of India's role[13] which I shall summarize. After March 1971 the paramount fact for India was that millions of Pakistani civilians had taken refuge in its territories, creating an immense administrative burden along with threats of civil unrest and widespread epidemics.[14] On this issue the attitude of the Indian Government was unequivocal. The refugees would have to go back. In June Yahya Khan asked all Pakistanis to return home 'irre-

[11] White Paper, *The Crisis in East Pakistan*, p. 46. The word 'latter' is an interesting admission.

[12] The White Paper (p. 48) explains, in a bracket, that 'them' means 'secessionists'.

[13] Op. cit. General Palit was once Director of Military Operations on the General Staff of the Indian Army. He is a good military writer and his account of the thinking that preceded General Aurora's 1971 campaign in Bengal is, leaving aside some ill-digested observations on politics and some unnecessary personal gibes, reasonable and convincing.

[14] There still exists between India and Pakistan a wide difference of opinion as to the number of refugees.

spective of caste, creed and religion', but there was no sign of positive response and, as we know, in the following August, the United Nations representative stated that refugees were still crossing the border into India. Mrs. Gandhi could say that the refugees would have to go back, but how can several million men, women, and children be made to do so? What could Yahya Khan do to induce their return and what could Mrs. Gandhi do to compel it?[15]

India's openly stated sympathy for Sheikh Mujib provided Yahya Khan with the rallying cry he needed, for although India made no explicit reference to secession but only to 'struggle' and although Mrs. Gandhi repeatedly stated that India had no territorial ambitions, no one in West Pakistan doubted India's aims and some who had once supported Sheikh Mujib and his Six Point Programme now raised the cry 'Resist India'. Perhaps Yahya Khan experienced a sense of destiny when he found himself compared with Turkey's Mustafa Kemal.[16] Pakistan newspapers began to heap blame on India although, to begin with, the tone was mainly restrained. Thoughtful people in Pakistan began to ask themselves the reason for this sustained newspaper barrage accusing India of hostile intentions and war-like acts. To regret India's pro-Awami League sympathies, or to protest against them, was very different from the creation of a war-psychosis, yet this seemed to have official inspiration. There then began the 'Crush India' campaign mostly evidenced by stickers on windscreens which bore these words or even more sanguinary exhortations.

It is clear that, after 1965, the Indian General Staff recast all its thinking with respect to the prospect of a war on two fronts—Pakistan and China. Moreover, Brigadier John Dalvi's description of the condition of the Indian armed forces in 1962[17] had underlined the fact that they were not ready for war, having suffered from the uninstructed interference of men such as Krishna Menon and from Jawaharlal Nehru's obtuseness with respect to China. The Indian Government thereupon embarked on a plan for expanding, re-organizing, and re-arming its forces,

[15] Moreover, Pakistan claims that the return of refugees was actually obstructed by India.

[16] *PT*, 11 April 1971.

[17] Brigadier J. P. Dalvi, *Himalayan Blunder*, Orient Paperbacks, Hind Pocket Book, Delhi, no date, Ch. VI and *passim*.

including the fortification of places which favoured enemy attack whether from China or Pakistan. General Palit states, however: 'Although expansion and re-equipment programmes were proceeding smoothly, the Bangladesh crisis blew up before they could be fully realized. . . . A few more months of crash programming were required before the armed forces could be brought up to full war readiness.'[18] This is the first reason he gives for the timing of the Bengal campaign. There are others, viz.:

(a) The formations deployed in West Bengal in March 1971 in aid of the civil power (cf. White Paper, p. 46) had left their heavy equipment behind and were not, therefore, operational at the time.

(b) A division had been deployed in the Mizo hills for security operations so that the two-front deployment had been extended to a two and one-half front commitment.

(c) Air bases for operations against East Pakistan had not been developed.

(d) If hostilities opened between the two countries, a Pakistani attack in the west could be expected.

(e) From April onwards the monsoon would develop and the climate would be adverse to air and ground operations.

(f) With the approach of summer the northern passes would open thus facilitating Chinese intervention.

These, then, are the reasons Palit suggests to explain the Indian General Staff's conclusion that before India could adopt any policy involving risk of war with Pakistan, three conditions must be fulfilled:

(a) The expansion and re-equipment programme would have to be completed and the armed forces re-grouped.

(b) It would be necessary to wait until the Mukti Bahini had acquired a degree of operational capacity since, if only for political reasons, these forces would have to spearhead the operations.

(c) It would be necessary to wait until any Chinese threat was minimized by diplomatic action and/or by choosing the season most unfavourable to any such threat, i.e. the cold weather.

Palit adds that for all these reasons November 1971 was indi-

18 *The Lightning Campaign*, p. 40.

cated as the earliest date for India to assume a positive military posture in support of a Bangladesh policy. The question then arises: Why should India pursue a Bangladesh policy involving a military posture with an implicit risk of war with Pakistan?

Palit answers the question by asserting that although there was no danger of immediate aggression by Pakistan, after the tensions created in February by the hijacking incident had abated, events had nevertheless created a threat to India's security in a wider and longer-term sense. This threat he attributes to the intolerable burden of the continuing influx of refugees, to the possibility of revolutionary strife in West Bengal and Tripura, and to nation-wide disruption of communal harmony. He repeats: 'The mass eviction of refugees was a deliberate act of demographic aggression. It constituted a clear threat to our national security.'[19] It is a pity that Palit spoiled a good argument by introducing the words 'deliberate' and 'aggression'. While Yahya Khan's pre-emptive action may have driven some millions of refugees into India, creating grave economic, administrative, and social problems, any deliberately aggressive intentions by Yahya Khan to this end seem extremely improbable.

It is difficult to accept the suggestion that Yahya Khan and his advisers actually planned to drive millions of refugees into West Bengal in the expectation of creating such a threat to Indian security as would bring that country to its knees or divert its interest away from Sheikh Mujib. If, indeed, such were the intention then only one of two consequences could be foreseen. Either the refugees would return of their own volition, and that was highly improbable so long as Yahya Khan and the army were in East Pakistan or, alternatively, India would adopt measures to compel it, with or without recourse to arms. It can, of course, be argued that a confrontation with India was what Yahya Khan and his military caucus desired in the belief that, with or without Chinese help, they could defeat India. But if that were also part of the plan, it can only be said that Yahya Khan's military dispositions scarcely bear it out.[20]

[19] Palit, op. cit., p. 38.

[20] There are good grounds for saying that not until about mid-October 1971 did the Pakistan Government accept the appreciation that India was, in all respects, prepared for a military solution in East Pakistan and that war must be anticipated.

However, General Palit's presentation of India's assessment of the situation is convincing on political as well as military grounds because it is consistent with:

(a) his explanation of India's Bangladesh policy.

(b) the statement of Pakistan's White Paper about India's plans for requiring East Pakistani insurgents to act first, supporting them as might be necessary from Indian soil, and undertaking more overt and extended action should that be necessary.[21]

(c) the thesis of the present chapter that in the events of 1971 India found the opportunity to execute the policy formulated after September 1965.

It is important to notice that this thesis was very nearly admitted by General Palit when he wrote: 'It was the crassness of the second-rate generals who controlled Pakistan politically and militarily that provided the opportunity India sought.'[22]

Thus, as events developed after 25 March, India was keenly appraising the situation and, referring to Mrs. Indira Gandhi, Palit says: 'Even as early as the first week of April—when the [Indian] armed forces were in a state of imbalance and hesitant to contribute to a policy that might lead to all-out war, she had taken action to assume a positive military posture along the Bangladesh border—albeit at a low level of confrontation.'[23] This, too, fits in with the Indian appreciation Palit has described, for there was no question of open hostilities, unless otherwise forced, earlier than November.

Generally speaking, in the diplomatic and propaganda démarches that ensued, India enjoyed advantages over Pakistan—for these reasons:

(a) There was a general, world-wide repugnance to the idea of soldiers making war on civilians even though some of the latter might be armed and in a state of rebellion.

(b) It was widely felt that the basis of the trouble lay in the fact that East Pakistanis had voted in a direction which Pakistan's military government did not like.

(c) Whatever the truth behind the stories of the night of

[21] *The Lightning Campaign*, p. 40.
[22] Ibid., p. 151.
[23] Ibid., p. 63. The expression 'low level of confrontation' is difficult to assess. Still, confrontation is conceded and signifies, perhaps, aid to the Bangladesh guerrillas.

25/26 March, the miseries of the refugees who fled to India were there for all to see.

(d) Pakistan is traditionally incompetent in propaganda, public relations, and image-building.

(e) Pakistan erred in relying excessively on the doctrine that what was happening in the eastern Province was an 'internal affair'.

(f) There was general recognition of the fact that India could not be expected to absorb millions of Pakistani refugees who would have to return to their own country.

However, to bring about the return of the refugees Indo-Pakistan co-operation was needed, but no element in the situation was more conspicuously missing. From the moment the evacuation into India began, relations between the two countries deteriorated steadily. Moreover, soon after 25 March the Soviet Union sent remonstrances to the Pakistan Government.[24]

As April passed, the Pakistan Government adopted precautionary measures and all Pakistanis visiting Indian High Commission offices in Pakistan were stopped at the gate by policemen; their names and addresses were recorded and the purpose of their visits noted. Indeed, it seemed as if India were trying to increase the pressure on Pakistan without going to war. By June the tension had visibly increased. In Pakistan there were constant references to 'escalation' and 'conflict'. At this time the Indian Foreign Minister, Sardar Swaran Singh, was visiting major powers to explain India's point of view and he appeared to be enjoying substantial success. The Indo-Soviet communiqué, issued at the conclusion of his visit to Moscow, revealed considerable Soviet support for India and this was further underlined, in September, when, at a lunch given in Moscow in honour of Mrs. Gandhi's visit, Mr. Kosygin said: 'The actions of Pakistan in compelling over eight million people to leave their country, land, property and to seek shelter in neighbouring India are impossible to justify.'[25] There was, furthermore, the question of the attitude of other powers and in particular the United States and China.

It was evident that, with the rest of the world, the United

[24] D, 6 April 1971.

[25] Quoted in D, 30 September 1971. The word 'compelling' is interesting since it suggests an intention, but, as we have argued, it is highly improbable that such an intention existed.

States viewed with dismay the military operations in East Pakistan from 25 March onwards, and the general feeling in that country was one of disapproval. Prior to 25 March there appears to have been considerable American contact, even at the official level, with Sheikh Mujib. However, the approach of Mr. Nixon's administration as the crisis developed seems to have been shaped by the following considerations:

(a) The desirability of a general policy of disengagement, coupled with the establishment of stable areas with governments congenial to American policy. These areas would enjoy American support although without formal alliance.

(b) The adoption of closer ties with China heralded, at that time, by the decision to allow trade with China in certain classes of merchandise.[26]

(c) An intention, stimulated by the Indo-Soviet Treaty of August 1971, to permit no Soviet political hegemony in the sub-continent, an intention of which the logical corollary led, in the circumstances, to closer relations between Pakistan and the United States.

An important factor was the change in the American attitude towards China during, as it happened, those crucial months in East Pakistan. It is difficult to discover any relationship between the two but it is the case that Dr. Kissinger's brief visit to Pakistan, in July 1971, provided a staging-post by which to make a secret trip to Peking. A few days later President Nixon announced his acceptance of China's invitation to visit that country. In this Pakistan claimed a vital role and Yahya Khan called it 'the event of the century'. Certainly, for Pakistan, it had claims in that direction, for twenty-three days afterwards the Soviet Union and the Indian Republic announced their Treaty of Peace, Friendship, and Co-operation.[27] It is by no means certain that American *démarches* with respect to China were a direct or even proximate cause of the Indo-Soviet Treaty but, whether foreseen by the United States Government or not, the shift in American policy towards China helped to tighten

---

[26] Decision announced in June 1971.

[27] General Palit wrote: 'India's intent in signing the Indo-Soviet Treaty ... was ... more in the nature of a surety than the forging of a coalition or bloc' (*The Lightning Campaign*, p. 66). Seeking a guarantor, in fact?

Indo-Soviet ties and added plausibility to the Treaty itself.[28]

The facts indicate that Mr. Nixon's policy with respect to events in the sub-continent was guided by his intention to thwart any Russian hegemony and, as 1971 wore on, this became increasingly apparent. Such an attitude, especially as regards Nixon's interest in Pakistan, was no new thing. His Secretary of State, Mr. William P. Rogers, had said he knew of no country more important to the United States than Pakistan.[29] Even so, the events of March 1971 rang with an ugly note for the American people, creating much misgiving, and Mr. Nixon's political opponents were not slow to use the situation to heap criticism upon him, so much so that, in September 1971, Mr. Rogers was obliged to make pressing requests to Congress not to withhold or limit economic aid to Pakistan. Later, Nixon's determination not to allow American influence in the sub-continent to be extinguished was underlined by disclosures made by Mr. Jack Anderson. These led the *New York Times* to comment severely upon the commitments made by President Nixon, with the aid of Dr. Kissinger, in support of Pakistan.[30]

Perhaps Nixon believed he exerted enough influence with Yahya Khan to ensure that Sheikh Mujib should come to no harm and that some acceptable settlement between East and West Pakistan could be reached. Perhaps it was with arguments such as these that he sought to persuade Mrs. Gandhi to moderate her policy, but she was not to be persuaded. This led Nixon into sharper criticism of India and warmer admiration for Yahya Khan's efforts to solve Pakistan's political problems, views which he expressed when Major-General Raza presented his credentials as Pakistan's new ambassador to the United States in December 1971. The American Government claimed to have organized secret negotiations between Yahya Khan

[28] Article 8 provided that the contracting parties would not enter into or participate in any military alliances directed against the other. Article 9 provided that each party to the Treaty would not give assistance to any third party taking part in armed conflict with the other. General Palit's view differs from that taken in this book. He wrote: 'One [surely not unintentional] by-product of the Treaty was the further neutralization of the Chinese threat . . .' (op. cit., p. 66). Much depended upon the evaluation of that threat and, as we shall see, India eventually concluded that it was not great.

[29] On the occasion of the oath-taking ceremony when Mr. Joseph Farland was appointed American ambassador to Pakistan, 10 October 1969.

[30] See Mr. Tom Wicker's comments in the *New York Times*, 4 January 1972.

and the Awami League dissidents. One wonders if Yahya Khan was ever consulted about this disclosure. Certainly, it did not add a single cubit to his stature. The belief that a crisis in the sub-continent could be averted led President Nixon to cancel $3·6 million worth of arms for Pakistan,[31] in an attempt to prevail with Mrs. Gandhi, but again he failed. Mrs. Gandhi's apparent determination might provoke angry comment from the United States Government, as in the passage: 'We believe that since the beginning of the crisis, Indian policy in a systematic way has led to perpetuation of the crisis, a deepening of the crisis and that India bears the major responsibility for the broader hostilities which have ensued.' But such rhetoric mattered little. The opportunity to execute a long-determined policy had arrived and, as is clear from what General Palit has written, the plan had been well-meditated. Nothing would be jettisoned now and why should it? Was it certain China would or could come to the aid of Pakistan? Was the United States Government, so deeply embroiled in Vietnam and facing much hostility because of it, about to undertake further military commitments in Asia?[32] Thus, while Nixon's policy of preventing Russian ascendancy throughout the sub-continent displayed a traceable consistency, it did not precisely correspond with what was felt and desired in Islamabad. Pakistan's attitude towards the United States therefore fluctuated a great deal, according to the emotion of the hour. As events turned out, Pakistan came to feel that the United States, under the leadership of President Nixon, had done much for Pakistan, although opinions may differ as to how much it really was.

India's stubborn refusal to listen to Nixon may have led him to believe that India intended to carry the war into West Pakistan, an issue on which a wide difference of opinion was to develop between the United States and the United Kingdom. On all political and military grounds it is still difficult to understand why India should have wanted to do what Nixon claimed, although, from what has been disclosed in the Anderson papers, as early as 6 December the prospect of India invading West Pakistan with a view to capturing territory was being seriously

---

[31] *The Economist*, London, 13 November 1971.
[32] Still, as the *New York Times* pointed out, Nixon went a long way towards doing so.

discussed in very high American circles.[33] President Nixon stated that his Government was in possession of 'hard' information to this effect and when pressed for details, as late as February 1972, Dr. Kissinger affirmed that the United States had information about India's plans to attack West Pakistan but declined to go further, on the ground that it would 'compromise sources'.[34] The claim to 'hard' and 'secret' information seemed to have no other purpose than to justify a policy concerning Bangladesh which was viewed with much concern in some American political circles.

China's attitude proved to be even more opaque than in September 1965. On 11 April 1971 the Chinese Government issued a statement supporting Yahya Khan's position in East Pakistan and on later occasions it accused India of expansionism. These fulminations apart, however, the Chinese attitude was equivocal and never more than lukewarm. It is extremely difficult to trace anything which might have satisfactorily persuaded the Pakistan Government that, in the event of conflict with India, China would intervene if only through diplomatic pressure. Perhaps Mr. Nixon, confident of his ability to persuade Mrs. Gandhi to abstain from armed measures, had in the course of his visit convinced the Chinese that he could ensure peace in the sub-continent, and he may have suggested that since China was about to assume a leading role in international affairs, it should not become too clearly a partisan in Indo-Pakistan disputes. This may read plausibly, but it is speculative nevertheless. The material fact was that, at the conclusion of Mr. Bhutto's visit to China in November 1971, no communiqué was issued. When asked about this, Mr. Bhutto explained that meetings between friends called for no communiqués. According to General Palit, however, the Indian interpretation was different, namely, that Bhutto's mission had failed.[35]

---

[33] See record of discussion on 6 November 1971 at a meeting of the National Security Council, Washington Special Action Group, reported in the *Evening Star*, Washington, 5 January 1972.

[34] The old 'sealed-lips' technique made famous by a former British Prime Minister, Stanley Baldwin. It never satisfies.

[35] Palit, op. cit., p. 65.

# XV

# War—December 1971

As with all fatal quarrels between India and Pakistan, the debate 'Who Started It in December?' is likely to be as interminable as it will be irresoluble. What is known with certainty of the conflict in Bengal in 1971 shows that soon after March, troops and Border Security Forces on both sides were exchanging fire. As Pakistani troops drove the Mukti Bahini before them, the latter sometimes took refuge across the border[1] and the Pakistani troops followed them. This inevitably led to engagement with Indian forces who supported the insurgents with counter-battery and mortar fire. As we know from General Palit's account, the Indian Government was committed at the outset to a policy of support for the East Bengal insurgents who were to spearhead operations against Pakistan troops. This policy depended upon how much support would be necessary and how far India would go, short of explicit war. But even that question was difficult to answer.

During 1971, as the months passed, the public in each country was fed with stories—doubtless often well-founded—of the other's shameful disregard of the sanctity of frontiers and territorial integrity. It seemed as if there was an intention on each side to intensify the scale of undeclared hostilities thus enhancing the prospect of full-scale war. It does not appear that such a possibility caused any dismay to the Pakistan Government. Newspaper propaganda not only became alarming in its tone but it also achieved a repulsive degree of vulgarity.[2] There was, moreover, deliberate misrepresentation of reports published in foreign newspapers.[3] Despatches by foreign correspon-

---

[1] Assuming, of course, that everyone knew where the boundary was.

[2] See cartoons depicting Mrs. Gandhi in the *Daily News*, Karachi, during September 1971. In its issue dated 11 September 1971 the *Pakistan Times* carried an extraordinary headline when reporting Professor J. K. Galbraith's comments on the situation. It read: 'Galbraith speaks a whole load of crap'—scarcely helpful to President Nixon's pro-Pakistan policy!

[3] Compare, for example, what appeared in *D*, 1 September 1971, with what was actually printed in the issue of the *Herald-Tribune*, Paris edition, which was supposed to have been accurately quoted.

dents in Pakistan were tampered with in the censor's office. The campaign of vilification and hostility towards India seemed to have official benediction, for there was not the least indication that the Pakistan Government desired to moderate or defuse the situation, notwithstanding a conciliatory message brought from Mrs. Gandhi by India's newly-appointed High Commissioner to Pakistan.[4] Some people concluded that not only would there be war, but that Pakistan might take the initiative. Indeed, it could be argued that India was deliberately seeking to provoke this. Yet the idea of Pakistan accepting the challenge or of intending to take the initiative appeared incredible. Did the Pakistan Government really believe it could wage war successfully in East Pakistan, encircled as it was by India, with no command of sea or air routes and where the population itself was hostile? Did it believe that a simultaneous attack in the west would succeed in drawing off Indian forces deployed in the east, and was it thought that this would enable General Niazi to achieve a counter-stroke in Bengal? Did it believe China would come to the rescue, or the United States, or the Security Council?

When the Pakistan High Command learned the shape of counter-insurgency operations in April 1971, met, as they were, by an increasingly positive Indian military posture, it should have been evident that pursuit of the rebels to the borders must lead to a confrontation with India and, in consequence, to the possibility of explicit war. Clearly, this was inherent in the situation but there is little evidence showing that this serious problem was either grasped or, if it was, that it received the degree of attention it deserved.

Yahya Khan's military caucus may well have accepted the possibility of war with India with comparative equanimity, although what grounds they could have had for such confidence is bewildering. Certainly, they did nothing positive to avert it. There is no indication that military precautions were taken or that tactics were devised for the eastern theatre, to meet the grave threats there. In India, on the other hand, planning for eventualities proceeded systematically. Not only was there explicit expression of the opinion that war must come,

---

[4] Yahya Khan was reported as making offensively belligerent remarks, in private, about Mrs. Gandhi as, e.g., 'That woman can't cow me'.

but operational planning was well in hand. It is strange that Yahya Khan either chose to initiate war, or allowed it to be initiated, at a time and season most favourable to India. It can be argued that if, from the climatic point of view, early December favoured military operations, it did so for India and Pakistan equally, but this ignores two points. It was late to open a western front to relieve pressure on the eastern and, of course, the northern passes were snowbound and more or less closed to China.

If India needed time to prepare, so, too, did Pakistan. Reinforcements had to be sent, mainly by sea, and this required time. These reinforcements amounted to one full division and one brigade group, in addition to units milked from formations in West Pakistan where it was necessary to make up by the induction of reserves. In the east, stock levels had to be built up along with a system of strongholds upon which considerable reliance was to be placed. In the west, too, much had to be done, principally in the organization of forward airfields, the preparation of defences, and the positioning of ground troops. Moreover, Pakistan's appreciations and decisions were, naturally, based on its intelligence sources which seem to have been poor and, in the end, to have broken down completely. This is proved, in part, by the speed of the Indian advance in East Bengal and, in part, by the resolute defence offered to Pakistan's attack on the western front.

Whatever the respective intentions and responsibilities of each Government, the path to war, for Pakistan, acquired an increasingly distinct definition. On 13 October Yahya Khan addressed the nation by radio. About three-fifths of his discourse had to do with India and its threatening attitude; rather more than one-fifth was about constitutional proposals; and the rest was made up of familiar, moralistic exhortation. A few days later it was widely rumoured that official papers had been evacuated from Lahore, while on 2 November Yahya Khan was reported as having said that war was 'imminent'. This assumed a more sombre aspect when the tale circulated that India would open its attack in the east on 20 November, on which day that year fell Id-ul-Fitr, most celebrated of all Muslim festivals. Indeed, on the night of 20/21 November reports reached Rawalpindi of intensified Indian military activity on

most fronts in East Bengal and these were interpreted as tan-
tamount to open hostilities. On 22 November Yahya Khan,
accompanied by his Chief of Staff, Hamid Khan, paid a visit
to front-line formations in the Sialkot and Shakarganj areas, an
event which acquired a significance it did not deserve since it
appears to have been nothing more than adherence to a previously announced schedule, although this was not then explained.

Next day, 23 November, a state of emergency was declared
in Pakistan, followed, in twenty-four hours, by a similar declaration in India. In Pakistan reservists were called up. About
the same time posters appeared on walls giving advice about
air-raid precautions. These measures led to some panic; people
began to stock food, and prices rose. In Karachi the District
Magistrate said he had issued instructions to special squads,
comprising magistrates and police, to administer a whipping to
traders who did not bring prices down to 'pre-emergency levels'.
With what authority he did this was not clear and, later, it
appeared that the flogging or whipping would be ordered by
the institution which had grown so lamentably familiar in
Pakistan, the 'Special' Military Court. The Sind Government
ordered hotels and restaurants to serve 'austerity meals' only.
On 30 November the Pakistan Government prohibited any
Pakistani from visiting India, while Gilgit and Baltistan were
closed to all foreigners because land convoys from China, bringing arms, were arriving by that route. On the late afternoon
of Friday, 3 December 1971, it became known that the two
countries were at war and the black-out descended.

India claimed that Pakistan had initiated hostilities on the
late afternoon of that day with pre-emptive strikes on the air-
fields of Srinagar, Avantipur, Pathankot, Jodhpur, Ambala,
and Agra, with a second wave the same night. However, in
reply to the question 'Who Began It?', it must be remembered
that East Pakistan had been under attack, or at any rate bom-
bardment, since 21/22 November, a period of thirteen days,
circumstances not of Pakistan's choosing. According to General
Palit the air strikes failed because the Indian aircraft were dis-
persed in bomb-proof shelters, of which precaution Pakistan
appeared to be unaware. The same night Pakistan's ground
formations were taking aggressive action along the western

front at many points, the Poonch and Chhamb sectors being particularly significant. For Pakistan it seemed encouragingly like September of 1965 with anticipations of a swift advance to Akhnur—and no cease-fire inhibitions this time—down to the plains of East Punjab and beyond. But things had changed and so had the beginnings of the new contest. What is more, India had made its preparations and, like Pakistan, intended to operate without inhibitions, regardless of world opinion.

For, plainly, in the east India intended to carry the issue to a final and successful conclusion. That was the campaign which really mattered. Accordingly, on the evening of 3 December, Lieut.-General J. S. Aurora, commanding three army corps, a communications zone headquarters and the Mukti Bahini, said to be about 100,000 strong, was ordered to attack.

Against Aurora's force, comprising nine regular infantry divisions, more than five regiments of tanks and a Border Security Force of thirty-nine battalions, Lieut.-General A. A. K. Niazi deployed three infantry divisions with artillery on a scale less than was normal for a Pakistani infantry division and, also, a para-military force, the Razakars, of doubtful worth and training. In artillery Aurora enjoyed a conspicuous advantage. Pakistan's forces were equipped with 105 mm. American gun-howitzers with a range of 16,000 yards and 3·5 inch Chinese mortars. India used the same American 105 mm. gun-howitzer and the British 25-pounder whose range was 13,000 yards. In addition, the Indian troops were armed with medium artillery including the British 5·5 gun and the Russian 130 mm. gun which had a range up to 30,000 yards. Aurora also had one parachute field artillery regiment. In armour, Niazi had five squadrons of the American Chaffee tank, a Korean war veteran first brought into service in 1944 and armed with a 75 mm. gun. The Russian PT-76, used by the Indians, was some four tons lighter than the Chaffee, but it was of later design. First introduced in 1955, it was an amphibian and it had a 76 mm. high velocity gun. In light automatic weapons, it is possible the Pakistani infantry battalions had an advantage, as Palit has pointed out, but this was offset, to some extent, by the four heavy machine guns, ranging up to 2,500 yards, with which India's infantry battalions were equipped. In the air, Niazi was hopelessly situated with one squadron of Sabres against ten assorted fighter-bomber squadrons at Aurora's disposal. They operated from a ring of air-fields around East Bengal and provided what amounted to a bomber shuttle-service. In addition, Aurora had helicopters with which to negotiate river-obstacles and launch airborne attacks. Excluding, therefore, para-military formations on either side, Aurora had a seven to four superiority in men which, according to Palit, was no more than was necessary to the campaign Aurora intended to fight. This may be so, but it is certain that, apart from men, he had an immense advantage in armament. The fact was that India fully intended to crush the Pakistani forces as decisively and, more important, as swiftly, as possible.

It appears to have been Niazi's plan to hold East Pakistan along its frontiers, for which purpose strong-points had been organized with anti-tank ditches. Acording to Palit, the strong-points had overhead concrete cover, six feet thick, minefields, and abundant dumps of supplies, but this is very doubtful. To be sure, as victors in the battle, India had every opportunity, afterwards, to examine the strongholds, but so far no evidence of Palit's assertion has been produced and it has been strenuously denied on Pakistan's side. The case appears to be that these strong-points had little or no overhead cover, and little in the way of mines. They were stocked with seven to fifteen days' supplies with rearward reserves amounting to a further fifteen to thirty days. Most of these were, of course, captured and may have given the impression of an abundance which did not really exist.

Such preparations as Niazi was able to make required time and it is certain that Indian intelligence was well aware of the construction of frontier fortifications and must have divined the reason for them. These fortifications may have been responsible for Niazi's statement that war, if it came, would be fought on Indian soil. He was, however, given to flourishes of that sort and liked to see his picture on the front page. But even if he could not, or did not, carry the war into India, the underlying strategy seems to have been that those fortifications would enable him to hold off the Indian forces long enough to enable foreign political intervention to bring hostilities to an end. Secondly, by denying East Pakistan's soil to an Indian advance, no independent 'Bangladesh' Government could be set up on its territory.

Whether or not this was a good plan may be debated. Clearly, political, as distinct from military, considerations were playing an important part. It must be remembered that in the preceding counter-insurgency operations Niazi's forces had inevitably been drawn towards the frontier. By stringing his troops round the frontier of East Pakistan Niazi lost some of the advantages of concentration, for it had always been the view of the Pakistan General Staff that the defence of East Pakistan could be sustained for only a limited period in the face of any determined assault by India and that the defence of Dacca would be vital. Certainly, the defence was aided by the terrain—the rivers and the poor roads, but these obstacles would also be adverse to the defence should recourse to rapid concentration become necessary. Palit takes the view that Niazi had troops enough for his 1,400 miles of frontier but this seems exaggerated. The forces at his disposal could be considered no more than barely sufficient for the linear defence which Palit, in fact, criticized. At best, Niazi could only have had in mind the possibility of creating reserves and manoeuvring them as striking forces with his strong-points as anchors, or as forces to occupy lay-back positions to assist an organized withdrawal to the 'Dacca bowl'.[5] What Niazi should have done is best left to the professionals to debate and the question that must occupy them is why Niazi, or his superiors at Rawalpindi, failed to appreciate, as soon as they discovered their forces were becoming inextricably involved in linear defence, that positive steps must be taken to secure the Dacca bowl at all costs.

General Aurora's problem was vastly different, for whereas Niazi could have chosen his time for the re-adjustment of his dispositions, Aurora 'must get to Dacca within a time-frame of 12–15 days from the declaration of war'.[6] As it turned out, Niazi stood committed by political considerations and, involved in his linear defence, left Aurora with the advantage of the initiative and the ability to concentrate at points of his own choosing. Of course, there was no declaration and, therefore, when Aurora received his orders, it was with the prior assumption that he was

[5] Meaning the plain surrounding Dacca where Niazi might concentrate and fight a standing battle.

[6] Palit, *The Lightning Campaign*, p. 100.

ready to move. But the crucial question is: why did General Aurora have to get to Dacca within twelve or fifteen days? Palit suggests, without actually asserting it, that Aurora needed to reach Dacca 'before the Pakistani forces pulled back to the inner defence line at the [Dacca] bowl'. This suggestion runs counter to all that is known of Niazi's intentions. If he had any plan to engage the enemy in that way, why should he string out his forces along the frontier with all the risks of never being able to catch up and concentrate in the event of a break-through on any one or more of the salients where the Indians had chosen to launch their thrusts?

· It is evident that Palit's suggestion was an unsuccessful attempt to conceal the real explanation. So brief a period had been imposed on Aurora because India was relying, no doubt by prior arrangement, on the Soviet Union's veto in the Security Council. It was plain that once hostilities began in earnest the issue would be raised in the United Nations, and India intended that there should be no interruption in the fighting until its purpose in East Pakistan had been achieved. But while the Soviet Union could, by means of the veto, hold the ring, it could not do so indefinitely, and the swift capture of Dacca, even if not the final destruction of Niazi's army, was necessary. The Soviet Union exercised its veto three times, thereby providing time for General Aurora to encircle Dacca and force a surrender. It was accomplished in twelve days and was no mean feat of arms. Had he not succeeded, the political situation might well have become adverse for India.[7] Further, if Yahya Khan and his advisers had been relying on China, or the United States, or the Security Council, they were cruelly undeceived.

Aurora deserves credit for the skilful conduct of his twelve-day campaign, but it is evident that Niazi fought under grievous difficulties. First, his strategy was dominated by political considerations, not always the soundest basis on which to wage war. Second, his intelligence did not seem to know that the Indians planned to neutralize the difficulties of the terrain by the use of amphibian tanks, helicopters, and paratroops which,

[7] On 6 December General Westmoreland, of the United States Army, expressed the view that Niazi might hold out for three weeks (*Anderson Papers*). There is the further point that India had to expect retaliation in the west and the sooner the task in East Bengal was completed, the easier it would be to give undivided attention to the battle on the western front.

in themselves, served well to overcome the defensive tactics on which Niazi was relying. Third, Niazi, after some two or three days, had no air cover and his troops fought the rest of the battle exposed to India's abundant air sorties. Fourth, he was fighting in a countryside where the civilian population was entirely against him and actively helped the Indians. Fifth, it is probable that the morale of his men was not high, mainly because of the dispiriting circumstances in which they had lived for eight months and were now fighting. There is evidence that, at some points, the Pakistanis fought to the last round and the last man but hard fighting means heavy casualties and the Pakistani casualties were light.[8] Still, it could not justly be said that they were wanting in valour. They were out-generalled, out-manoeuvred, and out-flanked from front to rear and thus it was that, on 16 December 1971, Niazi signed the Instrument of Surrender in Dacca.

Of the campaign on land in the west there is little to say. At first things went well from the Pakistan point of view. The Indians were obliged to withdraw in the Chhamb sector and it seemed as if September 1965 might be repeated until, shortly afterwards, the advancing Pakistani forces met with a check which they were unable to overcome or circumvent. The fact was that the Indians had learned their lesson. Their positions, now designed to repel the anticipated Pakistani attempt to break out through Akhnur, had been well prepared. Pakistan's assaults did not prevail against them, and losses, both in men and armour, were sustained. Elsewhere there was some cut and thrust, with the Indians taking large pieces of territory in Sind and smaller enclaves elsewhere to the north. However, upon Mrs. Gandhi's unilateral cease-fire, immediately after the surrender at Dacca, the military situation in the west retained importance only as material for subsequent wrangling at the political level. The contest was transferred to other arenas. In military terms, as later revealed, the net result on the western front was to leave India holding some 5,000 square miles of Pakistan's territory with 540 prisoners captured, while Pakistan held about 100 square miles of Indian territory (mainly in Kashmir) and 617 prisoners.[9]

[8] See Appendix D.
[9] These figures are based on the exchanges announced in December 1972.

The damage done by Indian aircraft in West Pakistan was by no means crippling although hits on the Karachi oil terminal destroyed twenty-two bulk oil tanks with the loss of about thirty-five million gallons of petroleum products. There was damage to the natural gas installation at Sui and to cotton ginneries and textile factories, as well as to some house property in Karachi. Shipping in Karachi harbour suffered slight loss, but there was no serious destruction and the numbers of aircraft deployed on either side were too small to cause major damage.

At sea, Pakistan lost a destroyer hit by an Indian missile craft of Soviet construction. These vessels were the most serious menace the Pakistan navy had to face. The result was that the Pakistan navy was virtually under blockade, and from 8 December onwards it was unable to take part in any operations. Perhaps the most interesting event at sea was the appearance in the Bay of Bengal of a task force sent by the American Seventh Fleet comprising the aircraft carrier, *Enterprise*, with nuclear-armed Phantoms, an amphibious attack ship, a guided missile frigate, dock-landing ships, and supply vessels. The United States Government explained that the presence of this force was to facilitate the evacuation of such American citizens as remained in the newly declared state of Bangladesh, but whether those citizens were present in such numbers as to require so formidable a squadron, whether they desired to leave, and whether they were in any real danger seems extremely doubtful. It is evident that the American ships were sent to remind the Soviet Union, then occupying a prominent position in the drama, that the United States was not indifferent to events in this theatre of war and had not lost interest in the sub-continent. As it happened, India declared a cease-fire and the American force steamed without ostentation towards other waters.

Meanwhile, on the evening of 16 December, Yahya Khan addressed the nation by radio for about thirty minutes, speaking in Urdu. He touched upon political matters and then said of the military situation that Pakistan would fight on till final victory. He made no mention of the cessation of hostilities in East Pakistan nor did he offer any comment on the Soviet Union

They included twelve Pakistani pilots and ten members of the Indian Air Force, presumably pilots. Such figures indicate the scale of the air war.

whose part had, for India, been decisively important. On the other hand, he thanked China and the United States for their support. The astonishing unrealism of this was disclosed, next morning, when the newspapers informed the public that, by agreement between the local commanders, fighting had ceased in East Pakistan and that Indian troops had entered Dacca. The newspapers added that India had informed the Security Council that it would observe a unilateral cease-fire on the western front on 17 December, at 7.30 p.m. local time.

It was learned that the United States had informed Pakistan that if India continued the war on the western front, they would give all material help and support, but that if India declared a cease-fire, Pakistan would have to accept it. The Soviet Union is understood to have informed India that, after taking Dacca, a cease-fire must be declared. Since, as it appears to me, India had no other intention than to do exactly this, the two super-Powers, each according to its own logic, made their respective contributions to crystallizing India's purposes.

Thus, for India, a victory;[10] for East Bengal a new life clearly fraught with immense problems and grave hazards; for the political generals of Islamabad, humiliation and disgrace;[11] for the old Pakistan, a bitter mutilation.

[10] Afterwards, it was argued in Pakistan that the war had not really been lost because Pakistan's ground troops in the west had not all been committed to battle and were still in being. However, much depends on how losing and winning are interpreted. As explained here, it seems impossible to deny that India secured what it had set out to do.

[11] In Peshawar, an indignant mob attacked Yahya Khan's privately owned residence and sacked it. Probably the mob would have burned it completely but cement-concrete does not ignite easily and the fire brigade turned up promptly.

# XVI

# The Disruption of Pakistan

With the onset of the autumn of 1971, and with the prospect of war casting a shadow across the sub-continent, it became evident that Yahya Khan and Zulfikar Ali Bhutto were discovering a measure of common ground. For some this confirmed suspicions of a secret collusion, although the true explanation seems quite different. In times of grave crisis men, although otherwise divided, may well deem it wise to sink less important differences and stand together. When the situation in East Pakistan acquired an aspect of menace, Yahya Khan evidently thought it necessary to adopt safeguards. One of them was to send a mission to China. Bhutto was invited to lead it probably because he was thought to be a personality readily acceptable to that country. The outcome of the mission disclosed no promise of material help or of other useful intervention but, for Mr. Bhutto, the visit was of great personal importance—for three reasons. It brought him even more prominently into the public eye. It earned for him a great deal of renewed public approbation. It recalled to people's minds his steadfast attitude in September 1965 and afterwards.

Mr. Bhutto must have been aware of this and of the promise it might hold for him because, on return to Rawalpindi from Peking, he travelled to Karachi by train, a method which, in the days of his quarrel with Ayub Khan, had enabled him to make dramatic contact with the masses. In the course of his journey he gave well-attended speeches at railway stopping-points and, on arrival at Karachi, a vast crowd gathered to meet him. Already, he was being spoken of as a prospective Prime Minister and he, himself, was using language clearly intended to appeal to those East Pakistan members of the National Assembly who, as the phrase went, had been 'cleared' by Yahya Khan's administration. Moreover, he was accorded a great deal of official attention. When he travelled by car in the cities, roads were cleared for him and other compliments were paid. By the time hostilities broke out, it was evident that Mr. Bhutto would soon be occupying an important role.

On 6 December the Soviet Union imposed its first veto, thus thwarting the Security Council's resolution calling for a cease-fire. Next day Yahya Khan announced the formation of a coalition government at the Centre with Nurul Amin of East Pakistan as Prime Minister, and Zulfikar Ali Bhutto as Deputy Prime Minister with, at the same time, the Foreign Minister's portfolio. Yahya Khan was to continue as President and Chief Martial Law Administrator, but he said that substantial power would be transferred to the new government. He also said that promulgation of new proposals for a constitution would go forward as planned. The conclusion seemed to be that Yahya Khan was already wilting under the turn of events. The ageing Nurul Amin who, so far as East Pakistan was concerned, re-presented no one but himself, would simply be a figurehead whose only qualification was that his presence might appease some people in the eastern Province, while Bhutto would be the effective political figure. In short, Mr. Bhutto had re-entered the corridors of power. His next move was to attend the United Nations on his country's behalf. At first his manner was mod-erate and persuasive, but with repeated Soviet vetoes facilita-ting India's offensive in East Pakistan, his attitude changed and, on 15 December, he made a bitter speech saying it would be the last time he would address the Security Council.[1] In a gesture of angry protest he tore up a Security Council paper and said, 'Why should I waste my time here? I will go back to my country and fight.' He then left the Council Chamber and, speaking to newsmen outside, expressed his hatred for 'this body'. Shortly afterwards, Bhutto set out for Pakistan, via Rome. It was at Rome that a new and different summons awaited him.

Meanwhile, on 12 December, Pakistan was disquieted to learn that Major-General Farman Ali, Military Adviser to the Governor of East Pakistan, had already sent a telegram to the Secretary-General of the United Nations, asking him to make preparations for the evacuation of West Pakistani soldiers

---

[1] Although Yahya Khan had no criticism to make of the Soviet Union, Bhutto referred to that country's conduct in harsh terms and he criticized France and the United Kingdom for not using their influence to halt events in East Pakistan.

operating in East Bengal. Further, as soon as he came to know of it, Yahya Khan countermanded the message. When questioned about this, the official spokesman replied evasively although the despatch of a message was not denied. Shortly afterwards, to make confusion worse confounded, Farman Ali said he had not sent anything.

Yahya Khan, with his political colleagues, was occupied with plans for the constitutional future of Pakistan, and he was busy preparing the speech in which he was to announce his proposals to the country. Between him and General Headquarters there was not a great deal of communication, partly because of his constitutional preoccupations. Moreover, Yahya Khan was so absorbed in these important but, at the time, not totally relevant matters, that he failed to notice what was going on elsewhere; for example in the higher ranks of the army in West Pakistan there was a growing sense of disquiet which was to show itself most notably at Gujranwala in the Punjab.

Among the formations held in reserve at Gujranwala was an armoured division, commanded by Major-General 'Bachu' Karim[2] whose position, because he came from East Pakistan, had become somewhat anomalous. He had, in fact if not by formal order, been more or less pushed aside. This may account for, or may have been due to, his concern for the safety and welfare of those East Pakistani (Bengali) soldiers stationed in West Pakistan who, in that moment of heightened stress, might become the object of attack by their West Pakistani comrades.[3] There is some evidence that General Karim gave expression to these apprehensions and was met with the reply that when the fate of so many West Pakistanis, including some 80,000 officers and men, hung in the balance in East Pakistan, a concern for a small number of East Pakistani soldiers who, at that moment, had no visible cause for alarm, seemed strange. In addition to this armoured division, there was an infantry divi-

[2] The same person mentioned in Ch. XIII who, as Brigadier Karim, advised Yahya Khan on East Pakistani affairs. The incident narrated here and the fact that this officer was Bengali may indicate that the spirit of provincial faction was already abroad in the army.

[3] Their number was in the order of 4,000. In April 1973 the International Committee of the Red Cross estimated the number of Bengali armed forces personnel in West Pakistan to be about 25,000. This figure can only be accounted for by the Navy and Air Force in which services the proportion of Bengalis was much higher than in the army.

sion, commanded by Major-General R. D. Shamim. The over-all command of these reserve formations was entrusted, on an *ad hoc* basis, to a senior Major-General, Bashir by name.

Quite apart from the question of General Karim's concern for East Pakistani troops, the situation of the formations held at Gujranwala was especially delicate because they were in reserve at a time when the Indian Army was attacking vigorously on the Sialkot–Shakarganj sector, capturing territory. To the local civilian population these formations presented the strange spectacle of soldiers, with their guns, tanks, and equipment, taking no part in the battle and showing no sign of any such intention. That these troops were being withheld on sound strategic grounds was not very likely to be understood by civilians and when the news came of the surrender on 17 December their indignation rose. They not only spoke slightingly of these uncommitted soldiers but even demonstrated it by a show of violence, throwing stones and hurling abuse. The fact of surrender in East Pakistan was, by itself, a great shock for the armed forces. For those unfortunate officers and men at Gujranwala who, plainly, had taken no part in the battle, to hear the contumelious scorn of their civilian countrymen was scarcely tolerable.

In these circumstances, some officers decided to raise the voice of protest. Among them were Brigadier Iqbal Mehdi Shah, of the Armoured Corps, and Brigadier Farrukh Bakht Ali, of the Artillery, both capable, unassuming men with high intellectual and professional reputations. Along with Colonel Aleem Afridi, they approached Major-General R. D. Shamim who expressed sympathy with their ideas, and they all sought an interview with Major-General Bashir. It seems that General Bashir impressed on them the need for moderation and unity at so critical a moment but these officers were not easily persuaded and G.H.Q. was informed of their opinions. Eventually they were invited to Rawalpindi where they did not prevail.[4]

---

[4] I must make it clear that the contents of this chapter form, in the main, an attempted reconstruction of events. Quite clearly, in times of great national crisis much happens that is not documented and much which people prefer to forget. The eventual fate of Major-General Shamim, Brigadiers Iqbal Mehdi Shah and Farrukh Bakht Ali, and three others was, in August 1972, to be compulsorily retired from the army following a Court of Enquiry into what was said to have been 'a plot to plunge the country into civil war two days before President Bhutto assumed power on 20 December 1971'. No details were given on the ground that

Whatever the conduct of these officers and whatever censure they might have earned, this incident was symptomatic of the grave doubts felt by many in the army about Yahya Khan's conduct of the war and of their apprehensions of an early and disastrous outcome. In addition, there was the question of Yahya Khan's political concerns and the part which the newly created government, under Nurul Amin's nominal Prime Ministership, was to play. Apart from what was being thought and said in Gujranwala much disquiet supervened at the highest level in the armed forces. At G.H.Q. in Rawalpindi Lieut.-General Gul Hasan, Chief of the General Staff, and Air-Marshal Rahim Khan, Commander-in-Chief of the Pakistan Air Force, were anxiously debating the course of events.[5]

The widening disassociation between Yahya Khan and his politico-military caucus on the one side, and General Headquarters on the other, may owe a great deal to the divergent courses of Yahya Khan and Gul Hasan. Although, in General Hamid Khan, as Chief of Staff, Yahya Khan had his representative and channel of communication with G.H.Q., it is by no means clear that this arrangement sufficed. One reason probably was that a strong antipathy had long existed between Gul Hasan and Peerzada. Another, perhaps, was that Hamid Khan's personal intellectual integrity would not permit him to support the irresponsible political preoccupations of Yahya Khan and his other colleagues. As events in East Bengal moved towards a climax and surrender in the Province seemed imminent Yahya Khan's immediate plan was evidently to promulgate a constitution drafted by his committee of experts, and to announce the broad outline of the constitution in a radio address. This plan was founded upon the assumption that East Bengal would continue to form part of Pakistan and even when it was known that General Farman Ali had sent his appeal for help to the United Nations, Yahya Khan was still absorbed with the finishing touches to his speech.[6]

---

it would not be in the public interest to do so, but the disparity between the gravity of the offence alleged and the comparative mildness of the punishment did not go unremarked. These officers seem to have been guilty of no more than insubordination, for which compulsory retirement could well be deemed an appropriate punishment.

[5] The Commander-in-Chief of the Navy played little or no part because his duties compelled him to remain in Karachi.

[6] The text of this address will be found at Appendix B.

To this atmosphere of impending disaster the top command at Rawalpindi could not be indifferent and there is no doubt whatsoever that the entire situation was the subject of very earnest debate. Among the principal questions was the future of Yahya Khan who was evidently imbued with the notion that in spite of everything he could carry on as President. At G.H.Q. the strong current of opinion was that he could not. However, on the question of his successor, there was a distinct difference of opinion. Some favoured the retired Air-Marshal Asghar Khan who had contributed to the departure of Ayub Khan and had built up a political following. Others, however, considered this a mistake. To introduce yet another armed forces man as President might well provoke stiff opposition in a nation which had no reason to feel any confidence in the political skill of men in uniform. Moreover, in the election of 1970, Asghar Khan had been soundly defeated—in a Rawalpindi constituency, veritable home of the armed forces—by a People's Party candidate of no great prominence.[7] Thus, Asghar Khan was not a member of the National Assembly and his party, the Tehrik-i-Istiqlal (a fair translation might be the Party of Steady Fortitude), had not a single representative there.

This second school of thought favoured Mr. Bhutto as Yahya Khan's successor. His qualifications were that (a) he was not an armed forces man; (b) he was an elected member of the National Assembly; (c) his party had a majority in the Assembly since Sheikh Mujib's Awami League had been banned and about half its elected members had been unseated;[8] (d) it was evident that Bhutto had emerged, in West Pakistan at least, as a popular leader; and (e) he was already Deputy Prime Minister. The course of events now becomes obscure, but it is evident that before leaving New York, and perhaps in Rome also, Bhutto received information from his closer political colleagues that events in Pakistan were taking an unpredictable course and that he would be well advised to return as soon as possible.

There still remained, however, the question of Yahya Khan's intentions and, on 17 December, Gul Hasan, along with Rahim

---

[7] Asghar Khan actually lost his deposit.

[8] This was not necessarily an overall majority and much would have depended upon the outcome of by-elections. Still, by 17 December, all speculation of this sort ceased to have any foundation in reality.

Khan, went to the President's House to confront Yahya Khan with the brutal actualities, to acquaint themselves with what was in train there and, if it came to the point, to inform Yahya Khan of the view held in G.H.Q. concerning himself. On arrival, it seems they found Yahya Khan still busy with his radio address. At the meeting, at which General Hamid Khan was present, Gul Hasan and Rahim Khan informed Yahya Khan that nothing remained but for him to go. At first Yahya Khan resisted this suggestion, but when they pressed him more firmly, he agreed and added that he would then go back to the army as Commander-in-Chief. This Gul Hasan and Rahim Khan treated as absurd and became even stronger in their insistence that Yahya Khan must go. In the face of this pressure it seems that Yahya Khan obliquely suggested that Gul Hasan might become President[9] and, more explicitly perhaps, that Hamid Khan might become Commander-in-Chief. At about this time, or somewhat later—so much is obscure—Gul Hasan became aware that the broadcast of Yahya Khan's address had begun and, at once, he ordered it to be stopped.

To the proposal that he become Commander-in-Chief Hamid Khan demurred and said he would not accept any such proposal unless he first met the officers at G.H.Q. to obtain their reaction to that idea.[10] He therefore called a meeting of senior officers at G.H.Q., i.e. lieutenant-colonel and above, for 20 December. Shortly afterwards it was announced that *all* officers at G.H.Q. would attend and, some thirty minutes before the meeting was held, all officers of the Rawalpindi garrison were required to be present. The circumstances which led to this significant expansion of Hamid Khan's audience are unclear and it may have been Gul Hasan who, as Chief of the General Staff, had these orders issued through the Staff Duties Directorate. It is believed that Gul Hasan advised some officers, who had consulted him, not to withhold their opinions or mince their words. The meeting was a stormy one in which strong language was used, and Hamid Khan was unable to satisfy his audience.

[9] With the intention of excluding Bhutto?
[10] The dangers inherent in such a move are obvious and one is reminded of the days when the Sikh sardars offered themselves to the Khalsa for acceptance. Still, it may simply have been General Hamid Khan's purpose to test the feeling that prevailed at G.H.Q. at a very critical time.

From 18 to 20 December the country was virtually without a government and Yahya Khan was more or less a prisoner; his coterie of political generals had been rendered impotent and the only person exercising authority was Gul Hasan whose orders were being obeyed. On his arrival at Rawalpindi Mr. Bhutto was met by Gul Hasan and Rahim Khan and, with them, went straight to the President's House where he took over office from Yahya Khan.

As described here, the impression may be left that Bhutto was simply a military nominee but this would do him less than justice. It is true that, in all politics, the final arbiter is the man with the pistol in his pocket (and political maturity can be measured by the ability to dispense with so drastic a recourse); nevertheless Bhutto had advanced himself by his electoral success—very much a personal achievement—and, as is clear from the reasons which motivated General Gul Hasan, Bhutto was as necessary to the army as the army's sanction was to him. It should be added that Mr. Bhutto has given some account of these events in his address on 20 December 1971. The words he used were 'summoned by the nation'.

Meanwhile, Pakistan's forces in the eastern Province had surrendered, the independence of Bangladesh had become a reality, and India, having announced a unilateral cease-fire, held its positions on the western front. In the new Pakistan it remained only for Zulfikar Ali Bhutto to enter upon the task of restoring the country's shattered fortunes.[11]

[11] The removal of Yahya Khan has been described as a 'mini-coup' and the part played by Gul Hasan and Rahim Khan as king-breakers and king-makers is not easy to assess. It is noteworthy that about three months after Bhutto became President, both these men resigned and afterwards went abroad in ambassadorial appointments.

# APPENDIX A

*Mr. Rezaur Rahman's Letter to 'A.G.'*

Dacca, 17 March 1971

Dear A.G.,

It is most heartening to hear from you. We seem to be living in a state of siege. Do you realise that we do not receive mail or cables or telephone calls from outside E.P. nor can one get out of E.P.—not that I want to at the moment—your letter was, therefore, most welcome.

In fact it was very analytical and I can only hope with you that we do not blunder now. In fact, I am feeling like discussing your letter with the Mujib group.

I have a new theory now. Let me put it to you so that you can find the weak points in it. It goes as follows:

(a) The Army never wanted to hand over power to the civilians without a definite say in future arrangements—constitution or whatever it may be.

(b) I know for a fact that they collected funds from industrialists well before the election. Some of our clients have paid. I presume others must have.

(c) Tajammul also knows that money has been paid out to various parties by the Army Intelligence.

(d) The Army Intelligence expected at least four to eight major parties emerging from the elections.

(e) With this expectation the LFO becomes really effective. The LFO can be helpful for the Army only if unanimity amongst political parties is lacking. If enough diversity could be created, the Army with its LFO could become the mediator.

(f) The first setback—the emergence of only two political parties.

(g) The silver lining—two parties from the Wings reasonably well-balanced.

(h) The honest broker goes into action—meets Mujib—declares him as the Prime Minister. Keeps the other military members in the background no pictures (covering them) in the papers. It is Mujib and Yahya collaboration.

(i) Bhutto annoyed. The honest broker now moves in with Bhutto. His military colleagues well covered in the Press. Bhutto and Yahya in the gardens. What the hell are Bhutto and Yahya up to now—says Mujib and his partymen.

(j) Up to now one can well question the necessity for Yahya to go flying all over East and West supposedly patching up differences between Mujib and Bhutto. Was he patching up? Or was he giving private and separate reassurances to both so as to ensure that differences are created? If you recall his pre-election speech, Yahya had asked all the National leaders to use the past election and pre-Assembly meeting period to get together to work out agreements. Did he allow enough time for this before taking up his honest broker act?

(k) Things are going well for the honest broker.

(l) Problems for the honest broker. There are dissents in Bhutto's camp. Bhutto named Mairaj and Khar as his successors. Yet the leftist group—possibly led by Mairaj—were quite prepared to sit in the opposition. They were also quite prepared to attend the Assembly meeting.

(m) Bhutto acknowledges that certain party members were in favour of attending the Assembly session—how big was this group— 20–25?

(n) Bhutto now threatens anyone who goes to E.P. for the Assembly. Then he threatens khaki-clads, etc. But is he really threatening the Army? They are not for the Assembly. Is he threatening Wali or Bizenjo or Daultana? Or is he threatening his own party people?

(o) Bhutto drops Mairaj and Khar. It is now Pirzada and Rahim making all party statements. What happened to the suddenly nominated successors? It would be interesting to meet these people.

(p) Bhutto has a long session with the honest broker. Did not the honest broker call him to 'Pindi 'for discussing national affairs'? Is the honest broker worried that if Bhutto's party breaks, then the mediator's role vanishes for the Army? The LFO becomes ineffective against an overwhelming majority.

(q) Something must be done to hold Bhutto's party in line. Bhutto makes his statement on 28th. He cannot demand postponement only. His party will not agree. So he throws in another alternative—withdraw 120 days' restriction.

(r) The honest broker picks up. Announces on 1st, the postponement. Refers to the major W.P. parties' refusal to attend but conveniently makes no mention at all to the party's other alternative. If the honest broker genuinely wants to resolve the problems and if Bhutto wants postponement, or 120 days restriction withdrawn, whilst Mujib does not want postponement, why not withdraw the restrictions? After all, this 120 days' thing is his own creation and there can be no objection from Mujib if his own condition is relaxed.

(s) Action 'R' taken—but with finesse. The 1st March statement is read out. Has the honest broker fallen? Mujib is led to believe so. He wonders about the alleged statement. Now in retrospect, one can wonder why the most important statement was read out. Frankly, Mujib had always stated to his colleagues that Yahya would not let him down. Even now he believes so.

(t)  Mujib reacts strongly. Takes up the challenge. Something has to be done. The honest broker now removes the velvet glove. He announces again. Now in no uncertain terms. He is very much in and challenges Mujib back. Puts all the blame on Mujib for failure of the RTC. Does not say anything for the failure of the 3rd March meeting due to Bhutto's action. After all, if you attack Bhutto also —perhaps people will wonder about that small 120 matter. He then insinuates that private understandings were there between him and Mujib. This could perhaps help to weaken and thereby annoy Mujib enough for him to take a rash action.

(u)  Having announced the Army now waits to see what Mujib will do on the 7th. Perhaps Mujib will after all take that one step that can now justify their plan—namely U.D.I.—no luck—although provocations were enough.

(v)  The waiting game cannot go on. The longer it goes the more established does Mujib become. A parallel government automatically takes shape. The world gradually realises that there are de facto two governments, two countries. This cannot help the Army's image of being an honest broker. If non-co-operation becomes the order of the day Mujib wins. But then Mujib is under tremendous pressure. How long can he hold out?

(w)  The Army decides the time is ripe for letting Mujib have a way out. Yahya announces that he will visit Dacca.

(x)  The pressure must, however, be kept on. So the delaying tactics start. Will he go? When will he go? Will he come? When will he come? Put the pressure on. Announce that Yahya will be opening a dispensary in Karachi on the 26th. Has he really given up the idea of the Assembly meeting on the 25th?

(y)  The honest broker arrives, but why is he not going straight to the meeting? Suspense.

(z)  They meet.

### The End.

Sorry if I kept you biting your nails. My Theory—The Army is the culprit. Bhutto and Mujib are but pawns well moved by them. If Mujib had realised this at the very beginning, he and Bhutto may well have arrived at a settlement which would have rendered the L.F.O. redundant.

What happens now? Does Mujib give ground? Can he bear the pressure a little longer? Can he call the Honest Broker's bluff? We have to wait for the next move.

So much for politics. Please keep this letter to yourself. Would hate to get into trouble over the first 'Play' I have written.

With regard to business—it is in another letter.

Reza

# APPENDIX B

*General Yahya Khan's Undelivered Address to the Nation,*
*December 1971*

Rawalpindi, 17 December 1971

The following is the text of President General Agha Mohammad Yahya Khan's statement issued here today:

As you may recall, in my address to the nation of 12th October, I had apprised you of the details of my plan of transfer of power and had stated that the new Constitution will be published by the 20th of December. In spite of treacherous aggression by India which she had hoped would completely disrupt my plan and despite certain serious set-backs that we have suffered, I am determined to keep to my programme of transfer of power. For its implementation I have already invited the leaders of the major parties representing both wings to form a coalition Government. The Government of the elected representatives of the people will assume the responsibility to guide the nation through this hour of crisis. The Constitution which I will briefly outline now will be released shortly, and will provide the framework for the representative Government to discharge its responsibilities to the people.

It is a matter of some sorrow for me that the process which I had initiated for the Constitution to be prepared by the elected representatives of the people was upset for reasons which are known. This unfortunate development has not deterred me in my resolve not to delay the transfer of power and it is this compulsion which has prompted me to present the Constitution to the people of Pakistan. At the same time, I have no wish to impose a Constitution. The Constitution, therefore, provides for the association and the participation of the elected representatives of the people through an easy amendment procedure in the first 90 days involving a simple majority and a consensus of 25 per cent of the representatives from the federating units.

I have been in constant touch with political leaders in the country and have taken into account numerous concrete suggestions which emanated from various sources. The object was that the Constitution should reflect the consensus and should meet the expectations of the people and the needs of the country.

I find that in the public debate on the subject general consensus exists on the following four broad elements which the Constitution reflects:

1. It should preserve and promote the ideology of the Islamic Republic of Pakistan.

2. The country needs a federal parliamentary system of Government enshrining fundamental rights of the people.
3. There should be maximum provincial autonomy within the concept of one country.
4. It should be an effective instrument for translating the new expectations of the people in the social and economic fields into a concrete reality.

The Constitution provides a parliamentary form of representative Government both at the Centre and in the Provinces. The President will appoint as Prime Minister a person who can command majority support in the National Assembly. The other Ministers will be members of the National Assembly, although a person who is not a member may be a Minister for a maximum period of six months. All will be responsible, as a Cabinet, to the National Assembly. The Prime Minister may be removed on only one ground, namely, that he has ceased to command the confidence of a majority in the National Assembly.

The Prime Minister will be assisted by a Vice-Prime Minister, who should belong to the other wing from that to which the Prime Minister belongs. The President is required to act in accordance with the advice of his Council of Ministers, except where such advice involves violation of his oath of office or interferes with the organisation of the defence forces of the country or their maintenance in a high state of efficiency.

The fundamental rights in this Constitution go beyond the provisions contained in previous constitutions. The directive principles of state policy have been reworded and strengthened in many respects. The state is to give special attention to improvement of the living and working conditions of the workers and the peasants.

Another major departure from earlier constitutions is the provision of a Vice-President. It has been provided that the Vice-President should belong to the other wing from that to which the President belongs and that his headquarters should be at Dacca. His principal function will be to be the Chairman of the Senate and this new House of Parliament forms the next major departure from the previous constitutions. A second House is a necessary feature of a federal state, and it has been missing from our constitutions for too long. Ordinarily, the function of a second House is to provide equal representation to the units constituting the federation and the Constitution provides that each of the Provinces shall have elected representatives in the Senate. In addition, to secure representation from among persons eminent in public and professional life, I have provided for nomination of fifteen such persons, of whom ten shall be from East Pakistan and the remaining five from the West Wing. The Vice-President of Pakistan, besides being the Chairman of the Senate, may have other functions conferred upon him by law and other duties may also be assigned to him by the President. The President and the Vice-President are to be elected normally by an electoral college composed of the senate, the National Assembly and all the Provincial Assemblies by the method of the alternative vote.

The Parliament of Pakistan will thus consist of two Houses, but the principal law-making body will be the National Assembly. The Senate has not been provided with a veto on legislation by the National Assembly, but may, nevertheless, propose amendments to any bill passed by the National Assembly which shall be transmitted to the latter Assembly through the President, who will have his ordinary powers of making suggestions for amendments himself. Thereafter, the power of putting the law into final shape is placed in the hands of the National Assembly. There will be joint sittings of the Houses for legislative purposes only when the Senate has disagreed with the National Assembly regarding amendment of the Constitution. In that case, there will be a joint sitting and besides a majority of two-thirds of the total membership of the two Houses of Parliament, there will be required a consensus of not less than twenty-five per cent of the total number of representatives from the constituent units to pass such an amendment. Among other occasions on which the two Houses will sit together will be when there is a motion for impeachment of the President or the Vice-President.

As I have spoken of the amendment of the Constitution, I may mention here that for the protection of the large measure of autonomy, which the new Constitution has given to the Provinces, it has been provided that any bill to amend certain specified provisions of the Constitution conferring such autonomy, when passed by the National Assembly, shall be forwarded not only to the Senate, but also to the Assembly of each of the Provinces for their consideration and recommendations. The views of the Provinces will be placed before the Senate which will thereafter formulate its own proposals for amendment and these will be passed back to the National Assembly by the President. In the event of disagreement between the two Houses of Parliament, there will be a joint sitting for resolution of the matter. A further safeguard for provincial autonomy has been provided by giving power to the President to withhold his assent if in his opinion any objection raised by a Provincial Assembly has not been substantially met.

Before I mention the matters in which provincial autonomy has been extended I would like to give a brief survey of the major features in relation to the Provincial Governments. An Assembly for each of the Provinces has already been elected. The Constitution provides that each Governor shall have a Council of Ministers and shall act in accordance with the advice which he receives from his Council. The leader of the majority in the Provincial Assembly is to be summoned to form a Ministry, and shall hold office subject to only one condition, namely, that he may be removed if he ceased to command the confidence of the majority in the Provincial Assembly.

Elaborate provisions have been made in that part of the Constitution which deals with relations between the Centre and the Provinces, which have the effect of transferring a large number of subjects from the central field to the provincial field. In relation to a few subjects such as post offices, stock exchanges and futures markets and insurance, where indeed central control is essential, it has been provided in the Constitution, in appreciation of the special position of East Pakistan, that at the request of that Province the Central Government shall transfer its executive functions to the Government of that Province. The powers of the Central Legislature have been expressly confined to matters which are provided for in this particular part of the Constitution. The provisions in the 1962 Constitution empowering the Central Legislature to make laws on provincial subjects under certain contingencies have been withdrawn. These purposes can now be served by the Central Legislature only upon request made by a Province or Provinces. In the financial field, very substantial powers of taxation have been transferred to the Provinces, but with this and with certain other matters such as the treatment of the subject of foreign trade and foreign aid, the making of grants to Provinces, inter-provincial trade, etc., I shall deal separately a little later.

The West Pakistan Dissolution Order 1970 provides that six autonomous bodies in the West Wing shall be managed by the President on behalf of the four Provinces. In the light of their operations during the course of the year it has been found that it should be possible to dissolve three of these corporations and their functions transferred to the four Provinces. These autonomous bodies are—the Agricultural Development Corporation, the Small Industries Corporation, and the Associated Cement Company. The arrangements envisaged in the Dissolution Order will now be restricted to the West Pakistan Railway, West Pakistan Power and Development Authority, and the West Pakistan Industrial Development Corporation with a restricted role confined to such important and basic industries which are of common interest to the four Provinces in the West Wing.

By the Constitution, the Centre will assume responsibility for protecting each Province from external aggression and internal disturbance, and for ensuring that its operations are conducted in accordance with the Constitution. For the implementation of this responsibility, two special provisions have been found necessary. One is that whenever the Central Government is satisfied that the Government of a

Province cannot be conducted in accordance with the provisions of the Constitution, it may authorise the Governor of the Province to assume to himself all the functions of the Provincial Government. Such a condition will not be permitted to last beyond one year. A provision has also been made for the Central Government to exercise a measure of control over a Province when it is afflicted with financial instability. As you are aware such provisions exist in many constitutions.

The subject which has most agitated the minds of the people concerns the relations between the Centre and the Provinces and the extent of provincial power consistent with the integrity and unity of the country. Consequently, it provides the Centre with responsibility in specified fields while all the residuary powers are with the Provinces.

Financial autonomy is an essential element in any scheme of provincial autonomy. Provinces should have command over their financial resources. The present position where the elastic sources of revenue were mostly with the Centre giving little scope to the Provinces to mobilise resources for their development has been radically changed under the new Constitution. The extremists, have, no doubt, advocated that the Centre should have no authority to levy any tax. This position is obviously unacceptable because if financial independence is essential for the Provinces, it is equally essential for the Centre to enable it to discharge its obligations under the Constitution. The new arrangement in the Constitution, therefore, provides for the complete transfer of the following sources of taxation to the Provinces in addition to the existing provincial sources of taxation:

1. Sales Tax.
2. All Excise Duties other than those on petroleum and tobacco manufacture.
3. Estate and Succession Tax.
4. Gift Tax.

Besides the complete transfer of the above mentioned central sources of taxation in favour of the Provinces, the Constitution also provides that the following three taxes will be collected by the Centre for the purposes of convenience but will be passed on in their entirety to the Provinces:

1. Export Duties.
2. Excise on unmanufactured tobacco.
3. Tax on natural gas and crude mineral oil.

In other words, the Centre will retain only the following sources of taxation:

1. Income, Corporation, and Wealth Tax.
2. Excise duties only on two items, viz. petroleum products and tobacco manufacturers.

3. Custom duties excluding export duties.

In addition to the transfer of these major sources of taxation to the Provinces, the Constitution provides for special grants from the Centre to the less developed Provinces. These grants will be not less than Rs. 70 crores a year, of which Rs. 60 crores or the entire amount of custom duties collected in East Pakistan whichever is higher, will be earmarked for East Pakistan. The NWFP and Baluchistan Province will get grants in aid of not less than Rs. 5 crores each.

The large special grant in favour of East Pakistan has been made to assist the development of that Province. The Central Government is on average collecting roughly Rs. 130 crores per annum from East Pakistan through central taxes. The arrangements made in the Constitution will give East Pakistan over Rs. 100 crores out of Rs. 130 crores which are collected from East Pakistan through central taxes. This will mean that East Pakistan's contribution to the central expenditure will be around Rs. 30 crores a year or about 5 per cent of the Centre's current total expenditure. This is indicative of the extent of the financial support which the Constitution provides to the resources of East Pakistan.

The allocation of these resources to the Provinces is now covered by constitutional provisions. The necessity for the establishment of a finance commission for periodic review will, therefore, not arise.

It has also been provided in the Constitution that Provincial Governments will be able to borrow internally within broad limits laid down by the Centre. This will obviate reference to the Centre every time a loan has to be raised. East Pakistan has been given a constitutional guarantee that it will be authorised to raise at least 54 per cent of the total public borrowings in the provinces.

In the field of external aid, which is an adjunct of the country's foreign policy, the Centre's role is restricted to the negotiation of the overall aid for the country. Here again, the Province of East Pakistan has been assured the minimum allocation of 54 per cent of the total aid negotiated in any one year. Within such allocations the Provinces will be free to negotiate directly specific projects and programmes.

The foreign exchange earnings of the country provide backing to the currency and, therefore, must be retained as a central responsibility. The Constitution, however, provides a system by which both East and West wings would use their own foreign exchange earnings after meeting the common liabilities.

The Provincial Governments would have powers to frame their own export promotion programmes and would be entitled to frame import policies in line with the availability of foreign exchange to their credit after meeting common needs and foreign aid allocated to them. These arrangements for West Pakistan will obviously be managed on a

regional basis. Since, however, foreign trade is an inseparable part
of the overall foreign policy, the Central Government would retain
powers to legislate and to lay down the framework within which the
trade policies have to be implemented by the Provincial Governments. The necessary institutional and administrative changes to
implement this constitutional provision would be made by transfer of
institutions like the Jute Board to East Pakistan and the setting up of
a Trade Board for coordinating trade policies in West Pakistan. In
the case of East Pakistan there is also a provision for appointment of
trade representatives abroad with the approval of the Central Government.

Inter-wing trade would be guided and regulated by a specially
constituted inter-wing trade board. It would be composed of representatives of all Provinces, half of which would be from East Pakistan.
The board would examine any questions referred to it on the initiative
of the Provinces. Thus, the Provinces would be able to ensure that
inter-regional trade is carried on in a fair and mutually advantageous
basis.

The currency has obviously to remain a central responsibility under
the State Bank of Pakistan but for the decentralisation of other central
banking functions the Constitution provides for the establishment of
two regional Reserve Banks, one in each wing. The Provincial Governments will be fully represented on these regional reserve banks which
will control commercial and cooperative banks in their respective
areas and will manage credit policies within the overall ceiling laid
down by the State Bank of Pakistan.

In the field of planning, there will be decentralisation permitting
Provinces to prepare their own development plans on the basis of
external and internal resources on which they will have full control.
The Centre will consolidate provincial plans for the preparation of
a national plan for any period specified by it. The decentralisation in
planning will involve the disbandment of the Central Development
Working Party for the Provinces and of the Executive Committee of
the National Economic Council as well as the National Economic
Council. The Provincial Governments will, therefore, have full authority to formulate and approve their plans without any monetary limits.

As regards the system of election, I might say that all the Assemblies
are to be those which have been elected by adult franchise under the
Legal Framework Order, and the same system of election is to continue under the Constitution. The Senate however will be elected by
the Provincial Assemblies by the method of the single transferable
vote, thus ensuring a wider representation than could be achieved
by the single vote under the party system.

I may mention too in relation to elections that provisions have been made in the Constitution to discourage multiplicity of political parties or their growth on narrow regional basis. I consider this reform necessary for the healthy growth of the parliamentary system and for the encouragement and growth of national outlook. These provisions would naturally apply to these elections.

The Islamic institutions which existed under previous constitutions are being maintained and it is also provided that branches of the Islamic Research Institution may be established in each Province if requested by the Provincial Government. In the principles of policy, at many places, the Islamic provisions have been strengthened.

At the end, I may mention that the Constitution provides that the Republic shall have two capitals at Islamabad and Dacca. The description 'Second Capital' in respect of Dacca has been abolished, and it has been provided that an adequate establishment shall be maintained at each capital for the discharge of the functions of the Central Government. The principal seat of parliament will be located at Dacca.

These are the main features of the Constitution, and its printed copies will be available on the 20th. I have attempted to synthesise the demands for maximum provincial autonomy with the imperatives of national unity. I have given fullest weight to the desire for decentralisation of functions and have accommodated this genuine desire up to the point beyond which I feared that the system would become unworkable. Decentralisation is required and has been provided but it obviously cannot be carried beyond a point which would become the starting point of disintegration. I feel that this Constitution is a bold measure in advance of almost any other constitution. But then our problems are unique and we have to find unique and bold solutions for the problems which this country faces. I earnestly hope and pray that this Constitution will help remove mistrust and bitterness which led us to the brink of a precipice and will herald a new era strengthening the unifying forces currently lying dormant in the national life.

PAKISTAN PAINDABAD.

# APPENDIX C

*Verdict of the Court in the Fokker Hijacking Case*

The trial continued into 1973 and, altogether, 133 witnesses were examined and the record of the oral evidence ran to 1,700 pages. In addition, a vast quantity of written evidence was produced. The judgement comprised 408 typed pages.

Of the six accused, one, Mohd. Hashim Qureshi, was found guilty as follows:

(a) under the Official Secrets Act, Section 3 (which relates to espionage) and sentenced to 14 years' rigorous imprisonment;

(b) under the Pakistan Penal Code:

    (i) Section 342, for wrongful confinement of passengers and crew of the aircraft—one year's rigorous imprisonment;

    (ii) Section 435, for burning the aircraft—two years' rigorous imprisonment;

    (iii) Section 120(B), for carrying arms, ammunition and explosives—two years' rigorous imprisonment;

all sentences to run concurrently. Qureshi was given leave to appeal to the Supreme Court of Pakistan.

The remaining accused were found guilty of an offence under Section 120(B) and sentenced to imprisonment until the rising of the Court.

The Court found that Hashim Qureshi was an agent of the Indian Government and that he organized the hijacking at the instance of the Indian Government, using the other five accused as his dupes. Unfortunately, the judgment, at the time of this writing, has not been published and the evidence establishing the links between Hashim Qureshi and the Indian Government and, more particularly, between the Indian Government and the hijacking, is not known. It is plain that Qureshi could have been guilty of all the offences, as found by the Court, without the Indian Government being involved in the hijacking. The further difficulty is that this latter issue was pre-judged, in Pakistan, by the Commission of Enquiry held in 1971.

# APPENDIX D

*Pakistan's Casualties in the Campaign of December 1971*

According to Major-General Fazal Muqeem Khan (retd.) (*Pakistan's Crisis in Leadership*, National Book Foundation, Islamabad, 1973, pp. 276 and 280) the Pakistan army's Order of Battle in East Pakistan comprised three infantry divisions, one brigade group, one armoured regiment plus one armoured squadron, six field artillery regiments, and five mortar batteries. There were also locally raised para-military formations armed with rifles and numbering about 73,000.[1] The same author states that Pakistan's casualties in East Pakistan from March to December 1971 were:

| | |
|---|---|
| Killed in action | 1,293 |
| Wounded | 2,539 |
| Missing | 35 |
| Missing believed killed | 340 |
| Missing believed prisoners of war before 16 December 1971 | 18 |

Casualties incurred near or just preceding the surrender may not be included in these figures which, in any case, bear out what is suggested in the text as to the severity of the fighting.

Major-General Khan states that Pakistan's casualties on the western front from 3 to 17 December were:

| | |
|---|---|
| Killed in action | 1,405 |
| Wounded | 3,078 |
| Missing | 126 |
| Missing believed killed | 134 |
| Missing believed prisoners of war | 215 |

When writing his book the General had access to Pakistan G.H.Q. records and after its publication he became Secretary to Government in the Defence Division.

According to the International Institute of Strategic Studies, however, the casualties sustained by Pakistan on both fronts were 7,892 killed and 9,547 wounded. The same source also states that some 15,000 of the prisoners of war were wounded. The disparity between these figures and those of Major-General F. M. Khan is considerable and it appears the Institute figures are mainly from Indian, non-official sources. It seems likely that General Khan's figures are closer to the mark.

---

[1] Their military worth was extremely doubtful.

# Index